Voices of the Voiceless
Person-Centred approaches for people with learning difficulties

Jan Hawkins

with additional material by
Vic Forrest
and
Michael Farrell

PCCS BOOKS
Ross-on-Wye

First published in 2002

PCCS BOOKS LTD
Llangarron
Ross-on-Wye
Herefordshire
HR9 6PT
UK
Tel +44 (0)1989 77 07 07
e-mail enquiries@pccsbks.globalnet.co.uk
www.pccs-books.co.uk

Voices of the Voiceless
Person-Centred approaches to people with learning disabilities

British Library Cataloguing in Publication Data
A catalogue record for this book is available from the British Library

ISBN 1 898059 41 1

Cover picture by James Brown
Cover design by Denis Postle
Printed by Bookcraft, Midsomer Norton, Somerset, UK

Contents

Acknowledgements

I wish to express my gratitude all those individuals who have learning disabilities who allowed me into their worlds. The journey to completion of this book has been supported by many experiences and people, thanks are due for every word of encouragement, challenge and every situation from which I learned. I wish to thank too, my sister Lynne, who painstakingly translated my handwritten scrawl into type, and my husband and children, who encouraged me, and gave me the space to write. Thanks also to those who contributed to the book, Vic Forrest and Michael Farrell, and to all the interviewees who so willingly gave their thoughts and time, as well as their passion to this book. And finally, to Michael Da Costa for listening to my voices of the voiceless.

The author can be contacted at:
The Foundation for the Developing Person
376 Hale End Road
Highams Park
London
E4 9PB
Tel/Fax: 0208 531 9760
Email: admin@thefdp.demon.co.uk
Website: www.thefdp.demon.co.uk

About this book

In this book I offer stories of those students and clients with whom I have developed relationships. It has been important for me to step back from direct work with people with learning disabilities in order to reflect on my experience and recharge myself for this special part of my working life. But though the stories I tell are of relationships long gone, the memories are as fresh today as they were from session to session. The people mentioned in this book have never faded but are etched forever, and with great clarity in my mind. I treasure many of the drawings they made that I will keep: however simple, they express intense emotions. My own experiences in counselling people or supporting people with learning difficulties have had a profound impact on me.

The book contains six sections where stories of therapeutic relationships and interviews reflect similar themes. The themes overlap, and dividing into sections does not lead to a neat and easy separation, but aims to bring together the dominant focus in a particular relationship or interview. I have also included accounts of some research I did to increase my understanding of how the Person-Centred Approach informs the work of others.

Use of language

The majority of the people mentioned in this book have severe learning disabilities, though a few are discussed who have moderate learning disabilities. There is still some confusion about what these terms mean. Since the 1920s the definition of 'severe learning disability' has referred to those with an IQ of less than 50, whereas those with mild to moderate learning disabilities are defined by having IQ scores in the range of 50–70 (Sinason, 1992). It seems unhelpful to me that people are classified in this way. In my experience IQ scores give very little indication of a person's functional ability. It is also very difficult to describe people who have learning and/or functional disabilities, as the description within the services which make provision for these clients continually changes. For a discussion of the euphemisms and labels applied to this group of clients, see Sinason (1992, pp. 39–54). I have chosen what appears to be the most widely accepted terminology, and throughout people will be described as having 'learning disabilities' or 'severe learning disabilities'. Some practitioners refer to those with 'learning difficulties', while others use the term 'learning disabilities', therefore both terms are used throughout.

There is not one person-centred approach — each contributor brings their own unique and creative application of the philosophy and theory articulated by Carl Rogers (1951). As each of the contributors brings their own particular person-centred approach, so too do they bring their own particular language with regard to people with learning difficulties. Wherever the Person-Centred Approach is referred to with capitals, this refers to the approach developed by Carl Rogers (1951; though Rogers uses the lower case), and those who work from the philosophy he described. When a person-centred approach is mentioned in lower case letters, this refers to the government's recommendations for working with people who have learning disabilities, where the person is placed at the centre of services, rather than fitting the person into existing services. It is also referred to with lower case where it describes an organic way of being which is not underpinned by theory, but which demonstrates the application of the Person-Centred Approach.

Contributions from other authors

Two additional contributions are written by Vic Forrest and Michael Farrell, whose work did not lend itself to the interview format. Once again I was keen to include the voice of the individual. Both these practitioners describe their application of the Person-Centred Approach with people who have previously been left by the wayside because of their particular difficulties. Vic Forrest describes his work in empowering people with severe learning disabilities through creative art therapy and in citizen advocacy projects, while Michael Farrell highlights the issues involved in day-service opportunities.

Interviews

In seeking contributions from other practitioners, I was eager to learn from others who are applying the Person-Centred Approach in a variety of settings. An interview offered each practitioner the opportunity to speak with their own voice about their work and what it means to them. The Person-Centred Approach is not limited to individual and group therapy, but can be applied usefully in any setting where it offers the possibility for growth and development within and between individuals. The five interviews range through a broad spectrum of services for people with learning disabilities, from individual counselling, to support in the community, residential care and support within families.

The interviews were tape-recorded, transcribed, and then passed back to each interviewee for consideration. This gave an opportunity for clarification or elaboration and for each person to gain a sense of ownership of their words, and they are produced without major changes, in order to maintain the immediacy of the spoken word. All names and identifiable details have been changed to ensure anonymity, except in the cases of organisations that have given permission for heir names to be included.

The first interview is with Bethan Jess Oliver, who talks of the dilemmas of her dual role as co-director of a specialist residential setting for people with learning difficulties, where she also offers individual therapy to some of the residents. Joyce Gardiner discusses her work in applying the Person-Centred Approach in supporting people with severe learning disabilities in the community, and describes the depth of love that is part of relating with her clients. Sara Watson describes her work in a house for people with severe learning disabilities who present challenging behaviours, and her desire to really listen to her clients so that they may have the opportunity to show what they have to offer. Carol Schaffer talks about her experiences as Chief Executive of *Kith & Kids*, an organisation for families who have members with disabilities. As a person-centred practitioner she shares how the approach is applied throughout the organisation. She stresses the enduring nature of many of the relationships that develop between families, people with learning disabilities and those who come as volunteers to support them. Carol also points to the need for the enduring relationship, which allows the person with learning disability to be known, and their likes/dislikes, needs and wants to be understood. Marie Cradock talks about her experiences of working with children with learning difficulties in a school and youth counselling setting, where her willingness to engage within the young person's framework allows for therapy to occur.

Consent

For many of the people whose voices have been included, any attempt at gaining informed consent would likely to have been met with agreement, though it would represent compliance rather than any kind of considered informed consent. James (p. 25 ff.) is able to understand what his consent means, when given sufficient time to explore it. His consent means that his experience, and my own within it, can be described more fully. Notwithstanding the difficulties of being unable to obtain meaningful informed consent, the desire to offer both a voice to those who rarely are heard, and encouragement to practitioners to embrace people with learning disabilities into their practices, has meant going ahead with stories of therapeutic and other relationships, with all identifiable details removed. My break from working with people with learning disabilities, and the varying referral agencies, means that the possibility of identification of individuals is further obscured. However, the voices herein speak of common experiences for people with learning disabilities

Research

I include in the appendices some research into the experiences of other Person-Centred practitioners who work with clients who have learning disabilities. I recognise that my interest in the experiences of other Person-Centred practitioners working with people with learning difficulties is, in part, about wanting to understand my recognition of deep connections that transcend speech or intellectual ability. It has been validating to learn that others share the dilemmas I have encountered in my work. The awe and wonder I feel when working at depth with someone who cannot speak, and whose intellectual ability and functioning are severely impaired, seem shared by those practitioners who contributed to the study, as well as by other contributors to this book.

For the interested reader, there is an academic exploration of the provision of services for people with learning disabilities and why I am advocating the Person-Centred Approach. I have left this discussion until the end in order to bring the voices of persons with learning disabilities into the foreground. It is my hope that through the stories of therapeutic relationships and applications of the Person-Centred Approach described, the arguments, when they come, will be recognised through the real lives of those who do not speak in academic ways.

Oliver still remains the most hopeless human being I ever met, the weakest human being I ever met, and yet he was one of the most powerful people I ever met . . . Oliver could do absolutely nothing except breathe, sleep, eat, and yet he was responsible for action, love, courage, insight. (De Vinck, 1989, p. 12)

And finally . . .

The Person-Centred Approach requires the practitioner to be continually open both to their own experiencing and to that of others. It can be deeply empowering and has a central focus on the tendency towards growth. Because of its emphasis on relationship it does not offer the quick fix or short-term results that are favoured by most funding bodies. People with learning difficulties may need more time in relationship to find their own potentialities. Certainly Person-Centred practitioners will want to take the necessary time to learn their client's language. This book is not about Hollywood endings where people caged within themselves suddenly learn to fly free. It contains stories of slow, painstaking work, and small changes. It is not about us and them. Emotional intelligence has little to do with intellectual intelligence. It is about people who, because of their limited cognitive or developmental ability, have been chronically emotionally undernourished. It is about listening to the voices of the voiceless.

Introduction

Danny's story

I was in my early twenties when I began volunteering in a school for children with learning difficulties. I spent only one afternoon a week there as my own children were still small, but that one afternoon each week changed the direction of my life.

After a year as a volunteer I was offered a job as a supply classroom assistant, and when my own children began school I accepted a permanent post in a department of the school for young people up to age nineteen with severe behavioural and communication difficulties. Most of the students were autistic, though some had been labelled psychotic. Many had no speech and little interest in the Makaton signing system we used, mostly staring into space.

I found early on that I had an affinity with those who could not speak. Somehow I recognised feelings in them which, when I gently checked them out, were often confirmed by brief (and unusual) eye contact or an even briefer nod.

As a classroom assistant it was my role to support the teachers in the team and to take care of some of the more personal needs of our students. In practice I was often left alone with a group of students and with no training I bumbled along, learning through experience how to interact without inciting problems or difficult behaviours.

It has taken me many years to understand my affinity with those who cannot speak and to find a language myself to speak of it and the stories of those I have met en route who could not speak for themselves. In essence, this book attempts to explore that affinity, and to encourage others to find their own affinities with people who have learning difficulties.

The school I worked in used the principles of behavioural psychology in attempting to offer relevant education to the children there. With no previous knowledge on the subject, I found myself at times saddened and enraged in turn by what I saw, and what I was sometimes required to do in applying programmes devised by the school psychologists. It was obvious to me that these psychologists were well-educated and had put a lot of thought and effort into devising programmes to address difficult behaviours. I frequently berated myself for my arrogance based on nothing but my feelings, for thinking what was actually happening was counterproductive and wrong.

Danny, a young man of eighteen and very tall with an athletic build, came to our department one summer term. As we got to know him, he proved generally cooperative and seemed able to follow quite complex instructions. He developed good relationships with staff members and certainly enjoyed and responded to me talking to him about what he was doing or what was happening around us. Danny's inability to speak seemed incongruous with his demeanour and expression: he shone bright and full of life. I often felt a great sadness in him as he would sometimes withdraw and screw up his eyes, looking sideways at the world. Danny often seemed to feel trapped in himself. He was a very affectionate young man, and would fling an arm around my shoulders, look deeply into my eyes and then quickly ruffle my hair before bounding off again. He was developing his sexual awareness and again I was struck by the cruel blow that he had been dealt. He was very good-looking and without his learning difficulties would have had plenty of admirers exploring their own sexuality. But this was not to be for Danny. For him the focus would be on learning to express his sexuality privately, with little opportunity for a relationship where it could blossom.

After the summer holidays we began the new term, the whole team feeling that Danny had settled well and a few of us having very good relationships with him. Two weeks into the term he had taken himself into an empty classroom and was taking things out of drawers. I went over to him and reminded him that it was break time and that we needed to be outside as I was co-supervising the whole group. Danny suddenly lunged forward and bit into my arm, his jaws so big he left a bruise six inches by two inches on my arm. It was a painful experience and quite unnerving, as Danny would not loosen his bite for some minutes. After this he went back outside, biting his own hand as he went. Danny had calluses on his hands from regular hand biting when he was frustrated. Though shocked, I felt that I was responsible. I had handled the situation badly. I knew, for example, that Danny must always have clear access to a door. He would simply blindly push away anyone in his path if he needed to get out. I thought I must have either gone too close to him in that moment or somehow seemed to him to be blocking the door.

But only a few days later he bit again, and this time it was another student. He was becoming regularly agitated and would slap his head hard with both hands and rock from foot to foot. Something was bothering him. Soon after the first two bites he lunged at me again and I signed a very clear 'no'. He lunged to my side, taking into his jaws the forearm of the quietest and most nervous boy in the group. Peter, too, was severely learning-disabled and had no speech. The sight of his eyes, wide with terror, but his absolute silence as Danny maintained his bite hold, was eerie beyond description. The resulting wound was dressed, and Peter remained silent throughout: the only impact, it seemed, was that he was quieter than usual.

The psychologist was called in to observe and advise us on how to handle things. I offered my theory that Danny might be suffering pain in his jaws because he had begun to chew things as babies do when teething. He was the right age for wisdom teeth to be erupting. This observation was brushed aside and the programme we were given was to isolate him if he bit and give him his favourite toy, which came with him to school each day. Each day the toy would be taken from him and kept in his bag until the end of the day, as he would otherwise fixate on it and be unable to be involved in anything else.

I raised a voice of dissent for this strategy, seeing it as rewarding the behaviour we were concerned about. My contentious remarks were treated as they usually were by the psychologists — I had no training or qualifications and was there to follow instructions.

Over the next few weeks Danny's behaviour worsened. If he slapped his head one, two, three times, the lunge and bite would follow. One day I was working alone with him on a task he clearly was uninterested in, and suddenly he slapped his head. I summoned up all my power and said, 'you don't frighten me, Danny', and he sat back and smiled! Sadly this approach never worked again, and it wasn't true. Danny now frightened both staff and students in the department. He was often isolated, playing with his toy, and the incident book was full of reports of his biting, though no-one ever informed his parents about what was happening. Everyone kept their distance from Danny but I refused to — it felt imperative to me to maintain our relationship. I just couldn't shake my belief that something was wrong and we were making it worse by rewarding him for biting.

The next bite I endured was particularly bad. Danny and I were sitting together, working on a task. Without any build-up or agitation — in fact things were going well — he suddenly grabbed me by the neck, strangling hard as he bit into my forehead, his jaws reaching from forehead to skull as far as behind my ear. I was quite faint when he finally let go and I was taken to the medical room to have the wound attended to.

It felt important to see Danny before he left at the end of the day. Somehow I felt that he was trying to communicate something, and we were all missing it. When he saw me back in the department his face was full of fear. I said, 'I'm alright, Danny', but the look of fear went home with him. The next day I met him at the bus to escort him into school. Danny would normally lumber up, fling an arm around my shoulder, ruffle my hair and bound into school. Not on this occasion. The look of fear was still there and he put both hands over his ears. He would not come near me. I said, 'it's alright, Danny, I still love you' and he gradually came to me. Slowly the hands came away from his face as we walked down to school. 'Bit Jan.' Danny had spoken, each word absolutely clear. I had never before, and never did again, hear him use words. When I told my team leader this, I learnt that Danny's mother had reported that he did occasionally say words, clear and in context, but this had never really been believed since he never did so at school.

Not long after, Danny did not appear for a few days. We got a message that he was in hospital with impacted wisdom teeth.

There was some degree of hope that when he returned he would not be so agitated and the biting would decrease. But why should Danny stop biting? He had been taught by us that if he didn't want to do something or if he wanted time alone with his favourite toy, all he had to do was bite somebody.

In the most awful incident to date, Danny had lunged for me, and I managed to sign an emphatic 'no'. He turned and bit another member of staff standing nearby and lumbered around slapping his head. He was distressed — desperately distressed. The air was filled with tension and fear.

The wounded staff member left for treatment from the school nurse while myself, and another member of staff, covering the lunch break, cleared the other students from the room as Danny was pacing in a corner of the room. Using a row of chairs as a pathetic barrier, we talked with him. The only safe thing to do now was to get him to the small padded 'eye room'[1] across the playground in another department. I wanted a nurse to look at him — I was convinced he was in pain. A male teacher came to help, but Danny lunged at the teacher, biting him in several places including one bite that went through to the bone.

The only option was to keep back from Danny, and using chairs held in front of them in the hope he would not attack again, more male teachers who'd come to help escorted Danny to the eye room.

I felt overwhelmed with grief and anger that it had come to this. The nurse did later give him some painkillers and recommended that his mother have him checked out. He had an infection where his wisdom teeth had been removed.

Danny's parents had still never been told about the biting and, though there was never such a distressing incident again, Danny continued to bite. After a term of this his mother was called to the school, shown the incident book and Danny's placement at school was terminated.

I felt that I had let Danny down badly. As the truth of his pain, due to impacted wisdom teeth, emerged, I realised that I should have been stronger and trusted more what I somehow knew to be the case. It was painfully obvious that Danny's behaviour was communicating something important. But behaviourism is not concerned with why or what feelings surround a behaviour. It is the behaviour itself which must be managed. But even if this is the case I could not understand at all why someone would stop a behaviour for which they are rewarded with something they like.

We let Danny down first by not really listening to the message behind his biting and then by teaching him that he could use biting as a way of controlling his environment. And for this he lost the familiarity and security of the place and relationships he had developed. Danny's records would always carry the reports of his dangerous behaviours. But those of us involved in pushing him further

---

1. This is a room padded on all sides, with a padded bench and a tiny eye-level window for staff to check on the occupant. This space allows for safe time-out where violent behaviour can be managed safely.

away from healthy relationships would not have reports of that on our records.

Danny, and others in my earliest learning environment with learning disabilities, is why I went into psychology and counselling training. I had the power of speech but no power to insist that people listen to my ideas. I reasoned that if I managed to collect pieces of paper that said I was qualified then I might have a chance to change things.

It is a sad reflection on our society that when I did have the papers — the qualifications — I was still saying the same things. My feeling that people with learning disabilities are finding clear and creative ways of communicating, is no different now than it was then. I now can speak the language of behaviourism, and other theoretical approaches, but what I speak in theoretical terms is as nothing to how people with learning disabilities find ways to speak their feelings.

Danny's teeth hurt. He showed that by leaving teeth marks in others. If only we had, before discussing behavioural programmes, had him checked by a dentist. It would have been so simple.

Dilemmas

This section focuses on just a few of the dilemmas in being with people who have severe learning disabilities and includes an interview with Bethan Jess Oliver who juggles two roles within the same organisation. Though this section has a focus on dilemmas, other dilemmas appear throughout the book, as listening fully to people with learning disabilities continually raises challenges and additional dilemmas that are less apparent when working with people whose capacity to initiate change in their lives is not hampered by complete reliance on others.

When I asked other practitioners (see The research study, p. 180 ff.) about the dilemmas involved in offering counselling services to people with severe learning disabilities, the responses reflected experiences I have had in my own practice. It is difficult sometimes knowing that any client may leave the session to go back to an abusive or hostile relationship/environment. The hope I have though is that, as the client grows in connection with self, s/he will be empowered to make changes and choices that give her/him more of what s/he needs. I live in that hope because people whose cognitive apparatus is reasonably intact have the ability to think in a consistent way about what they want and need, as well as varying degrees of independence. The dilemmas in work with clients who are hindered by cognitive impairment or deficits, are of a different nature, often relating to harm to self or others.

People who have severe learning disabilities, or even those with mild to moderate learning disabilities, often are reliant completely on carers, or systems of care, for their everyday basic needs. Some who are more able and who challenge carers may have been threatened that they will lose their homes, carers, friends, everything if they do not shut up. What place, I often ask myself, does empowering therapy have in those situations? Two particular people come to mind when I think of these dilemmas and difficulties. One story remains a dilemma, whilst the other speaks of the power imbalance that is inherent within most systems of care.

Simon (see p. 90 ff.) shared with me his experiences of sexual contacts during our sessions. Initially he talked of 'Uncle Ken', who I knew had died many years before. From what Simon was able to tell me, his sexual experiences were likely to have occurred when he was a child or young teenager, and would be labelled in today's world as 'sexual abuse'. Simon described these experiences happily, and I endeavoured to remain open to him and his pleasure in it, whilst acknowledging my own anger towards anyone who would use a child for his own sexual gratification. As a vulnerable middle-aged adult, I was concerned about what had happened to him and took these concerns many times to supervision. The fact that Uncle Ken was dead made the holding of confidentiality an easier issue. With the support of my supervisor I explored my concerns and feelings, and concluded that Simon deserved the right to have his own confidential material honoured, despite being a vulnerable adult. Simon's story is more fully told in The asexual myth section, p. 79 ff.

Patrick's (p. 31 ff.) experience shows how the dilemmas in counselling are also present in the care system. If people had listened properly to Patrick, much of his abuse, and that of others, could have been prevented. Instead when he told what was happening to him he was either ignored, or his story was held confidentially and he continued to experience abuse. When he came to me, my dilemma was how to respond to his desire to sue the perpetrators of his abuse at a time (twelve years ago) when survivors of abuse generally were struggling to be heard, and they were not constrained as he was by severe speech impediment. He so needed me to help him take legal action and I knew this was because I understood the impact the abuse had had on him. This was important to him as no-one had truly heard and understood before. Part of me wanted to lay down my therapist's boundaries and take on an advocacy role for him. Again, supervision was my haven for working through my own entanglements with Patrick's need for help. I solved this particular dilemma by making an appointment for him (his speech was barely intelligible by phone unless one had really tuned into him) with an advocacy project so that he could take that part of his work forward, leaving us free to focus on the legacy the abuse had left him with. Patrick's living situation then was safe and he felt happy being there, unlike his previous homes in the care system.

Working with clients who have severe learning disabilities means listening on a regular basis to experiences of overt abuse, past and present, through to simple but obvious bad practice. It is hard for me at times to remain open and hear the fullness or restrictedness of my client's experiences when I am in touch with a part of me which would like to arrange for those 'carers' to experience what they inflict on their clients, just so they might develop some more empathy or at least humanity and compassion. Remaining open, and willing to connect with my clients though, is the goal in my work, but it brings with it openness to my own grief about man's inhumanity to man.

I am reminded here of recommendations from a psychologist on Pat's notes: 'When she talks about her abuse or cries, ignore her, she is just seeking attention'. It is that kind of remark that causes me to despair for humanity — Pat's experiences of abuse were causing her distress in the here and now, but it had been deemed reasonable to ignore her pain. My dilemma again is how to know these things and not fly into reaction on behalf of my clients, because that is not my role as a therapist.

The question remains — whose role is it?

How long is a counselling session supposed to be anyway?
May's and Paul's stories

It has long been a tradition in the therapeutic world to speak of 'the fifty-minute hour'. I have never really got to grips with the reasoning behind this, other than making practical sense for the therapist. There seems to be an idea of discipline for the client — the expectation that they will come to pace their process within the confines of the fifty minutes. In my own practice, I prefer to offer a full hour, there seeming to be something rather powerful in referring to a fifty-minute hour that offends my sensibilities.

I offer sessions of one-hour duration and negotiate different times to those clients who need them. For example, some clients travel long distances and we meet less often for longer. So far the longest individual or couple session I have experienced as a therapist is four hours, once, for a particularly delicate and fragile piece of work with an individual who needed that degree of contained space. More usually, long sessions last up to two hours, for those for whom one hour simply is not sufficient space to deal with the particular issue safely. I am open to negotiation if a client feels a longer time period would allow them to work on particularly difficult issues. This approach to flexible time contracts is especially important in my work with adult survivors of childhood abuse. Where dissociation and fragmentation is what an individual lives with, the inevitable defence structures which enabled them to survive need space to be honoured so that the whole person, in all their parts, may be allowed to speak. It feels important to me to be willing to make room for flexible time-contracting too with people who have learning difficulties.

All of my clients with severe learning disabilities, so far, have experienced abuse of different types. Yet all those with learning disabilities that I worked with also had limited attentional abilities. Some, like Carl (see p. 150 ff.), always used his full hour, settling into the rhythm of the session from the start. Others began with twenty minutes building up to their hour over time. It was one of the only opportunities to give over power with these clients, to allow them to end their sessions when they chose to. Those clients who were brought to my private practice by care workers knew that the worker would return, and I reminded them at the beginning of each session that 'Sarah will be back for you in X time and take you back to — [name of their home or day centre]'. With those who found time and attention extremely difficult, I would remind them that when they were ready to finish I would 'phone Danny on the mobile phone and he will come straight back for you and take you back to — [name of home or day centre]'. Repeating this same information at each session was important, as most of my clients would not retain information from week to week. When a client spontaneously told me that Sarah or Danny (or whoever) would collect them, I knew that they had grasped the safety of the situation, and their own power within it. Some, like Simon (see p. 90 ff.), regularly for many months, wanted to leave after a relatively short time. He told me this by going to the front door! Others, like Rachael (p. 118 ff.), Keeley (p. 142 ff.) and

Carl (see p. 150 ff.) would have stayed longer if they could.

Once a week, I spent a morning offering a counselling service within a day centre for people with severe learning disabilities. Many of my clients there had been institutionalised for many years in a long-stay hospital, here called Longwood. The Government's decision to 'disperse' people into the community meant that my clients spent their weekdays at the day centre, and went home to group houses, instead of hospitals.

May came every week to the drop-in counselling sessions. She was a small woman, who was probably in her sixties, though no-one really knew her age. May would say she was a different age from time to time, and was equally convinced each time she said it that she really was that age. May liked to show me the contents of her handbag in most sessions and was very interested in money, especially counting it, if she had any, with my help. Our work was disjointed and things that worried her would be inserted between exploration of the bag and telling me who would be on duty at her home that evening. May's story was of being in Longwood: she wasn't sure if she had parents or other family. No-one visited her in hospital and no family visited her at her new home in the community. She told me about leaving the hospital. 'Auntie Hilda' (a nurse she liked) 'put my clothes in a bag and I got on the bus and I don't know where Auntie Hilda is now'. I asked how she felt about leaving the hospital. She described her bed in the ward, her locker, and the other patients who she never saw again. She gave me an 'it's alright, dear', which I wondered whether she had cultivated for herself or for others. In myself I had a vision of a stark, grey ward — yet secure and known home for May for many, many years. Suddenly her case is packed, she's put on the minibus and sent off to a house in the community, with her own bedroom, a real house instead of a hospital. If any of us could choose for someone like May, I have little doubt it would be a real house rather than a hospital. For me the sadness is that so little recognition was there for that transition. May is not someone who'd complain: 'it's alright, dear' is her refrain. She told of beatings she had witnessed, of other residents who frightened her, of wanting a new handbag and wishing for a watch. In two years I worked there she never had either of those things. May was living in the community, but her clothing, shoes and personal care remained institutional.

May loved her sessions, always asking on my arrival at the drop-in, 'do you want to see me today, dear?' and a certain air of pleasure when I responded, 'I'd be happy to see you May, if you'd like to come and talk'. It was as if our sessions gave her a small sense of importance. She began talking of her wish to have a family and not being happy in her home. I encouraged her to tell her social worker when she said he was coming to visit. I encouraged her to say when she's frightened at home, though the picture of that particular home I gained from May and others did not give much hope of her being heard there. It was four years after I finished at the day centre that a supervisee (who took over from me) told me that May had finally moved in with a family. She looks well cared for now and has a new watch and handbag at last.

My shortest session with May came one day when we had begun by counting her money — she hoped she had enough for an ice cream. This task finished — and joy of joys, there was enough for an ice cream — we moved on as she drew an upsetting incident that had happened at her home on the previous evening. She was focused for longer than usual and I felt we'd moved to a deeper level, when suddenly an ear-piercing jolly tune filled the air. Only fifteen minutes into this session May dropped her pencils, her mood lifted and she jumped up, grabbing her purse — 'I've got to get my ice cream', she said. What more therapeutic thing could there be, it seemed to me, as I followed her to the ice cream van and back to our room. My empathic responses have rarely been so well-received — her joy is with me now. I could feel a paper coming on: 'Ice cream, a therapeutic intervention to connect with joy'. We shared the time of the ice cream and May left uplifted!

Paul holds the record for the shortest ever therapy session with me. He dropped in to the counselling sessions only rarely and usually in a frustrated state. Being profoundly deaf with no speech or discernible vocalisations, we communicated in pidgin sign language. This was complicated further by his ingenious, personally idiosyncratic signs which took me a very long time to understand. One of these signs confused me for ages and I resorted to asking one of the day centre workers if they knew what it meant. Paul would point and place his hand on his hip — this was his sign for mum!

Our sessions were always short, focused on today's frustration and beleaguered by the fact that it was difficult for me to understand his signs. What was more difficult was that Paul was so intent on telling his problem that he rarely attended to my responses, and I'd have to somehow stop his flow to let him know I'd understood — or didn't, whichever the case was. We had the beginnings of understanding, which would have been enhanced, I am sure, by regular contact if he had chosen that.

One day Paul came into the room very agitated and excited. He was signing that he had new hearing aids. I understood right away! Paul, in his excitement, was signing the same thing over and over and I couldn't get him to stop long enough to concentrate on my response. After a few minutes, in desperation I drew a simple face with enormous smile, and huge hearing aids. I wrote, 'Paul is happy, he has new hearing aids'. I wasn't sure if the words would mean anything, but his reaction was clear — he felt understood. He gave me an emphatic thumbs up (good sign) and raced off with his picture showing everyone in the day centre. Later, a staff member told me he'd been trying to tell them something all morning, but they hadn't been able to understand.

In a whirl, as ever, Paul came, went, and I was left at the end of this five-minute session wondering whether the purpose of Person-Centred Therapy really came down to this — a full understanding of the other's communication. No frills, no pleasantries, no need to go deeper or make connections — Paul was off doing that for himself.

How often can you hear it?
Hope's story

Hope presented an ongoing dilemma for me, which I struggled to articulate in my supervision at the time. Essentially the dilemma centred on whether continuously listening to a repeated story would actually be more harmful than healing. Hope was referred by the day centre team, who were concerned generally about her. Always appearing well cared for, with clean clothes which fitted properly and clean, well-groomed hair, she was always something of an enigma to me. She would talk of quite complex feelings and issues relating to her here-and-now situation, and yet more often seem stuck in some fixed fears and concerns of a much younger developmental phase.

Hope's story, like most, came in snippets, building up over the fourteen months that I saw her. She did not always come to sessions, and after several in a row would come sporadically for a while, before going back to a pattern of coming for several sessions in a row — that was her chosen pattern. I would mention this from time to time and each time received the same genuine response that she liked to come, wanted to come, would come every week — somehow it seemed the response Hope thought I might want. It felt important then to accept that this was her pace, her choice, and to allow her drop-in time, rather than the fixed sessional spaces, so that she could freely choose and I could allow the regular session time for another who really needed that.

Like the others at the day centre Hope had been in Longwood Hospital for a long time, and moved into the community to a house only three years before.

She remembered her mother and sister and often talked of them, usually sadly repeating, 'I don't know where they are'. She talked of her sister having been on a different ward at Longwood, and Hope would be allowed to visit her sometimes when she lived there. One day a nurse came in and packed her bag with her worldly belongings contained in her bedside locker, and left her by a minibus at the steps of the hospital to 'go to my new house'. Hope did not know from that day what had happened to her sister. She remembered her mother visiting her in hospital but had not seen her since and she didn't know what had happened to her either. There was just a sad shaking of the head, 'I don't know where they are'. This was a regularly repeated issue in our work and it never went beyond the same expressions, and my attempts to communicate my understanding of how sad and lost she felt and how she found it so hard not knowing. Though I know she said the same to anyone when that issue was around for her, people tended to ignore it — they'd heard it so many times before.

I did check with the staff if there was any information for Hope about her sister and mother but — like so many others — very little information came out of the hospital with them. It seemed that Hope would never know about what happened to the people she loved most and the best I could offer was to hear and let her know it mattered.

Another frequently repeated issue was her fear that she was pregnant. She relayed, on many occasions, her experience of living rough on the streets for a while and a man giving her fish and chips and then having him 'do sex with me'. She hadn't wanted that and hadn't liked it, but he gave her fish and chips so she had to. She thought she was fifteen when that happened and she thought she was pregnant but didn't know what happened to the baby. Another loss, and unknown. From the streets she remembered being in Holloway Prison before hospital. Her snapshots of her history were snapshots in time and Hope found it difficult to move beyond repeating them over and over, either in the same session or repeated ones. She was in her sixties when I knew her and I tried a little input on what pregnancy would feel and look like in the hope that she'd feel clear about the fact that she was not pregnant — that might, I thought, help her to resolve what had happened for her. She never retained the information so the repetitions were the same, save for the variance in my efforts to respond in a way that would connect for her.

Hope, through demonstrating compliance at every level, would sometimes express anger. Sadly, most of my clients with severe learning disabilities were so busy complying or guessing what I would be wanting or assuring me they were fine, that few ever expressed or even seemed to feel anger.

Hope would express anger about money and wanting a job. She didn't want to be in this day centre, she didn't want to live with other people with learning difficulties, she did not identify herself as having learning difficulties at all. She wanted a job, money and freedom (see also James's story, p. 25 ff.). Despite her very real difficulties in caring for herself and understanding certain things, she desperately wanted to be 'normal'. She had had a few jobs which had always broken down because of her difficulty in staying on task, or following instructions. Hope wanted to be able to do things alone and could not make the step of having support first then working alone — so she remained stuck in the day centre routine.

Hope's 'stuckness' in her repetitive stories was hard to stay open to. She desperately needed to say the story and be heard. Yet her need to know, as in where her sister and mother had gone, and whether she was (or had been) pregnant, could have little resolution without the evidence to ground her. Unlike people without severe learning disabilities, Hope was unable, during our work, to do any research, or access any information about her history, that might help her to resolve some of her confusion and 'lostness'. She was never able to reach a place of acceptance — that sometimes there are questions we never find the answer to, but we move on anyway.

Hope may always need to talk about her losses: my hope is that there will always be people who will listen.

Though I still find no easy or clear answer to the dilemma of how often one should listen to the same story before it becomes more a rigid trap than a process of developing understanding, I feel that for Hope the connection with someone willing to listen was what was therapeutic, rather than achieving resolution. Hope taught me that person to person relating is what she needs.

She could have no 'goals' or 'measurable outcomes' in terms of letting go of painful memories, or working through them. Hope had been rehearsing the same stories for years, but had never felt listened to. When she did feel listened to, maybe it was too late for the stories to loose their painful grip on her, her confusion and bewilderment had been set for so many years. Hope's 'measurable outcomes' are her gradually relaxing posture throughout and after a session, her smile when she knows she is to spend time with someone who really wants to understand how her world is for her. Hope is stuck. It requires great effort and respect to really hear her, no matter how often. The value for Hope (and for me too) is in the relationship and the process of sharing and being heard. In our product valuing rather than process valuing climate, it is not always easy to let go of others' expectations of change within a client.

Interview with Bethan Jess Oliver: dual roles

Bethan is co-director of an independent organisation that provides residential care, community support and day services for people who have learning difficulties and emotional, behavioural or mental health needs. Her primary role within the organisation is to direct and monitor the delivery of care through supervision and training of managers, training of staff and the development of appropriate systems and approaches to care. She also offers therapeutic support and individual counselling to service users.

Jan: I'm wondering why the Person-Centred Approach attracted you, and what attracted you to offering counselling to people with learning difficulties?

Bethan: On my way down to here tonight, I was thinking about where my desire to work with people with learning difficulties came from, and I think it has its roots in my having grown up amongst and around people with learning difficulties and emotional difficulties. That is my background which has had a significant impact on me. I was also thinking about your title for this book, the voice for the voiceless, because, for me, people who have learning difficulties represent a whole section of society that in many ways have no voice and I have always felt strongly about that.

Jan: From your own experience with people with no voice, but also your own experience of yourself having no voice.

Bethan: Yes, my own past involved many situations in which I didn't have a voice, where I felt both overpowered and disempowered, and I guess I relate to that aspect in others who live either in an environment or within a society where they are marginalised or pushed into the background. For me, its about visibility, inclusion and representation. I encounter many people through my work who talk to me about people with learning difficulties and I am still, sadly, very often surprised and staggered by where they're coming from and what they're saying. I find it quite hard and frustrating at times because people say things to me like, 'of course all people with learning difficulties are like this or that, they can't help it. It's just the way they are'.

They think of the person (if they think of a person at all) as being very much secondary to their disability. Even when people talk about disability, they talk about whether somebody is able-bodied or not — the emphasis is placed on the body, which again completely excludes people with learning difficulties. In that sense they are often not even acknowledged within disability movements or the language used by disabled groups. My own response is that I have always seen myself in them and them in me, I relate in the same way I relate to anyone else, some of my closest friends as a child were people who have learning difficulties, they were my peers, and the vast majority of what I know about myself and what has helped me in my work is what I have learnt from people that I now also work with.

Jan: That's interesting: that far from feeling like the one that's given everything, you feel that you have been receiving.

Bethan: I feel I have learnt and gained far more than I have given in the work itself. I have found many insights that I have taken within myself that have helped me grow and move and change, and they have been based on something that someone with learning difficulties has done before me, regardless of whether that was balancing across an imaginary river in the back garden, or bridging a gulf between emotional denial and free expression. For me the work is about being flexible and creative, being willing to open yourself up to another so they can learn from you and you can learn from them. I approach my work with each person from the standpoint that I know nothing, they are the expert, and implicit in that is the understanding and belief that they will teach me, over time, what I need to know and how to be in order to help them get to where they need to or become the person they want to be.

As a society I think it's time we actually started opening the door and saying, 'hang on a minute, what happens to you, happens to me, happens to us, happens to everyone, we're all human'. That's how I feel and as far as my desire to work with people who have learning difficulties and my passion for the work is concerned . . . it comes very much from their passion, their determination and their courage. I have seen over and over again people who, let's face it, have the odds stacked against them from the start, who, despite this, struggle in the most amazing ways with things that so many of us just take for granted.

For me that has been a very powerful and often humbling experience. Sometimes the struggle is a defiant one — they lash out at our attempts to control them and throw chairs at the professional shields we hide behind; sometimes it is passive, a silent retreat from a tokenistic world that makes little sense that isn't at some level patronising; and sometimes it's a hilarious parody in which their every action seems to deliberately mock and stick two fingers up at a society that by comparison takes itself far too seriously.

Jan: Can you say a bit about where you work, the context in which you work with people with learning difficulties?

Bethan: I work with people with learning difficulties on a one-to-one basis, I also do some group work with people, and more recently I have been particularly interested in creating environments that are supportive of the therapeutic process that people with learning difficulties, like anyone else, have to go through to get to where they need to be. I think that is important, because often the environments that people with learning difficulties find themselves in and also society in general is not always supportive of that process. By that I mean it is not generally supportive of, nor does it tend to facilitate the natural ability and tendency towards, self-directed growth and learning that people with learning difficulties share in common with others. Very often the people I work with come from situations that far from being empowering are in fact extremely disempowering. I've had people that have come to me from abusive and restrictive backgrounds or extremely institutional settings, also people that have been in police cells, who have been arrested and charged, and I've taken people with learning difficulties from prison.

Jan: Creating the residential environments that can be supportive and that can allow the process to happen and in that context you offer one-to-one and group work.

Bethan: Yes, when I started off working therapeutically with people with learning difficulties, I found over and over again that very often the obstacle wasn't the person themselves, it was what they were contending with in the outside world that was making it impossible for personal growth to take place. I tried to imagine myself into a position where everything I did was questioned or controlled, where I was dependent on others that were trying to modify my behaviour one way or another, where my adult self wasn't acknowledged or I was being responded to in this very professional setting but not being related to as a person, and some of my past experiences are similar to that so it helps me to be able to make that leap.

My aim was to try and create environments that were nurturing and supportive of the person being who they are as a person without the pressure of having to be 'normalised'. For me there doesn't have to be a pressure either to alter or control anybody's behaviour all of the time, which I think is an emphasis that still exists to some extent within the work. Very often people within the care profession talk about behaviour modification — they talk about controlling challenging behaviour and managing situations, they talk about independence training and appropriate behaviour, they talk about normalisation. All those concepts, to me, add up to really directing the way a person's life goes and I feel that for the most part the people I encounter through my work are people who have for all the best intentions and reasons been completely and utterly disempowered. Yet everybody who has been working with them is convinced they have been working towards their empowerment, but for some reason it doesn't happen.

For me it's about allowing the person to be first, to have enough time and space to decide what they want to be and to have the space they need to become themselves, when and how they want to. To give ourselves time and space enough to discover that person, for ourselves, the creativity, the resourcefulness, the beauty, the everything that makes the person. I think sometimes if we don't, we miss that. I think sometimes we are so keen to get someone to learn to get up, to dress themselves, to learn some budgeting, to learn to go and buy things from the shop, say the right things to the shop keeper, and unless the people we work with are consistently making progress, achieving physically visible goals and meeting practically measurable targets in a predetermined sequence, you know, learning to sign the names of objects in Makaton or attending so many activities a week, then they are somehow not doing what they're supposed to and so by proxy the implication is that we as carers are also failing in our job. Less visible and measurable achievements like the building of trust, individual expression, establishing a sense of safety, developing a personal sense of space and boundary, the uniqueness of the person are rarely considered or held to be as valuable or important. I think sometimes we can miss the person altogether. They get shut out by our expectations of what they should be, rather than being free to be what they are as people. I feel very strongly about that. For that reason, I suppose a lot of my work is very . . . it could be described as loose in some ways. I believe that it is very important for me to have flexible boundaries, because very often the people I work with have not grown up with the same kinds of expectations or acceptance or freedoms or even relationships that the vast majority of other people take for granted and would be quite horrified to imagine as being missing from their lives.

A lot of my work in the past has been done just walking round the grounds with somebody. It's been sitting watching a programme with them. It's been discovering something new together. It's been as part of just relating, because very often that's what I find people with learning difficulties have never been offered the opportunity to do, to just simply relate to and be in relationship with another human being where there is a sense of acceptance and equal worth.

Obviously I recognise that like the rest of society I am in a position of power in relation to the people I work with, but I try very hard to ensure that in other ways the relationship is as equal as it can be. For me that is very important, as is being myself within the relationship. I know from my own experiences what it can be like to be given the disrespect of being a non-person and to confront a face and a smile and a voice that really may as well not be there because although the person doing it may be making all the right noises and gestures and what have you, it is blatantly apparent they don't want to be there and for me that sincerity is important.

Jan: A genuine and real relationship where they are accepted, that is what you're trying to offer the people you are working with, something real and genuine where power is acknowledged but is not used and wielded and not used over them. Acknowledged and then set aside somehow, so that you can be who you are with your clients.

Bethan: Yes, and they can be themselves with me: hopefully I don't make any attempt to cover the fact that I sometimes find things difficult or to withhold unnecessarily; for me, working with people with learning difficulties, there has been such a lack sometimes of real response. The realness is very important because it is shared experience of mutual trust, as is disclosure.

Self-disclosure is something I use a lot in my work with people with learning difficulties because at the end of the day it is about them being able to see me too. And I think very often their perception has been that they are an imperfect person in a perfect world and I am very careful that I never consciously attempt to hide any imperfections within myself. Obviously therapeutically I try to be aware of where my own issues and problems lie and try not to let them interfere with the work but I think that is very different to making them invisible and I think it is very important to be very visible when you are working with somebody that has been so invisible.

Jan: I know that you work with people who have quite challenging needs, with quite dangerous and violent behaviours, and that you said that behaviour modification is what you are challenging in your work. You've taken people from prison cells, you've taken people with serious histories of violence, and I suppose what I'm wondering is how, with your person-centred approach you work with them . . .

Bethan: I suppose that it is about honesty and openness. I think it is very important. The work I have done with people in the past has involved many that have no concept of right and wrong, and have a completely confused idea of really how the world works. It is because, as I say, they haven't been offered the same opportunities and experiences to actually build a stable, rather than a shifting, interpretation of self that is grounded in a solid sense of self-worth rather than dependent on whimsical and often conflicting validation from others. It is very often so with people who have learning difficulties, because they have not been consistently responded to as adult, knowing, understanding, feeling individuals — very often their interpretation or the way that they respond to the world is seemingly without feeling, without understanding, without knowledge.

The work is about first of all trying to build between us a foundation of basic understanding of how things are and that can take a long time. I worked with one young man who firmly believed he could go to prison for swearing, but if he was to hit a three year old that was fine because the three year old had hit him — so his understanding of right and wrong was completely at odds with the world around him.. So a lot of the work with him was straightening some of that out and as I said, honesty was very important. The people that I have worked with, very often are people that have hurt other people. When they finally do begin to see and understand and realise that they actually are able to have an impact on other people and other people have an impact on them, because they are both people and because they are relating, the actual shock of realising the impact of some of the things they have done can be very traumatic. It's like, 'hang on, I was this non-person, invisible, that didn't have any impact on anyone, I had to beat that person in order to make them listen to me. Actually they could hear me but my experience was of not being heard' and then 'this is what I've done to that person' because suddenly the person is able to see themselves as a person, and therefore is able to begin to let in the person of the other, or whatever. That, for me, is very much about honesty and openness, open listening and open speaking. I don't hide the fact that I have an opinion about what they do or don't do.

What I don't do is personalise that opinion, I don't allow it to become the lens through which I respond to or relate to the person. My greatest concern is with them, and helping them to be able to take what they need to learn from that experience themselves. I have found that it's a bit like you've learnt to bang a drum so loudly that you deafen everybody around you and it's not until you start to not need to bang the drum so loudly that you can hear the drumming of others and differentiate it from your own, then you can begin to make a rhythm, to relate, to blend, to listen and to be heard.

Jan: There is something then about the real encounter between you and your client that somehow encourages real encounter between them and others. What you are describing is a situation in which these values are implicit in the whole environment, that people are first, relationship is all, and learning from experience is important. So, if you have got somebody who is violent, how can the environment be safe for everybody, whilst the learning happens? Is there a place, do you think, sometimes for control and restraint?

Bethan: Absolutely, certainly any environment needs to be safe. I suppose in reality all I am doing is extending the boundaries of the therapeutically 'holding' environment, to actually include the immediate environment the person lives in, so they can continue to be 'held' in a similar way when I'm not there and that has to be in the same way safe. They need to be able to be angry or lash out or express whatever and the resources need to be there in terms of staff, skills and training in order to contain that. It is at times difficult and it can be difficult to find what is needed in order to create that kind of resource, that kind of environment.

Very often we are working with people for whom most other things have failed, because with those individuals there is often more willingness to look at funding in a realistic sense, what's needed to achieve that, but yes, there is a place for physical restraint, there is a place for it in the short term as a form of containment, as an aid to the process of helping that person to get from A to B with the minimum risk of damage to them and other people along the way. I don't see a place for physical restraint unless that is actually underpinned by a need to look at the causes of behaviour and a need to find out what that underlying need may be. I think there is a danger though in allowing a place for physical restraint that it could be used more widely purely as a means of control, rather than as a last resort for safety reasons.

Jan: Kind of like a punishment sometimes?

Bethan: I am not sure in the present climate — I think things have moved forward. It is outlawed as a form of punishment now, but I think there are still some environments in which it is sometimes seen as a form of control and I think it is sometimes along with medical restraint seen as a form of control that is effective by itself. I was in a meeting only about a month ago that was a meeting of professional people who were discussing the problems that one person with learning difficulties was experiencing, and the comment made at that was, 'well of course they behave like that, they have learning difficulties'. I was stunned. So was everybody else in the room, so despite tremendous steps forward there is still sometimes a tendency for some individuals and professionals to see some people with learning difficulties as being somehow apart from the rest of humanity. Somehow uncontrollable. Somehow, with this challenging behaviour which seems to be innate to their being, and the fact is we are all human. You get angry because there is a reason you are angry. You lash out because something precipitated you doing that. There is always a trigger, reason and emotion that that it is linked with.

Jan: So your approach then is trying to understand that, to try and get to the root of what that might be for the person.

Bethan: Yes, and I think often part of the problem for the person is the way they have been responded to. Over and over again I have worked with people, and they have sat and reflected themselves back to me through the eyes of the people that have cared for and worked with them.

Jan: The naughty boy, naughty girl kind of message . . .

Bethan: Yes — either that or 'I am just evil; I am ill; I have a problem; I will never get better because this is what I do — this is how I am'. I think, 'I beg your pardon!' It's like this myth is generated and taken into themselves and that can be a good part of the work itself, actually undoing, disentangling, helping the person to disentangle themselves from the myths that have been created around them. Because that is so strong. More than anything that comes across in the voices of the people that speak to me is a kind of, 'well, I thought I was a person and I thought I was here, but I can't be because nobody else thinks I am, so I can't be'.

Jan: Like a complete lack of trust in organismic being, like a total disconnection.

Bethan: That's very often been my experience. I suppose for me it's very much about trying to help that person to make a connection with themselves as a valued, caring, feeling, knowing, understanding human being. Before it then becomes possible for them to actually decide, 'OK, that's what I am — this is what I want to do with my life'. It's the recognition that, 'I have a life which is valuable and I can do something with it'. I think a lot of the stigma of how people with learning difficulties are responded to within our society is very much taken on board, in many different and subtle ways. It's seeing yourself as useless, seeing yourself as a burden, responsibility for other people — 'I make life difficult for others'. Hundreds of examples that are really people who lack a concept of themselves as being valued for who they are, and so therefore subsequently sometimes there is perhaps an inability to value other people around them.

Jan: So somehow you mean because they haven't themselves experienced being valued, then that model is how they view the world and others around them, as if there is no other possibility for them . . .

Bethan: If I hit you or kick you, I'm just hitting or kicking a mannequin because that's how you are, that's how you respond to me.

Jan: Not as a real human being who says, 'ouch — I don't like that'. So there is something about the way the language is sanitised and simplified to the point of sterility.

Bethan: And I know from years ago, my own training when I worked as a carer, it was about being professional, about keeping your emotions contained and detached. At work not allowing your personal feelings to interfere with what you are doing. I think that sometimes it got to a point where you approached work from a perspective of, 'I step through the door and leave my feelings outside', which, to a certain extent, I'm picking up on what you were saying earlier about your own experiences.

Jan: Having no way of doing it because that was the environment . . .

Bethan: I guess that is what I'm talking about — that's what that leads to — the 'leave your feelings at home' makes for that kind of atmosphere.

Jan: I think certainly one thing I have reflected on is how I felt disempowered and voiceless in the same way as the people I was trying to support — I would be trying to say, 'hang on a minute, that doesn't make sense', but it was as if I was insignificant, just a care assistant in the same way as the people I was trying to support were insignificant because they were just people with no power or authority. I think that that is something you were saying earlier on, about having a sense from your own experience of having no voice, having been disempowered and having recognised that and understanding that . . .

Bethan: I suppose for me the one thing that really sticks in my mind is someone a long time ago that I worked with who rang me to say that she had taken an overdose — she was at the time receiving psychiatric input and help. She had mild learning difficulties but was living semi-independently with one or two other people with learning difficulties, but it was a matter of supportive people popping in and checking that things were OK. She rang me about 7 o'clock in the evening, I rang the people that were responsible for her treatment and asked them to send an ambulance because she had taken an overdose. I was assured that they would get on to it and sort it out — I was met with a very sceptical kind of attitude. It was kind of like, 'oh no, not again, this happens all the time'. I thought, 'it might well happen all the time, but it needs dealing with'. I don't know why, but about an hour later I rang her back as I was concerned. I just felt something wasn't right. I had to get the girl who was living with her to take the phone over to her and by this time the girl couldn't wake her up. Eventually, with a lot of shaking and shouting, she managed to get her to speak to me on the phone. She was very slurred. I went round obviously and sorted things out. I got an ambulance myself, but I was furious. When I eventually later on rang back and spoke to the people that were at that time responsible for her care, I was again told, 'but she does this all the time, and, well, you know what it's like'. I thought, 'I don't know what it's like, actually'. To me that was the kind of — there was no value or trust of her as a person — it must have taken a lot for her to ring me, a lot for her to tell me that — that in itself involved a lot of trust. That trust was not returned in her life — generally it was a matter of her trusting others and them not trusting her. Basically it was a case of her not being believed.

Jan: The old attention-seeking view.

Bethan: Yes. They were really quite shocked when I rang back again and they realised that she wasn't crying wolf, but to me it was the willingness to take that gamble.

Jan: That they could be that willing to take the gamble.

Bethan: Yes it made me question, if I hadn't rung her back she could have died. There are no two ways about that. It made me wonder how many people are in that position. I found out later that I wasn't the first person she had called — I was the fifth or sixth down the line and she had actually been calling around for a long time and had been ignored, which made me absolutely furious and I went through the complaints procedure but didn't really get anywhere.

Jan: It's that complete devaluing of her as an individual. Also a lack of recognition that if she's doing this, there is a need not being met. How easy it is to say, 'oh, she's just crying wolf, she's just doing this again'.

Bethan: Yes, and similar things have happened a lot with people I have worked with. Another young man had a problem with his bowel, basically it wasn't functioning at all and he had Hirschsprung's disease. Again we got to this point of going to the hospital and 'yes there is an operation that he could have but he's got learning difficulties and he's had a good life, it will be very traumatic to have the operation. How would he cope with a bag? We don't think we should do it'. On that particular occasion some of my colleagues actually ended up at the hospital camping out in casualty with him, refusing to move until something was done, because basically he had been sent back, and he had been given 48 hours to live with the message that what will happen is that the bowel will perforate and he will either have toxic poisoning or he will begin to vomit and choke.

Jan: And that was it — send him home?

Bethan: Yes, he wasn't given any painkillers — he must have been in agony. And again it took tremendous pressure for anyone to act. The same young man now leads a perfectly active, happy life — he has a normal life expectancy. It took a lot of effort from a lot of people to actually get an operation

Jan: It seems from your experience that you perceive the devaluing of people with learning difficulties that they are actually brushed aside in all manners — and what you are trying to do with your work is actually value each person first.

Bethan: I think it's about environment — in many ways the devaluing is an endemic part of the culture and society we live in, it's about people being disempowered in both overt and covert ways and needing to feel generally valued, because everybody is of value. It's about challenging the status quo about taking risks, about actually getting involved, and that's what I find more often than not. Very often people want to work with people with learning difficulties, or they want to work with people that are violent, or they want to work with people who have suffered and been through trauma, but very often they are unwilling to get involved and risk confronting in a real sense their own internal assumptions and socially acquired prejudices that continue to reinforce and play a part in maintaining a 'safe', 'sanitised' distance that allows the professional to demarcate a difference and draw an invisible but impenetrable line between themselves and the people they work with. A bit like going swimming without wanting to get wet. I have been hurt many times in the process of having got involved, because I have got involved and I have lost someone, I have got involved and they have moved on and maybe not as successfully as I would have liked them to have done.

Jan: You have a willingness to accept failure, loss and perhaps imperfection.

Bethan: Yes. I think I have to take the risk of caring enough to want to get involved. Very often I find that, as far as somebody reaches back, is as far as you reach out to them. I know what I am saying here is a very simplistic logic, but very often it's the way it works. If you are willing to take a risk, get involved and to risk obviously what happens in that process of whatever you discover together, of whatever comes of that, it will have an impact on you as much as it will on them. I think sometimes when somebody has been so disempowered — when somebody is so far at the bottom of the heap — I think it takes tremendous courage for that person to even begin to be able to reach back up, to force themselves through the layers that have been imposed upon them. Therefore I think anybody working with that person has to be prepared to breach certain layers themselves and to risk feeling hurt, frustrated, angry, whatever, in the process because that is what getting involved is about.

Jan: It's as you're saying, this has to be a full-on relationship, for the person with learning difficulties to have the chance to grow within it.

Bethan: I suppose I am, yes.

Jan: On that note, thank you very much for your time.

'I just want to be normal'

James's story

By way of introduction to this section with the theme of desire for 'normality', I offer James' story, since it highlights some of the more subtle underlying themes in supporting people with learning difficulties. James's story is of a more personal nature than the rest of the relationships mentioned in this book. James is my son. After I had written this, and read his chapter to him, he was pleased to have himself included in these pages.

Like all mothers, I have been called upon to respond from many roles during my children's lives: mother, nurturer, teacher, ally, boundary-setter, facilitator of communication and so on. I bring James's story to this book because it shows the feelings of a young man with complex needs. James's learning disability is moderate, but his epilepsy is complex, and severely interrupts his life on a daily basis.

Like many parents of children with disabilities, I have had to, and still have to, battle to have my son's needs met, and in addition have been called to be his care manager during a year at home when his adult residential care placement became unsafe for him. James is not 'voiceless' in the sense that many others mentioned in this book are. James can, and does, speak up for himself. However, his very ability to speak, reason (much of the time), and verbalise his wants, needs and rights, often mean that his difficulties in understanding, rigidity in thinking, anxiety-provoking fixations, and personality changes (affected by frequent sub-clinical epileptic activity) are viewed as bad behaviour, and within his control. This view frustrates and confuses him, as he very much wants to be liked, and accepted, but cannot understand why people do not understand him. For these reasons, and the difficulties resulting from them which cause negative patterns to spiral out of control, I am often in the uncomfortable position of trying to explain my son to people, and having to encourage and support his support workers not to give up on him.

James is a young man with aspirations. He wants a job, he wants to drive, he wants money and the freedom to come and go whenever he pleases. In short, he wants what most young men of twenty-five want. James looks about the world and constantly is reminded of what he cannot have. He is aware of what there is, and what he is denied, in a way that I hear people with physical disabilities talk about. Yet James is not physically disabled.

If his learning disability were more severe he would, bizarrely, probably suffer less in that he would not constantly be aspiring for 'normality' and constantly be denied it.

Throughout his life from age five, there have been continual attempts to control his seizures with every new drug on the market. All attempts have failed in the ultimate goal for all people with epilepsy — to be seizure-free. Being seizure-free for a year allows people with epilepsy to apply for a driving licence. The world opens up.

James has never been seizure-free. He has a complex type of epilepsy with a variety of different seizure types. Some drugs reduce a certain type of seizure while not affecting other types, whilst sometimes the benefit of reducing the frequency of one type of seizure is countered by another type being exacerbated. Currently James takes high doses of three different drugs and is still liable to up to four seizures in his sleep and varying numbers and types of seizures during his waking hours.

Most of the time James manages every day by getting on with things between each seizure without complaint. On good days he is a delight to be with: funny, compassionate, creative and up for trying most things. Whilst there are areas of difficulty, he is able to receive support and use it positively to stay focused on what he has chosen or agreed to do. On badly affected days he becomes belligerent, confused, rigid, argumentative in a circular, persistent manner and completely unable to get himself together to do anything. Often he must sleep or take additional drugs to calm down the epileptic activity. With the frequency of his seizures and the effects on his mood and disposition — to say nothing of the effects of the drugs he is taking — we all recognise, apart from James, that a 'normal' job, which is what he wants, is a goal to be held whilst realistically he actually still needs 24 hour care and supervision to ensure he is actually able to live safely. This is a painful and regular dilemma.

Whilst James wants to be 'normal' he does thrive on care and support, and if it is not there becomes quite anxious. He has a degree of developmental delay, which on the positive end gives him a spontaneous and fun-loving character and on the negative side can lead to very young and demanding behaviour.

Again, those of us who love him, and the team who support him in his new home, recognise the complexities and how these prevent him from attaining the independence he so wants — and we all want for him. But James, on the whole, does not recognise the complexities. For him it is a simple matter to have a job, a flat on his own (failing his real desire to live at home with us always), and money to buy videos, video games and CDs.

Through Kith & Kids (see p. 122 ff.) we found a consultant who understood James's rare and complex type of epilepsy and it was he who was instrumental in getting James a place at St Elizabeth's School in Hertfordshire (for address see p. 30). The school specialises in educating children with severe and complex epilepsy and learning disabilities. My instinct was to keep him at home and educate him there after dreadful experiences in mainstream education had caused him to miss healthy supported opportunities to socialise with other children. Yet, I feared that keeping James at home would necessarily restrict his independence and give him fewer opportunities to find himself in the world. In a world where not only are there frequent and unpredictable changes — which James finds extraordinarily difficult to cope with — there are continual and unpredictable interruptions in the normal functioning of his brain. It is small wonder then that he seeks to be with me wherever and whenever he can, and if he could he would live with me, and spend more or less all his time with me, because I seem to provide the one predictable, sure element in his life.

For James the world was confusing and unpredictable. Due to absence seizures (these look like daydreams, but the individual is actually unable to receive or respond to any stimulus — the brain is unconscious for seconds), things, people and objects would seem to have moved position by magic — he having switched off whilst the move was made — and this frightened him.

Due to bullying in his previous school and humiliation by teachers, James learned that he was 'slow' and 'lazy' and 'stupid'. It took years at St Elizabeth's for him to find his self-esteem through encouragement and one-to-one support for learning new concepts.

We have encouraged him to go for his dreams step by step and I sometimes wonder if our approach has been more cruel than saying to him, 'you can't do that', because he really does want to be 'normal'. No matter how many times I have offered my empathic understanding for that desire, nor how many times he has cried in my arms, or slapped his own head to make it 'stay still' or I've wept quietly with him when he's sad about it — or challenged his idea of 'normal' or encouraged and affirmed all is great qualities — the bottom line is that James wants to be 'normal'. For him that means no epilepsy, not being confused and unable to understand, and finding his own words and having a job, money and freedom.

The Person-Centred Approach is not just how I practise as a therapist. When I read my first Rogers book — *On Personal Power* (1978) — I finally learned that I was not alone. Rogers put into words what I had felt and struggled with my whole life until that first reading. I was 29 and a divorced single parent raising James and his younger sister. I was working and studying for a degree in psychology. The way I had lived my life and struggled to be with my children was person-centred. Rogers spoke in that book about the threatening nature of personal power and much fell into place for me. Congruence, empathy and acceptance were the antitheses of my childhood environment. In retrospect I can see that I was displaying always-embryonic core conditions of the Person-Centred Approach which, in a hostile environment, left me vulnerable to attack, ridicule and humiliation. Somehow, despite this, I held fast to my belief that being genuine, accepting and understanding were parts of me that I could not, and would not, lose. My parenting style has certainly been the applied Person-Centred Approach.

As a result of growing up in a culture of respect, James has a very good sense of how he should be treated. Unfortunately, his ideas about his rights overshadow the other important part of social living — that other people have rights too. Our efforts at encouraging him to negotiate and compromise are ongoing.

At times James becomes overwhelmed and depressed and has needed time at home to feel those feelings and then to try to get a sense of what the difficulties are. At these times, we sit and do a 'problem page' as I do sometimes with clients who have learning difficulties or very occasionally a client without learning difficulties, overwhelmed by the endless issues and problems they have to juggle. It has always helped James to calm his head from spinning. I got the idea from asking him what he was feeling and he responded that everything was 'spinning around' in his head. On the first occasion we tried this, he and I sat at the kitchen table. He was so full of epileptic activity that he frequently blanked out momentarily and held his head in his hands and then hit his head on the table crying. Having understood that everything was spinning I got a large sheet of paper and drew a stick figure with down-turned mouth, arms up, and several large plates spinning around his head. I invited James to try to name the 'spinning' things and he began telling me all the problems he felt overwhelmed by.

We filled the page with the problems and James began to visibly calm as each problem was written. I asked him to say more about each problem and wrote down each of his words clearly so that he could not only hear he was understood, but could see it. I realised how useful this was as he was calming, but also as I knew that at times when I had heard him and understood, he had not received that validation because of epileptic interruptions. Having it all in front of him in his own words — no summarising or tidying up for grammatical correctness — helped him to see things more clearly and know I understood. He was also able to take the page with him to show, if he needed to, his care staff or social worker. It proved to be a useful way of helping him to communicate when things became too much and he might otherwise fly into a rage and attract more of the negative responses he hates.

We have used the 'problem page' idea only three or four times over the past five years, and there are some hardy perennials that appear as painful issues. His epilepsy, and fear of dying during a fit, is a realistic fear borne of reality. Ten young people James has known have died from their epilepsy since he was twelve. This fear comes up for James when his seizures are particularly frequent, and it is most often only with me he feels able to say he is frightened. His desire to be 'normal' is another regular issue and it is most important at these times of overwhelming distress for him to feel he is understood, simply and plainly — he is desperate to have a 'normal' life.

At various times, James has told me he wishes he could die and be born again 'normal' without epilepsy. The last time he came into contact with someone his own age who died during the night, most probably in seizure, it was when James had moved into his first adult residential house. Only after two weeks as a resident there, a young man, here called Colin, died. James's initial reaction was as usual — concern for everyone else — 'I didn't know him, Mum, but the staff did, so I gave her a hug'. The first of our problem pages came, when a few weeks later James became depressed and needed to be at home. After some days we tried the 'problem page' idea.

I knew what was going on for him, but waited until it came out one evening when he said, 'Mum, would you be upset if I died?' 'Of course I would', I responded. He then talked about having been to Colin's funeral and felt so 'upset for his mum'. He went on, 'I wouldn't mind dying but I'd be upset, because I wouldn't be there to give you [me] a hug'. These deep and painful issues rarely face a young man, then aged nineteen, but James was working it out in one of his amazingly philosophical ways. Beneath the spinning and as the epileptic activity subsided for a while, he reached his wonderful inspiring self.

We shed tears together in our shared unspoken knowledge that James and I might be parted prematurely as Colin and his mother were. And afterwards we went to get ice cream from the shop. Taller than me by then, James flung a hefty arm around my shoulder and said, 'Thanks for listening, Mum'.

James, and many like him, does not fit into the world of learning disabilities, but neither is he able to fit into the world of 'able' without continual support, empathy, and acceptance. Because of staff shortages and other lacks of resources in the care field, people who are more able are expected to get on with things alone, or need less than those who have more severe learning disabilities. James has certainly experienced anger from support workers who find his demands and needs exhausting, and expect him to manage his needs and behaviour far more than he is able. It is difficult to balance the needs of those who cannot ask for them along with those who can, without assuming the latter are being wilfully 'demanding', 'selfish' or 'attention-seeking'. Frustration escalates all round. A person-centred approach requires resources, including more staff, as well as opportunities for those staff to deepen their understanding and empathy for the people they are supporting. In an environment where people are met as individuals, development is possible, rather than simply caring for or managing. People like James are vulnerable because complex needs are often very difficult to recognise and respond to. In the care field, it is much easier to know how to respond when people's needs are clear too.

James articulates very clearly what so many with complex learning difficulties communicate. 'Normal', for them, holds the possibilities they know they are denied. 'Normal' looks easy and fun, and the 'normal' fantasy includes the possibility for autonomy. Even when the concept of 'normal' is not directly mentioned, there is a sadness and frustration, as well as confusion about why the 'normal' world seems an exclusive club. When I stand in James's shoes I know that my occasional attempts at challenging the idea that there is any such thing as 'normal' are futile. He, and others with complex needs, knows the reality. They are denied access — they are forced to live on the border of able and disabled. Limited though they may be cognitively or developmentally, they do know that, and therein lies a major source of their sadness.

It behoves all of us who claim to be capable of living a 'normal' life to welcome, encourage and support all people, whatever their degree of disability. We have much to learn from those who, like James, clamber over obstacles just to get started every day, and keep on going despite endless interruptions to their abilities and consciousness.

St Elizbeth's School and Centre
Much Hadham
Hertfordshire
SG10 6EW
01279 843451

'No-one ever listens'
Patrick's story

The first time I met Patrick was at the college of further education where he attended a course for people with severe learning disabilities. I was asked to spend time with him as he was in an extremely agitated and upset state.

It took a while to find an empty room and I pulled two chairs close together and invited him to sit with me. Patrick had cerebral palsy but was able to stand unaided and he stood tearing at his hair and crying. His speech was quite severely affected by his cerebral palsy and was even more difficult to understand while he was upset.

The best I could do was let him know that I was there and that I did want to understand what was making him so upset. I saw Patrick several times in this phase of our work together. Years later I saw him again for twelve more focused sessions.

Over the initial sessions I gradually listened to Patrick's story. A man in his thirties he had been placed in a hospital for the 'retarded and insane', he told me, from when he was a very young child. He knew that it was because he was unacceptable to his parents, and yet he accepted this. As a teenager he had been moved to a smaller institution where he felt very unhappy. He wanted freedom and money and felt that the manager of the institution was keeping the patients' money and letting them have very small amounts of what they were entitled to. He complained and was threatened with going back to the hospital. Things were difficult for all the residents, he said, but one young woman confided the worst to him. She told him that she was being forced to have sex with the manager. Patrick vowed to protect her, and went with her to the manager to tell him never to do that again. Subsequently Patrick was forced to witness the manager raping the young woman and then had to endure being raped himself.

Patrick's tears and hair-tearing, drawing blood on his head and face, accompanied the telling of his awful experiences. I worked with Patrick early in my counselling experience and I did my best to understand and support him. I sometimes wonder if I might have helped him more with my later knowledge and understanding of the legacy of abuse. It was painful to allow myself to enter his understanding of his world. He had no-one safe to talk to, and had to endure several years of abuse along with threats of going back to hospital if he made any fuss.

Like many people with severe cerebral palsy, Patrick had never received education, the assumption being that his speech could not be understood and he was physically so impaired, then he *must* be learning-disabled too. As a result of lack of education he would, like others, perform as predicted. And like many with speech and communication difficulties he relied on others to actually spend time tuning into his particular speech patterns. When I had tuned into his draining efforts to articulate his words, I realised that his choice of words, and how he created the sentences to express himself, were poetic and beautiful. But to hear the poetry I had to listen carefully to each struggled syllable and put it together with the others, just to gather together the words he was saying.

Patrick was experiencing flashbacks and nightmares due to his experiences of abuse. He would try to tell staff in the new home where he lived, but they always told him to 'forget that, it's past'. 'No-one ever listens', he wept to me one day.

He felt guilty for telling the abusive manager that he knew what he was doing to the young woman, because it seemed so much worse for her after that. He felt frustrated and angry that he hadn't been able to stop his own abuse. He was angry that he needed physical care and support because it trapped him.

Patrick told me he'd once gone out for the evening from the abusive institution and had tried to tell a policeman what had happened. The policeman took him back and nothing changed. I wonder if the policeman didn't understand Patrick's speech or simply didn't believe him.

The manager had moved to a different home after some years of abusing Patrick and the new manager allowed the residents more of their allowances. Patrick had tried to tell about the abuse but no-one wanted to hear it. When he moved recently to his current home, no-one there would listen either, he felt. For Patrick the most important thing was to be able to say what had happened to him and to have his experiences acknowledged. That I could do.

Sometimes he would be triggered into flashbacks or intrusive thoughts and imagery, common problems for people who've experienced abuse (Sanderson, 1995). He just wanted someone to listen to him. Through being listened to he would come back to himself and made contact with his anger about what had happened to him.

After leaving the college, some years later I received a call from Patrick's social worker asking me to see him again. We agreed to twelve sessions.

Patrick came with his wife and we worked on some sexual issues – both needed support in developing their relationship. He now wanted to sue the man who'd repeatedly raped him, but again 'no-one would listen'. He also wanted to trace his family. He felt people were not interested and didn't want him to talk about it.

During the course of our work I observed that he wanted me to be his advocate. Actually, I suggested to him that he wanted me to do more than listen — he needed practical help. He agreed. I explained again the 'boundaried' relationship we had, and offered to make contact on his behalf with an advocacy service. That is how we ended our work, with Patrick clear about what he really wanted and also knowing that he could have someone whose role it was to listen and support him in taking back some power in his life.

Creative groupwork: towards self-advocacy
by
Vic Forrest

Vic Forrest has worked with people with learning difficulties for over twenty years. In 1993 he completed a Diploma in Client-Centred Counselling, Psychotherapy and Applications of the Person-Centred Approach. Vic undertook this training to help him become clearer about how to support people with learning difficulties to do what they want. He is currently working towards a PhD at the Centre for Citizen Participation in Brunel University, while supporting people with learning difficulties to undertake the research of their choosing.

Introduction

People with severe learning difficulties needing support can find themselves referred to various educational or 'improving' institutions. Those attending day centres, colleges and charitable schemes, etc., are often directed towards certain goals that others may have for them. They may not, for example, have chosen to be part of a group that is being taught specific skills or have decided to be in any sort of learning situation whatsoever. People with severe learning difficulties may be afforded a limited amount of choice over many other day-to-day aspects of their own lives, if indeed they are offered any choices at all (Wertheimer, 1996).

I became interested in Person-Centred practice during a time when supporting people with severe learning difficulties to access visual art methods was part of my weekly workload. Initially I was aiming to understand and develop, often in conjunction with other supporters or group facilitators, conditions that would maximise the degree of choice and control that could be made available to participants within creative groups. This chapter discusses aspects of a particular way of facilitating Person-Centred creative groupwork that I have been involved in developing and practising and moves on to describe the development and implementation of an approach to supporting self-advocacy within the confines of a time-limited group or session.

One of the main values of the practices that are described in this chapter is that, within the limitations of the particular sessions that are mentioned, they support people with severe learning difficulties to choose or direct how they spend their time. They also allow people who are supporting people with severe learning difficulties to find out more about the preferences of the people they are working with, and to develop ways of supporting people with severe learning difficulties to get what they are indicating or directly communicating that they want. The practices described in this chapter can be applied within any environment that aims to support groups of people with severe learning difficulties, where there are enough workers, facilities and space to carry out the activities that are discussed.

Visual art and people with severe learning difficulties: what is it?
Bearing in mind the meaning of the term 'Person-Centred' as defined by Rogers (1951), it seems reasonable to state that the facilitator of a Person-Centred visual art group for people with severe learning difficulties (who have chosen to participate in it) aims to support the self-directed creative responses of others. Although the materials that are available will to some extent influence the appearance of the work, what the finished result actually is will depend very much, or completely, upon how the person, or group of people with severe learning difficulties, responds to those materials. So the art that is the end-product of this process is, in short, designed or conceived by group participants and not the facilitator. That is not to infer that participants will necessarily conceptualise what they are going to create prior to engaging with the materials, but to make clear that the finished result is a record of the self-directed responses of group participants to a range of art materials and implements.

Not being in control of the finished result can be a challenging position to stay in for people who are working with people with severe learning difficulties. The creative group facilitator may be working in an institution that is managed or staffed by people who have strong views on what art should or should not look like, and who disapprove of Person-Centred working methods. Indeed, the basic concept of supporting people to be in control of what they are choosing to do, or not do as the case may be, can be difficult to grasp for people who are used to 'motivating' or directing people with learning difficulties to undertake tasks that they or their managers perceive as being beneficial for them in some way. Even without the pressure of external judgement the facilitator may be tempted, as I have mistakenly been at times in the past, to judge the success of the creative groupwork on how the finished work matches up to her or his own idea of what an attractive or clever piece of work is.

Mess?

'Mess' and 'messy' are words that are rarely used in a positive context within a 'professional' environment. The word 'mess' can be used to describe the physical presence of unwanted or misplaced substances or materials, i.e. a lot of paint in a person's hair or on their skin, or used to describe a chaotic or, in relation to the work that this chapter describes, what can seem to be a chaotic, process. The 'messiest' situations can appear to be occurring when working with people who have intensive support needs.

I have had quite a lot of experience of facilitating groups that contain numbers of support staff who are there to enable service users to participate in the creative session. Some support staff can have strong emotional reactions to situations where they are aiming or expected to aim towards following the lead of people with severe learning difficulties. This is especially the case when there is paint and glue around and group participants are responding in very different ways to the situation, i.e. some people are getting lots of paint on their hands and arms and other people are apparently doing nothing. However, using paint as an example I would like to write something in praise of offering some 'messy' materials. Paint can be used to make dramatic and arresting marks with a relatively small or 'uncontrolled' gesture. A person that doesn't move towards a pencil, a felt-tipped pen or piece of gummed paper who may not be able to grasp them without a lot of 'support', and who may see no point in touching them anyway, may revel in getting their hands in a generous selection of paints, being absorbed and fascinated by their intervention with the materials and motivated to make something visual occur.

Situations like the one that has just been described can leave support staff very edgy and uncomfortable and the group facilitator feeling responsible for the distress of the support staff. This can have a knock-on effect on the people with severe learning difficulties involved in the session. It is important to develop strategies that enable people with severe learning difficulties, support staff and group facilitators to feel as comfortable as possible within the session.

Some practical physical considerations

Creative groupwork sessions for people with severe learning difficulties will inevitably be less tense and risky if the materials used in the session are non-toxic. While in my opinion it would be unwise not to discourage someone from actively eating non-toxic art materials (boundaries will be discussed later in this chapter), if all the materials used are non-toxic this eliminates the risk of people with learning difficulties being poisoned, and makes room for support staff to feel more relaxed about allowing people with severe learning difficulties to freely explore and react to the materials used.

It can also be very helpful if the art materials that are used are washable and fairly easy to remove from people's skin and clothing as well as the surrounding environment. All the people involved in the art session including facilitators and support workers will probably feel more comfortable ultimately if they are wearing old clothes and/or protective clothes and aprons. It makes for a much more relaxed session and eliminates or minimises the need for the people without learning difficulties to control some people's movements in order to protect their own clothes and those of people with learning difficulties. Carpets, upholstery and other surfaces that are difficult to wash can be moved out of the way or protected if possible. Ideally it is best to do 'messy' art activities away from such materials but this is not always possible. I have also found it useful to cover tabletops or floors with a large sheet of plastic as this reduces the amount of time it takes to clean up after a session.

It is important to build in a realistic amount of cleaning-up time after a session and ensure that the way that this will be implemented has been discussed with support staff and service users wherever possible. It is essential that service users who will need to be supported by others to clean themselves or cleaned by a supporter are not rushed through this process or treated brusquely. The time spent cleaning up and in particular the time when people with severe learning difficulties are either washing themselves or being washed can be a relaxing and pleasant experience. Soothing music can be played to support and perhaps further encourage gentle and subtle communication between support workers and people with severe learning difficulties engaging in what can be a relatively intimate and physically interactive part of the session.

'What are we doing?'

It is important that, in addition to the group facilitator, any support workers who are working in conjunction with her or him are clear about what their role is in supporting the unpredictable situation that is Person-Centred creative groupwork. The facilitator can begin the process of defining their role by explaining some of the benefits of person-centred ways of working. They may, for example, want to raise some of the following points:

• Person-Centred creative groups can create opportunities for participants to make informed choices and to develop their ability to make and communicate their decisions.

• Person-Centred ways of working can give the support workers and group facilitator/s opportunities to further develop the skills they have around being sensitive to what group members are conveying and to further understanding group members' preferences, interests and abilities, both interpersonally and in relation to the choice of activities that are on offer.

• People with severe learning difficulties can, because of past experience, often lack confidence (Sinason, 1992) and may be used to waiting to find out what is required of them rather than initiating a move of some sort. This way of working can enable service users to become more confident and interested in taking self-motivated courses of action. Some people with severe learning difficulties may have a limited range of activities they choose to actively initiate. Person-Centred ways of working give people opportunities to safely discover different activities and their own self-motivated ways of responding to a situation.

• Ultimately, Person-Centred ways of working enable people with severe learning difficulties to be in control of what they are doing and, perhaps even more importantly, what is being done to them.

The facilitator may also choose to discuss how important it is for the supporters to pay attention to the service user or users they are supporting, and to respond to any attempts that they are making to communicate with them or other people within the group, as well as any interest they are showing in materials or equipment. The facilitator can also encourage discussions to take place around supporting people with severe learning difficulties to make informed choices. It is important that support workers fully understand that they do not have to actively 'motivate' or direct the person with learning difficulties and that it is acceptable for both the person with learning difficulties and themselves not to be engaged in some creative task or other as the art choices are only an option.

In my experience the support staff who are unfamiliar with this way of working can readily adopt this approach to supporting people with learning difficulties, allowing and actively supporting the person with learning difficulties to be in control while engaging in an attentive and responsive relationship with them. Others can find this approach very difficult to grasp and not know how to behave, or continue behaving in an overtly controlling manner. They may feel that their 'normal' working methods are being undermined, and uncomfortable with accepting that there are times when they will be required to do nothing. This approach requires people to open up and utilise their capacity to empathise with people with learning difficulties and develop their ability for feeling what can be a painful truth: that people with severe learning difficulties are no less feeling and valuable human beings than anyone else. I have found it useful to gently direct those support staff that continue to behave in overtly controlling or directive ways with service users, for example by telling them that it goes against the aims of the session to tell people with learning difficulties what to do. It can also be useful to model ways of being with specific group participants.

Materials

One aspect of supporting people with severe learning difficulties to have the option of participating in a Person-Centred creative art group is to aim to maximise the amount of choice and flexibility that is available to them. A starting point for a discussion on the above subject could be what materials and implements or tools are made available to people with severe learning difficulties participating in the creative session. An important factor within such a discussion is how materials can be used in conjunction with each other. The following, by no means exhaustive, list is an example of just some of the materials, implements and tools that in my experience can, broadly speaking, be used in conjunction with each other: chalk, oil pastels, wax crayons, water-based inks, water based paints, graphite sticks, pencils, coloured pencils, PVA glue, felt-tip pens, cartridge paper, tissue paper, crepe paper, metallic and patterned papers, sticky-backed papers, fabrics, i.e. felt, net, cotton, silk etc., wool, string, glitter, polystyrene, straws, sponges for printing or sticking down, objects that can be dipped in paint and used for printing shapes, i.e. the rims of small jars, etc., brushes, rollers, palette knives, scissors (although many people prefer to tear paper or fabric to use for collage work, etc.) and water pistols.

When offering paint as an option I have always chosen to give people with intensive support needs a range of colours that mix to form clear colours, i.e. reds, yellows, pinks, oranges and white or blues, greens, yellows and white etc. A full range of colours across the spectrum when mixed together will form muddy browns or greys. Obviously when someone is aware of the consequences of mixing colours or able to understand that the grey or brown they have produced is a consequence of two or more specific colours being mixed together I would not limit the amount of colours that were on offer. There is a possibility that perhaps part of my reason for adopting this limitation is my own fear of the reactions of the support staff and the managers of the various venues I have worked in to what would often inevitably be produced, i.e. a series of muddy, dark paintings, where distinctions between different surface areas would be difficult to discern to both the person who was viewing the completed work and the person or persons with learning difficulties who were engaged in the process of working on it. However, I feel that the major determinant in the decision I have made is the wish to enable people with learning difficulties who are participating in the session to be able to make paintings that contain an array of colours and have distinctly different surface areas. As people can often work over a period of weeks or months on a single piece of work they can eventually get to use the full spectrum of colours, while building up layers of colours. Other facilitators could choose not to set up this particular restriction and even argue that this practice is unnecessarily controlling.

Making art

As far as the facilitator of the Person-Centred creative group is concerned there are no 'right' or 'wrong' ways for participants to construct their work. The way a participant decides to respond within the boundaries of the session is very much up to them. However, when working with a new group of people and particularly those with severe or 'profound' learning difficulties who have little or no understanding of language, it is important to start from a position that maximises the potential of all the participants to successfully interact with the materials (and their supporters and each other if they so choose) and create something on their own terms.

The following practical strategy is by no means offered as *the* way to set up the environment for a new group. Rather, it is one example of an approach that has been effective for certain groups of people with 'severe' or 'profound' learning difficulties that I have supported. I myself have addressed the 'setting up' of the working environment of a new group in a variety of different ways that have been influenced, for example, by the nature of the group, the number of support staff, the availability of particular materials, the time span of the project, what is known about the interests of the group participants, and the restrictions of the working environment. However, in my experience, it is sometimes useful to be given a practical example of one response to a particular theoretical concept, and that is all this is.

I have found it useful on several occasions to firmly attach a large white cotton bed sheet to a large table, or a group of smaller tables pushed together, and put a lot of materials and implements in the centre of the table, ideally within the reach of all of the group participants. People can reach for what they want or be offered choices based around what they might be showing interest in by looking at or touching. The positive aspect of using a cotton sheet is that people cannot easily accidentally wear a hole through it or tear it. If someone chooses to work on a piece of paper they can put one on top of the sheet. However, if someone repeatedly drenches the same area with layers of paint that they have applied with their hand in, for example, a strong snatching movement, as a group participant I once worked with did, a sheet will withstand this and hold up to being worked upon session after session.

Over time both the group participants and their supporters or facilitators can become more aware of what participants are interested in and the nature of the particular support that individuals want in order to create their own work. Also the interests and motivation of participants will become clearer. In short, what is made available to specific participants both in terms of the materials and implements that are at hand, and the nature of the support they receive, will vary as participants are supported to follow their particular line of interest. People's work can, over time, become increasingly sophisticated and unique in approach. Work can be an individual or group activity, large or small or even a combination of both, i.e. small individual pieces of work forming an integral part of a larger construction. It all depends upon the individuals and how they respond within any given group.

While I have supported people with severe learning difficulties to work on reliefs or three-dimensional pieces, it is important to acknowledge that many traditional three-dimensional approaches require that complex technical strategies be applied in response to structural dilemmas, and as the facilitator aims to support people to be in control of the direction of their own creative responses to materials, three-dimensional options can often only occur if structural complications are not present. For example, it can be really difficult to make a large structure that stands up and doesn't collapse under its own weight.

The following account of work developed by a woman within a person-centred creative group for people with severe learning difficulties I facilitated is a good example of three-dimensional work that did not present a structural problem for its creator. Over a period of time this group participant built up heaps of broken polystyrene pieces held in place with PVA glue. Structurally all this involved was her dipping the pieces of polystyrene in glue and placing them in a pile. Also she chose to mix paint in with the glue and to paint the surface of her creation. Over time she created brightly coloured mounds. Each time this particular group participant came back to the work the glue had hardened, enabling her to build the mounds taller.

Towards self-advocacy

While facilitating creative art groups for people with severe learning difficulties I found myself growing increasingly interested in ways of supporting people with learning difficulties to explore their interests on their own terms. In addition to the visual art groups I was involved in supporting, I had started working with musicians and drama and dance/movement therapists in multimedia sessions that aimed to maximise the choice of opportunities available, within a session, to children with severe learning difficulties and challenging needs, and I had become involved in an established multimedia creative group for adults with severe learning difficulties. I was also working for a People First organisation as a supporter of various 'talking' self-advocacy groups and committees for adults with learning difficulties, that were working on changing the circumstances for people with learning difficulties outside of the group.

The above groups and their participants as well as the people who supported and/or developed or initiated them influenced the direction I took when aiming to develop a self-advocacy group for people with severe learning difficulties who were users of an intensive support unit. In addition, the Severe Learning Difficulties Self-advocacy Development Group, where I subsequently worked in conjunction with a People First organisation and their supporters and associates to explore the issue of self-advocacy in relation to people with severe learning difficulties, provided the support and stimulation to carry on developing and clarifying the form of self-advocacy group support for people with severe learning difficulties that is described in this chapter.

It is important to mention that the knowledge of the group participant's key workers and support staff was utilised in the development of the self-advocacy group. I found that they knew a great deal about the way that the people with severe learning difficulties they supported communicated their needs and interests, and that they were, in the main, concerned about and committed to the idea of supporting the service users they worked with to define the activities they engaged in within the new self-advocacy group. I met with all of them to find out what they knew and what their views were. The quality of the support we were able to offer was informed by their collective expertise.

A way of working that support and key workers agreed with and felt par of was developed. This was particularly important, as it would not have been possible for the participants with severe learning difficulties to become as involved as they did within the sessions without their committed support. Also, without the understanding and willing involvement of support staff and key workers, information that came out of the sessions about participants' interests, etc. could not be acted upon within other sessions that took place in the centre. Support staff and key workers also kept us well-informed about what group participants were showing interest in within other groups and what significant events had occurred within the lives of group participants who were unable to tell us themselves.

Self-advocacy support for people with severe learning difficulties remains comparatively underdeveloped, as historically the self-advocacy movement has largely involved the participation of people with learning difficulties who are comparatively articulate, and excluded many people with more severe learning difficulties and or challenging needs (Walmsley and Downer, 1997). Traditionally self-advocacy groups involve people sitting together and discussing issues. This way of being is not an option for many people who are defined as having severe learning difficulties and even today very little has been written about how to support this particular grouping of people to participate in self-advocacy processes.

Self-advocacy in an intensive support unit

While working closely with staff and key workers within the intensive support unit where the structure of the first self-advocacy group for people with severe learning difficulties that I was involved in were developed, the following points were accepted before the group ever began to meet (upon reflection it would have been a good idea to have invited advisors with learning difficulties from People First to these initial discussions):

- People who use the service have the right to maximum control over their own life, and the service that is there for them.
- Self-advocacy should be supported throughout the entire centre, and attention not just be paid to its support during the time when the self-advocacy group was occurring, i.e. two hours a week.
- Clear and effective communication between the staff and the person/s facilitating the self-advocacy group is essential.
- We need to think carefully about how we interact with service users. We want to support them, not direct them.
- We need to create a relaxed environment in which service users can interact with each other and with a range of materials and activities.
- It is important that group participants feel safe to try things.
- It is important that people with severe learning difficulties are controlling what is happening within the self-advocacy group, not the support staff or facilitator.
- People with severe learning difficulties are used to other people controlling them. We have to actively work against this.
- We will demonstrate or model activities but not direct the group participants to undertake any activities.
- We will provide a range of activities, i.e. art, musical instruments, tapes, books and magazines, mirrors, food, drink and anything else that we think people would like to have in there. Some people have very specific interests (e.g. one person is interested in makeup).
- If someone shows an interest in something we will try and support them

to achieve what they want, i.e. if a service user walks up to a cup and touches it and then seems unconfident or unsure around how to proceed, we will try and find out if they want a drink and if so what particular drink and then we will support them to get the drink that they want.

- We will try and ensure that all the activities and materials are accessible and always in the same place so that service users can help themselves (the centre ordered open-plan shelving in order to achieve this aim).
- We will use multicultural books magazines and tapes.
- We will be supportive of group participants' communication with each other and us. We will make empathic responses to this communication.
- We will not tell people what to do and only assume control or say no if someone was about to get hurt (later this was revised and will be discussed on the section on boundaries).
- We can teach skills only when someone is showing or has shown an interest in learning about them, i.e. when someone is holding a paintbrush and asking directly for help, or appearing to be trying to convey they want help non-verbally, i.e. holding a paintbrush and looking at us as though they want us to help them.
- We are supportive of self-motivated activity and communication.
- The group participants are free to do what they want at any given time. This includes leaving the session (this is very important as none of the participants have agreed to stay for two hours or appear to understand the concept of 'an hour').

Boundaries

At first, as the group facilitator of a *self-advocacy* group for people with severe learning difficulties, I did not see it as my place to be involved in the setting of any boundaries upon the behaviour of group participants. Upon later reflection (and certainly by the time a second self-advocacy group for people with severe learning difficulties was developed) I decided that by adopting this position I was avoiding the issue of addressing the boundaries that were being set for service users anyway, often apparently at random, by support staff and service managers. These boundaries could be formal (where all staff had been directed by a service manager or a psychologist, for example, to respond in a certain way to the behaviour of specific individuals) or much more commonly, informal, i.e. the differing individual responses from support staff towards the behaviour of group participants that they perceived as being challenging. In addition, by not addressing the issue of boundaries both myself and support staff, working within the self-advocacy group, were also not openly acknowledging the existence of our own personal boundaries that we were not allowing service users to overstep.

In many self-advocacy groups the participants are able to communicate in ways that enable them to define the boundaries or 'ground rules' of the group. This is not always possible for groups of people who are defined as having severe learning difficulties, as often significant numbers of group participants are not able to communicate a great deal, if anything, verbally. In addition, within this particular grouping of people there are sometimes those who can overstep the boundaries of others in a physical way, i.e. by hitting or very roughly grabbing other people, etc., and it is important that attention is paid to the well-being of all group participants.

The people I co-worked with supporting the group and myself chose not to say 'no' to group participants. We did this in order to further support people with learning difficulties to make moves that were neither criticised or directed by us. We also thought that by adopting this approach we would make it easier for people with learning difficulties to feel safer around saying 'no' to us in whatever ways they chose to, e.g. by pushing a hand away, moving to another part of the room, or just by looking uncomfortable and ill-at-ease with an intervention of ours. Obviously if any of us had seen someone on the other side of the room attempting, for example, to hit someone over the head with a heavy object we could drop this rule and shout 'no' at the top of our voices if it would prevent the violent act from occurring, but excluding circumstances like this, which were virtually nonexistent in the particular groups I worked in, we stuck to this rule. We saw it as our responsibility to provide a safe and flexible environment that allowed for the maximum amount of self-directed responses from the people with severe learning difficulties.

When subsequent discussions around boundaries led to us defining and consciously implementing boundaries we never lost sight of this original aim. We agreed that we would start from a position of no rules or boundaries, excepting that we would do whatever was reasonably necessary to prevent group participants being hurt or intimidated by others, and then together add, if necessary, the absolute minimum amount of ground rules for service users. We discussed together with service staff involved in the group, and on some occasions with service managers, every single situation where we may be required to intervene, and how we could least disempower the service user during our intervention.

The ground rules or boundaries were comparatively easy to agree upon when we were unanimous in believing that there was a need to react directively to the situation. For example in the second self-advocacy group one of the women group participants sometimes chose to remove her clothes during the group, especially if the weather was warm. We were working in a room that had windows that overlooked a busy shopping centre and apart from any other consideration that we may have needed to address in relation to this dilemma we were aware that the large numbers of people walking past the windows would be able to see the woman naked if we left the situation unchecked. Everyone agreed that whenever this situation occurred one of the female support workers, while explaining the reason for intervening, should gently and with good humour calmly cover the woman's nakedness and try and encourage her to put her clothes back on. Other situations were not so easy to agree upon. It took us a longer period of time to discuss and decide how to react to situations when opinions around whether to respond directively or not were divided. Adopting this approach to the setting of boundaries ensured that in reality there were fewer rules that were defined by us as group supporters, and that any directive interventions we initiated were carried out in the least disempowering ways that we were able to collectively think of. It is important to add that, on occasion, issues around the setting of specific boundaries were also discussed within the Severe Learning Difficulties Self-advocacy Development Group.

We also discussed our personal boundaries and the balance we needed to strike between allowing group participants to communicate with us, as they wanted to, and extracting ourselves or disengaging from particular forms of communication we didn't like. Some of us were more comfortable than others around, for example, being touched or hugged or getting the saliva of certain group participants on us. While we agreed that it would be helpful to support the ways that group participants chose to communicate wherever possible, we recognised the importance of being aware of our own limits and the ways we would express these to group participants. It was important that we owned our feelings and reactions and when necessary were openly congruent about them. So, for example, if a group supporter was being squeezed harder than they were comfortable with, rather than blaming the person who was squeezing them they could explain that they realised the person wanted to hug them but they were getting hurt by the hug and that is why they were stepping back on this particular occasion from the person. This particular form of response was also used on any occasions when a group participant was behaving in an apparently aggressive or physically rough manner. We aimed to empathise with the distress that often appeared to accompany the aggressive behaviour while openly acknowledging that, for example, being spat at was unpleasant for us, etc. If it seemed like the person was really guarding their space we kept back and gave them the room they needed. Although I have discussed some problematic situations that could arise within the self-advocacy groups, generally the groups seemed to be both relaxed and interesting for service users and group supporters alike.

Influences on the direction of practice

While being involved in the development and support of the groups that are discussed in this chapter I was, at times, called upon to justify the way I was choosing to work to employers, co-workers and funders. Also, I have sometimes noticed or been told that the ways of working I have chosen to be involved in have been seen as incompatible with 'programmes' of 'support' or 'education' that various individuals or teams of professionals have been adhering to. It has been important to be able to find a way through the maze of theoretical perspectives that can impact on the lives of people with learning difficulties and construct arguments for an approach that supports people with learning difficulties to be in control of their own agenda. This process has often been very rewarding as certain political and theoretical perspectives have challenged and enriched my understanding of how best to support people with learning difficulties. Understanding other perspectives has enabled me to further comprehend why it has often been so difficult to get permission to work in ways that aim to afford people with learning difficulties control within their own lives. Bearing this in mind I have selected the following information to be included on this brief section on key theoretical and political perspectives, and how they relate to self-advocacy and the Person-Centred Approach.

Person-Centred ways of working or aspects of the Person-Centred Approach can be entirely consistent with ways of supporting self-advocacy. Brechin and Swain (1988) have commented on this issue. However, although Rogers' has written about the broader political or emancipatory element of the approach he developed (Rogers, 1978) it seems important to state that Rogers Person- Centred Approach is fundamentally therapeutic in as much as the aim is to facilitate personal growth. Self-advocacy on the other hand has a history of being concerned with addressing civil rights issues and the oppression of people with learning difficulties (Williams and Shoultz, 1982), although in my experience this political aspect of self-advocacy can be denied by some service providers, who choose to interpret self-advocacy solely as a process that enables people with learning difficulties to develop interpersonal skills.

In recent years many key players within the self-advocacy movement have assimilated the social model of disability into their perspective on the oppression of people with learning difficulties. The following quote explains briefly both the history of and the argument behind the social model.

The social model of disability . . . pioneered by the radical network union of the physically impaired against segregation in the early 70s, and given academic credibility by the work of Vic Finkelstein (1980) and later Michael Oliver (1990) . . . challenges the traditional view of disability as a medical tragedy, and replaces it with a view of disability as a social oppression. In sociological terms this is about arguing that disability is socially constructed not biologically determined. (Shakespeare et al., 1996, p. 2)

However, within the majority of services for people with learning difficulties the focus is firmly on 'improving' the person with learning difficulties who is seen as flawed. Their position in society and the responses of others towards them is rarely addressed. This way of perceiving the situation has been called the 'individual model of disability' by Oliver, who has summarised the situation in the following way:

Firstly, it locates the 'problem' of disability within the individual and secondly it sees the causes of this problem as stemming from the functional limitations or psychological losses which are assumed to arise from disability. These two points are underpinned by what might be called 'the personal tragedy theory of disability' which suggests that disability is some terrible chance event which occurs at random to unfortunate individuals. (Oliver, 1996, p. 32)

Goodley (2000) has discussed, in detail, the social model of disability in relation to self-advocacy and people with learning difficulties.

The concept of 'normalisation' has greatly influenced and to some extent continues to influence the nature of the support that is offered by the majority of services for people with learning difficulties (McCarthy, 1999). The original definition of 'normalisation' by Nirje is the most positive. This interpretation of normalisation is compatible with self-advocacy and the Person-Centred Approach. However a different interpretation of normalisation by Wolfensberger, that is not compatible with either the Person-Centred Approach and self-advocacy, has been at least, if not more, influential than Nirje's. The following quote outlines the differences in the two approaches:

The original concept of Normalisation as articulated by Nirje . . . is really quite simple: mentally handicapped and other handicapped people should be given the opportunity to live a life as similar in nature as possible to that of others, with similar rights and responsibilities. Just as (within certain limits which vary from society to society) a 'normal' individual may engage in unpopular, nonconformist or even 'deviant' behaviours, the normalisation principle implies that the same right should apply to mentally handicapped people. Normalisation emphasises clearly respect for the individual and his or her right to be different. As Dybwad (1982) has indicated in his own critique of Wolfenberger, it is normal to be different.
Wolfensberger (1972, 1980a), on the contrary, interprets normalisation as specifying various standards of behaviour to which a mentally handicapped person must conform. He speaks openly of 'normalizing' people through 'eliciting, shaping, and maintaining normative skills and habits' (Wolfensberger, 1972, p. 32; 1980a, p. 17) or even through the use of force: 'Normalizing measures can be offered in some circumstances, and imposed in others' (Wolfensberger, 1972, p. 32, p. 28, italics in original) . . .' (Perrin and Nirje, 1989, p. 224).

Within services the concept of independence is often presented as an aim for service users. Staff can interpret independence as being able to deal with a task or situation with less or no support and aim towards this goal. They may spend time directing people with learning difficulties to learn a task, regardless of whether the people with learning difficulties are interested in learning it or not. As one commentator has put it: 'The non-disabled world uses the term in a specific ideological context; it means both physical and emotional autonomy and the focus is on the individual's ability to achieve this autonomy' (Morris, 1991, p. 139). Many policies and good practice guidelines mention the importance of people with learning difficulties being 'independent' but do not define the meaning of the word, for example the Government's new white paper on services for people with learning difficulties, Valuing People (Department of Health, 2001).

The following quote illustrates a redefined meaning of the word 'independence' developed by people involved in the Independent Living Movement: 'we use the word in a practical and common-sense way to mean simply being able to achieve our goals. The point is that independent people have control over their lives, not that they perform every task themselves' (Brisden, quoted in Morris, 1991, p. 140). Interdependence is an essential component of human existence. Barnes, writing on the subject of empowerment in relation to people with learning difficulties and their families, has developed this point:

> It is at best unhelpful, at worst damaging, to pose dependence and independence as dichotomies with one bad, the other good. It is also both inaccurate and unhelpful to assume that an individual always occupies one position in relation to others within their family or in other relationships. Empowerment needs to be understood as relating to the nature and quality of people's relationships with others, rather than as a feature of unconnected individualism (1997, p. 73).

Describing what happened in one of the self-advocacy groups

As I have stated previously, the self-advocacy groups I am describing contained a variety of activities that people could get involved with if they chose to. It is also important to explain that group participants could choose to *not* get involved in any of the activities that were available. Some people came up with activities or ways of spending their time that we had not considered and were supported to follow their interests. However the following is a list of some of the different activities that were available for people to choose from within the groups: art (including painting, printing, collage, drawing etc.); participating in making music (including being involved with percussion instruments, an electric organ, and a karaoke machine); listening to music (including choosing tapes to play and radio stations); massaging hands and feet and shoulders etc. (including choosing what part of the body to be massaged, what perfumed oil to use and whether to receive or give massages); using sports and games equipment (including a trampoline, balls, skittles and bean bags); using a computer with an educational games programme that was aimed at people with severe learning difficulties; making snacks and drinks; consuming snacks and drinks; using various grooming products (including makeup, nail varnish and perfume); brushing and styling hair; looking at magazines or books and dancing.

We kept records of what happened in the groups. The purpose of keeping the records was twofold. Firstly I was only able to achieve funding for the groups if I was able to demonstrate that group participants 'progressed' in some sort of way, and having records of what they chose to do and how they chose to do it was one way of demonstrating their 'achievements'. A second reason for recording the responses of group participants became more apparent as we started to document their reactions within the group. We realised that by keeping these records we were able to support people better, to get what they wanted out of the groups. For example if a person was showing a particular interest in a specific activity or appeared to enjoy or appreciate being responded to in a certain way, we could keep track of this and provide support that was specifically tailored to them, by ensuring that what appeared to interest or engage them was accessible to them on successive weeks.

We were documenting how group participants were choosing to spend their time within the group. Then we were recording if what they had chosen to do had been initiated totally by them alone, or whether they had been supported to make a decision to do something by us in some way, and how they had been supported. We were also trying, as far as was possible, to identify just what facilitated their particular responses if anything, and finally we were aiming to record anything new that group participants were choosing to do.

The following accounts (taken from the records that myself and others kept while supporting the second self-advocacy group for people with severe learning difficulties) of how group participants responded within one particular session give some idea of how the groups could be used. I have not identified individual support workers or myself in this section, choosing instead, for ease of reading, to use the term 'a supporter' to cover all of us. However I have given the service users false names to differentiate between them while maintaining confidentiality:

Dave chose to spend the entire session making art. He had asked to paint and spent about half of the session using a brush. Then he decided to make printed marks across his paper by dipping sponges and the rims of jars in two colours of paint. When it ran out he asked for more of the blue paint that he had chosen, and when he had decided that a picture was finished he requested that a supporter should deal with the wet object by saying 'make it dry'.

Mike spent the first half of the session flicking through a particular book. He had been offered several alternatives and was very clear about wanting to look at the book he chose. At one point he got hold of a supporter's hand and placed it across his forehead as if to soothe a headache. Mike had been to see the dentist the day before and was less lively than usual during this session. During the second half of the session Mike 'played' with a large specialist activity for people with severe learning difficulties that consisted of several plastic covered foam rubber discs that fitted together on a foam rubber pole. He decided to look through the discs at people and speak through the hole while putting the disc near the ear of a supporter who was being with him and then he put his ear to the hole in the disc. The supporter spoke to Mike through the hole and this seemed to be what Mike wanted. He was obviously amused by this game he had devised. After being engaged with Mike for quite a while with this activity, the supporter thought he heard Mike say, 'go away' to him but he wasn't sure so he asked Mike 'do you want me to go away?' Mike very clearly said, 'go away' and waved his hand in a gesture that indicated that he wanted the supporter to go away. Later he approached the same supporter and made it clear that he wanted him to kick the foam rubber discs across the floor with him.

Pearl chose to do a little bit of crayoning early on in the session. She took the crayons off the table where the art materials were along with a small piece of paper and put them where she wanted them to be. Pearl, who can only use a few words, called across the room several times and seemed to be just greeting people. The people who worked full time in the intensive support unit said that Pearl does 'chat' when she is feeling good. She smiled at the people who looked at her when she did this. Later on Pearl approached the table where the bottles of massage oils and the towels were and indicated to a supporter that she wanted her hands massaging by touching her own hands in a mime of massaging. She seemed to really enjoy receiving the massage and put forward her hands and withdrew them when she wanted to. We noted that Pearl had chosen to stay in the session the entire time on this particular week. On other occasions, especially when the group was first made available to her, she spent time outside of the group in other rooms.

Ellen started the session by picking up and playing a set of bells for a short while. Then Ellen, who had chosen not to paint for several sessions and involved herself in other activities, decided to paint by grabbing hold of a bottle of paint when she sat down at the place she wanted to sit. When a supporter had helped her to get the paint out of the bottle she initiated taking her jumper off. When offered an apron by a supporter she chose to accept it (Ellen sometimes had clearly refused an apron). Ellen initiated a painting and carried on painting for three quarters of the session. She covered a piece of paper with paint and then drew round shapes with different coloured paints on the top. Then she decided to stop painting and play the set of bells again. She was making singing sounds that seemed to accompany those made by the bells. When a supporter accompanied her by making compatible or similar sounds to Ellen she looked at the supporter and maintained eye contact. The singing and eye contact was sustained for about ten minutes, until the session finished.

Wayne left the table he always chose to stay at and came over to the other side of the room to join supporters and other service users at the massage area. He originally asked for moisturising cream, but when shown the cream he didn't want it for some reason. He stayed at the table, so a supporter asked Wayne, who is very capable of saying no and clearly communicates when he doesn't want to do anything, if he wanted a massage. Wayne said 'yes' and pointed to his shoulders and took his sweater off. A supporter massaged Wayne's shoulders. Wayne stood up and started to put his sweater on when he wanted the massage to stop. Later on Wayne was looking at Pearl playing skittles. Pearl was smiling at Wayne. A supporter said that Wayne could come over if he wanted to and join in. Wayne came over and played skittles for a while with Pearl and the supporter.

Stephen came over and got hold of a particular supporter at the start of the session and several times during the session. He seemed to want to be with her. There was some bubble pack on the floor and he enjoyed rocking from foot to foot on it. The supporter that he had chosen to be with was supporting him to remain upright while he did this and mirroring the movement that Stephen had initiated. Stephen put his arms round the supporter on and off throughout the entire course of the session. Other people were playing music in the session and Stephen clapped about six or seven times during this time. Stephen left the room and came back of his own accord twice. We thought he might have been looking for another service user who he liked to sit next to. She was not in the intensive support unit at the time. At one point Stephen went across the room and sat on a different supporter's knee. Stephen made quite a lot of eye contact with the two supporters and smiled several times during this session.

Margaret looked 'fed up' or 'down' at the beginning of the session. A supporter read a book which Margaret was known to like and later played a Bob Marley tape that Margaret was also known to enjoy. She had been shown the book and other activities and she looked at the book (people who had spent a lot of time being with Margaret had told us that they believed Margaret communicated what she was interested in by looking at it). This was the way a supporter had deduced that Margaret might like to hear the Bob Marley tape. Margaret smiled a lot for thirty to forty minutes during this time and when the supporter sang to her along with the taped music she laughed several times. During the time that Margaret was being read to she reached out and held the supporter's hand twice. Later on Margaret looked at some pictures on the wall. The supporter followed her eyes and wheeled her closer so that she could see them better. For the last ten minutes of the session Margaret was looking fed up again. The supporter gently tried offering different choices to her but was not able to offer anything or behave in any way that interested or engaged Margaret at this particular time.

Choosing a change

The purpose of the self-advocacy groups was not specifically to support the development of skills within group participants. However I was amazed at the skills that group participants developed. The following section will outline some of the changes that occurred in four of the group participants, from the second self-advocacy group, throughout the first two years that they attended, or more accurately some of the changes in how they were choosing to act (the other participants either came to the group later or attended infrequently due to ill health). I am not intending to infer that the learning of skills by group participants is the most important element of the groups that have been described in this chapter. They are a by-product of working in this way. The most important aspect of the groups was that people were being given the opportunity to define how they spent their time and being supported to do what they wanted to do.

It is also important to note that not only participants learned within group. We supporters learned too. Some, if not all of us, learned to do the following things a little better: to listen and just be in the moment, being responsive without having to try and make something occur; to understand more about the people we were working to support, what made them tick, and both what they liked and what they were really like; and finally to feel and understand what group participants were giving us. Many times my mood was lifted by the affection, friendliness and empathy that group participants displayed to each other and to us as their supporters. Also, there was no shortage of times when one or another of the group participant's sense of humour about a particular event would provoke laughter in other people as well as themselves.

It would be irresponsible of me to suggest that the following accounts of how group participants changed their actions within one particular self-advocacy group was totally to do with what they were experiencing within the group. For example they were being supported both inside and outside of other groups by the same staff members that acted as supporters within the self-advocacy group. However I think it is fair to state that discussions in connection with the self-advocacy group, that took place around the nature of self-advocacy and Person-Centred ways of supporting people, as well as the type of support that took place in the self-advocacy group itself, played a significant role in further developing practice within the Intensive Support Unit that gave control to service users.

Dave was always primarily interested in art and spent most of his time within the self-advocacy group following this interest. Although one time, towards the end of the two years, Dave brought a book in from home and asked for it to be read to him throughout the course of the session and fairly soon afterwards he brought a water pistol from home to the session and had a great time squirting us all. When Dave first started the self-advocacy session, and during the earlier part of the first two years he attended it, he used a brush to paint over and over a small area of the paper he chose to work upon, and even when he had worn a hole in the paper he still carried on working the same very small area. In addition he made no direct requests and didn't help himself to materials. After one year Dave was moving freely from one art activity to another i.e. from painting to printing. He was asking for specific things i.e. red paper to stick on top of his work, a bowl of water to wash the table with and different coloured paints. Towards the end of the two years he was calling supporters over to make requests of them and helping himself to a range of different materials. He was covering the whole piece of paper, often three or four in the same session, with paint and deciding when one piece of work was finished and moving onto another. He was making increasingly complex work with clearly defined circular spots, or 'balls', as he called them, on the paper and had developed the ability to place paint on small specific areas of his paper i.e. on top of sticky labels he had placed over the painting or inside of printed circles. Dave was doing all of the above things completely unaided although at his request he had been supported to learn the skill of being able to paint inside circles and on top of sticky labels.

When we first started working with Stephen he was often unwilling to come into the group and frequently left the room. When he was in the room he would sit on a beanbag, rock, flick his fingers in front of his eyes and occasionally masturbate. He showed virtually no interest in other people or any of the objects around him and he would not look at anyone. On the rare occasion that someone, spending time with Stephen, did manage to make eye contact with him he would look away within a second or two. Towards the end of the two years Stephen was spending very little or no time flicking his fingers in front of his face or rocking and masturbating within the session and had become very outgoing. He wanted to be around the supporters and was readily approaching them and other people in the group. Stephen was smiling at people and confidently initiating looking into their eyes. He initiated hugging people and was leading supporters by the hand to places where he wanted them to be. Stephen was also beginning to show interest in some objects, i.e. a balloon filled with warm water. The change in how Stephen was choosing to spend his time in the session was really remarkable.

However about a month before the end of two years Stephen started to become more withdrawn again. Not to the extent he was in the beginning but the change was noticeable. We speculated on the reasons why. It could have been because the supporters prevented him being with a service user in the room next door. Stephen wanted to sit next to her and she had hit him very hard in the recent past. It seemed he was attracted to the loud screaming noises she made when distressed and Stephen sitting next to her made her even more distressed. It could have been that Stephen came to regard the supporters within the self-advocacy group as people he was increasingly in conflict with rather than people who were there to help him achieve what he wanted. Also Stephen had moved house and no longer came into the centre every day. In addition the staff in the new house were trying to change his habit of sitting on the floor (normalisation at its most negative). At one time a worker from his new house 'escorted' Stephen into the session and immediately started dragging him up off the floor and towards a chair very roughly while shouting at him to stand up and sit in a chair. It took some discussion to prevent this worker doing this within the session and to get her to leave the session as she thought it would destroy their 'programme' if we didn't do the same to Stephen. Finally because of space problems within the centre we had changed the layout of the session and Stephen may not have liked this.

At the beginning of the two years Wayne wanted to do the same thing every week, cutting up birthday cards and sticking them down and clapping. He chose to work on a table away from everyone and although Wayne may not have been incontinent he would wet himself frequently throughout the session and then go and get changed. Often Wayne would get very agitated and upset. Towards the end of the two years there were sessions where Wayne had not wet himself at all and at times he signalled with Makaton that he was going to the toilet. Also when he did wet it was only once or twice at the most within a session and much less frequently than in the beginning. Perhaps it is important to remind the reader here that we were not offering any kind of training to Wayne around this subject and that he had known the Makaton sign for going to the toilet for years but just wasn't using it as much.

Towards the end of the two years Wayne rarely got agitated and not to the same extent. He also became much more sociable, wanting to join other people in what they were doing. He was spending lots more time with other people away from his table. He started to initiate a whole range of different activities including singing, dancing, massage, playing tapes, helping other group participants and playing the electric organ. Wayne started to make requests more, i.e. to have his pictures pinned to the wall or for a particular tape to be put on, and as his use of language was limited he would often lead a supporter to what he wanted. Generally Wayne enjoyed the company of others more and became much more playful, interactive and interested in trying different activities.

When we first started working with Ellen she chose to play with a child's activity centre that she carried around with her to use whenever she could. Ellen's key worker informed us that Ellen had been playing with the 'spinning' part of the activity centre for years and that she only did a maximum of twenty minutes different activity before she went back to it. At the end of the first year Ellen was leaving her activity centre in another room and coming in without it. During the second year she never brought the activity centre into the group. Ellen moved from making twiddling or spinning movements with objects such as small paintbrushes to exploring and enjoying a whole range of activities. She was periodically interested in painting throughout the two years but when she first cautiously got involved with paint she wanted to wash her hands if she got even a small amount of it on them. In addition she made small marks for a short period of time. Later on she made large expansive paintings often with delicate details on them and became relaxed about paint getting on her hands, washing them at the end of the session. At first she did not choose to wear an apron. Towards the end of the two years she was going and getting an apron to put on before she stared painting.

Ellen also came to enjoy playing percussion instruments and singing, and could spend entire sessions doing this. Occasionally Ellen chose to spend the session doing nothing. In the beginning we used to ask Ellen if she wanted to come into the session and it could take her a long time to decide to come in. Sometimes Ellen would decide to stay in the adjoining room for the entire session. Before the end of the first year Ellen was choosing to come into the session without being asked if she wanted to. Ellen progressively got more adventurous and confident within the group. At the end of the second year she was initiating a wide range of activities for herself, often because she had seen other people doing them, and moving around the room helping herself to different materials and objects. She also became much more communicative, laughing with and looking at people much more and even using spoken phrases that she may have known previously but did not use in the group for over a year (she hadn't spoke at all during the first year) such as 'that's enough' when she wanted a massage to stop and 'thank you' when a supporter commented on her nail varnish.

Conclusion

People with severe learning difficulties can benefit a great deal from Person-Centred support. Much has been written about the oppressive and controlling attitudes, behaviours and institutional regimes that people with learning difficulties can be subjected to while receiving what was supposed to be support (e.g. Ryan and Thomas, 1980; Booth and Booth, 1998). Because of their higher support needs people with severe learning difficulties can come into direct and intimate contact with these negative aspects of 'support' more intensely and often than other people who are described as having learning difficulties. Wholeheartedly adopting Rogers' non-directive stance and core conditions of empathy, positive regard and congruence (1967) can enable us to develop ways of supporting that are of particular value to this grouping of people.

For example those of us who adopt a Person-Centred Approach actively aim to identify with the people we are supporting. This can lead to us challenging destructive and prejudiced perceptions of this grouping of people we may encounter in others and ourselves, and further recognising the equal value and worth of people with severe learning difficulties. In addition Person-Centred ways of working enable us to support people with severe learning difficulties to spend their time as they wish at a pace that suits them. Person-Centred ways of working also enable us, at best, to be honest and open and offer a support that harbours no hidden agendas. In addition all the above aspects of Person-Centred practice are consistent with the support of self-advocacy (Dowson and Whittaker, 1993), and can be combined with a political perspective that recognises people with learning difficulties as an oppressed minority within society (Williams, 1989). They can also be used when supporting people with learning difficulties to counteract this oppression and have their rights taken seriously.

Valuing People (Department of Health, 2001) actively directs service providers to ensure that services are developed in conjunction with people with learning difficulties in order that they may fulfil their self-defined needs and interests. Now is a good time for challenging older established systems and promoting and developing those that genuinely aim for people with severe learning difficulties to be in control of what happens within their lives. We still have a long way to go towards finding and implementing ways of supporting people with severe learning difficulties to lead the sort of lives we might wish for ourselves. While writing this chapter I have been increasingly aware of the limitations of the sessions that are described within it. For example they all took place within a day centre, and lasted no more than a couple of hours a week; the times they happened were dictated by the time that the participants' minibus arrived in the morning and when their 'meals on wheels' lunch was available; and what group participants could do was limited by what the service could afford to provide and the numbers of support staff that were available on the day. However having written this, the interpersonal aspects of the support relationships that have been described in this chapter and the underlying principles that have informed the development of these support relationships can be applied positively in a wide range of different settings and situations.

I hope that what has been described and discussed in this chapter is of some use to other people who want to or are already facilitating the development of support that helps people with severe learning difficulties to move towards living the day-to-day existences of their choice. It was with this in mind that this chapter was written. By describing the sessions that along with other people I have been involved in developing and supporting, and focussing on some of the issues that initially challenged us (and still do to some extent because they are complex and open to differing interpretations and responses) I have aimed as much to provide material for discussion or further development as to comment on specific areas of practice.

References

Barnes, M. (1997) Families and empowerment. In Ramcharan *et al.* (eds) *Empowerment In Everyday Life: Learning Disability.* London: Jessica Kingsley

Booth, T. and Booth, W. (1998) *Growing Up With Parents Who Have Learning Difficulties.* London: Routledge

Brechin, A. and Swain, J. (1988) Professional/client relationships: creating a 'working alliance' with people with learning difficulties. *Disability, Handicap & Society,* **3**(3): 213–25

Department of Health (2001) *Valuing People: A New Strategy for Learning Disability for the 21st Century: A White Paper.* London: DoH Publications

Dowson, S. and Whittaker, A. (1993) *On One Side: The Role of the Advisor in Supporting People with Learning Difficulties in Self-Advocacy Groups.* London: Values into Action

Goodley, D. (2000) *Self-advocacy in the Lives of People With Learning Difficulties: The Politics of Resilience.* Buckingham: Open University Press

McCarthy, M. (1999) *Sexuality And Women With Learning Disabilities.* London: Jessica Kingsley

Morris, J. (1991) *Pride Against Prejudice: Transforming Attitudes To Disability.* London: The Women's Press

Oliver, M. (1996) *Understanding Disability: From Theory To Practice.* London: Macmillan

Perrin, B. and Nirje, B. (1989) Setting the record straight: A critique of some frequent misconceptions of the normalisation principle. In: A. Brechin and J. Walmsley (eds) *Making Connections: Reflecting On The Lives And Experiences Of People With Learning Difficulties.* London: Hodder and Stoughton

Rogers, C. R. (1951) *Client-Centered Therapy: Its Current Practice, Implications And Theory.* London: Constable

Rogers, C. R. (1967) *On Becoming A Person.* London: Constable

Rogers, C. R. (1978) *Carl Rogers on Personal Power.* London: Constable.

Ryan, J. with Thomas, F. (1980) *The Politics of Mental Handicap.* London: Penguin

Shakespeare, T. Gillespie-Sells, K. and Davies, D. (eds) (1996) *The Sexual Politics of Disability.* London: Cassell

Sinason, V. (1992) *Mental Handicap and the Human Condition: New Approaches from the Tavistock.* London: Free Association Books

Walmsley, J. and Downer, J. (1997) Shouting the loudest. In: Ramcharan et al. (eds) *Empowerment In Everyday Life: Learning Disability.* London: Jessica Kingsley.

Wertheimer, A. (ed.) (1996) *Changing Days: Developing New Day Opportunities With People Who Have Learning Difficulties.* London: Kings Fund Publishing

Williams, F. (1989) Mental handicap and oppression. In: A. Brechin and J. Walmsley (eds), *Making Connections: Reflecting On The Lives And Experiences Of People With Learning Difficulties.* London: Hodder and Stoughton

Williams, P. and Shoultz, B. (1982) *We Can Speak For Ourselves.* London: Souvenir Press

Interview with Joyce Gardiner: Supporting people with severe learning difficulties living in the community

Joyce Gardiner has many years' experience of supporting people with severe learning disabilities in residential settings, as well as managing teams in those settings. She trained as a Person-Centred counsellor, and has offered counselling to people with severe learning disabilities in a variety of organisations. Currently, Joyce manages a supported living project for people living in the community, and talks here about her experiences in supporting adults with learning disabilities living in the community.

Jan: I'm interested in how you apply the Person-Centred Approach in supported living projects for people with severe learning disabilities. In addition, how you fit into a field where so many practitioners are working from the behavioural approach; would that be your experience as well?

Joyce: I would say so. Certainly when I was in the respite unit it was the behavioural approach. Anything that was challenging, the focus was on the behaviour: why was it happening; monitoring it; coming up with a way of dealing with the behaviour, and, depending on the individual, that would include some plan about what would happen when this behaviour came up, and that occasionally was useful. But I feel my experience with Susan [woman with learning disabilities living in the community, for whom Joyce was a support worker] in the community was that she had lots of behaviour that would be considered challenging.

A behavioural programme with her would have been totally inappropriate, and would never have been helpful at all in expecting any change from her. She herself wanted to change things and it would only work if she wanted it to work. So it was finding out from her what she was doing and exploring with her what was happening when she might be shouting or cursing or swearing or getting upset, crying, and it was basically going back to where she was at, and actually exploring with her what was happening. That was just basically spending time with her and trying to appreciate what was going on for her, and just appreciating who she was as a person, and appreciating her experiences of her life full stop. How other people, family members, the community, had treated her, social services, everybody she had come into contact with, which was sort of squashing her I suppose.

She needed to be listened to, to be able to express things in her own way and be able to reflect on some things she was saying. To be able to reflect on how things could be different and just being in a place with people who weren't going to reject her or judge her for the way she was behaving. Not to say you would accept some of the stuff that she was doing, because it was unacceptable, but within limits. Be able to actually allow her to tell you what was going on to try to understand it. To say, 'I don't like what you are doing but I'd really like to understand why you are behaving like that, what's happening for you right now?' Then, and only then, would she able to actually get down to the roots and most of the time it would be a big explosional behaviour with a lot of shouting and a lot of having a go at you, and then a period of quiet. And then it usually came out as, 'are you going to leave me?' and, 'don't you like me any more?', and actually just accepting that, 'no, I am not going anywhere, I'm staying here with you but I'd like to understand what is happening with you', and that's the point where she would break down and then a whole load of old material, old feelings that were very, very raw and fresh would be there as soon as she knew she was going to be understood and listened to, accepted. She was able to tell what was actually happening and would cry and cry and cry and would just want to be held. Almost like wanting to be mothered, rocked, hugged, and told that you cared for her and you worried about what was happening for her. That you want to be able to help and that you are going to stick with her and know that is going to be difficult at times, but knowing that I'm not going to run away from her.

Jan: So communicating a genuine sense of concern for her and what she is doing.

Joyce: She brought that out in me as well, but it's almost like for me, it wasn't just about telling her, but demonstrating in all sorts of ways. The trust that she had in me — you couldn't allow yourself to let her down — in very practical ways and then she would perform. If you promised to take her somewhere at a particular time, then you always made sure you did it. If you were going to meet her, you met her on time. If you were going to be five minutes late, making sure that you rang and said you were going to be late because if you didn't turn up, even if it was only five minutes late — or even two minutes — there was an instant sign of, 'you don't like me, you were late because you don't like me, it's because I am a horrible person'. So it was instantly taken as that, a reflection of how you felt about her.

She would pick up on when you met and if you were really tired when you went to see her, if you were more quiet than normal, she was absolutely on the ball with the fact that you were different and immediately assumed that was to do with her, rather than to do with that you were tired or you'd had a late night or thinking about something else. She would pick up on every single thing — she was very sensitive to everything going on and took it back, thinking it was all her fault, and I felt that that was not just with me but with people. If you were on a train and somebody got up and walked and went and sat somewhere else, it couldn't be the fact that perhaps that they had gone to sit with their friend who was on the train, it was to do with the fact that they had got out of that chair because they didn't like sitting beside her. And it was constantly having to give her alternatives. Offer alternatives as to why people were doing what they were doing so that she wasn't stuck with that constant, 'it was me, it was me'. Everything was her fault, no matter what was going on. If somebody fell down the stairs, it was like, 'what did I do, did I do something wrong?', and she needed to constantly hear these messages — that she was a good person, she was a nice person, that she was kind.

These are true things about her, it wasn't that you say it for the sake of saying it, but because I felt that I was genuine with what I was saying. I did feel these things, and I realised what a hard time that she had had and the racism that she experienced when she was growing up as well. She would apologise to people if somebody ran past and bumped into her and it was their fault the way they had rushed past her, and she would be the one to apologise. I can remember saying to her, 'that wasn't your fault, that was their fault because they were rushing, they should have been apologising to you, not you to them', and finding out that that is what she had been told to do because it stops things getting into a bad situation. Her family had believed that if you apologised first it just took the heat out of it with that person. It was less troublesome for you, that's how you survived. Even if it wasn't your fault. It was like getting to the nitty gritty stuff with Susan to try and understand where she was coming from, but she's grown, she's grown a lot, accepted for her whole self, you are not going to reject her.

Jan: It's as if what you are offering in your one-to-one support work is a therapeutic relationship spread over a longer time period rather than the one-to-one, this is your space, this is your hour, let's sit down and talk about your problems. It sounds as if what you are describing is on the hoof with the issues.

Joyce: Yes, and I think with somebody like Susan, she also gets counselling — Person-Centred counselling — and I think it is as important as the counselling in a sit-down situation — there is an awful lot to be gained from having the skills and using them on the hoof, as you say. With somebody like Susan, who has quite a high support package[1], it's those messages that you get in a counselling session for one hour a week that she was getting all the time on a regular basis. I've seen her in the morning, seen her in the evening, at different times of the day and that wasn't just with me, it was with her other support worker and a person at the day centre who was also very into giving her very good messages. So she was getting it all the way round her and for me I think that Susan would gain more from that than she probably did in that one hour because she was getting the messages in her everyday life. So it wasn't just about talking about it but doing it and picking up what upsets her, picking up when she feels bad so you would be able to deal with the different issues that come up for her in community life, and you are able to support her with this. Not

1. Support package refers to the individual's assessed needs to include their needs for one-to-one support

just dealing with her emotional side but also helping her to cope with the practicalities of living in the community, which are hard. I think she needed more than one-to-one sit-down counselling could do for her — it wouldn't have been enough, I don't think.

Jan: So just to clarify, in the supportive living situation and being a support worker, many people will just do the practical things and help the person with those practical things to try to help keep them on task and so on, but what you are advocating is something different, is actually being with the person.

Joyce: Yes. In terms of the practical things, there were lots of practical things that I had to do with Susan: going to the bank, dealing with writing her cheques, dealing with people behind the counter, going shopping, doing the finances, a whole range of things, how to keep her flat tidy, cooking. I was doing all those things, but my feeling was that Susan in many ways had a lot of those skills. What stopped her from being able to perform those skills was her emotional state, so by being able to support her emotionally we were able to give her positives about her other skills in a way you would never be able to do by just talking. So, for instance, going into the bank, Susan has difficulty writing but desperately wants to be able to do it on her own. Being able to stand by her while she writes her cheque and telling her every single letter that she writes on there, what letters, when to make the break, where she puts things. Quite often, you know, after a time where she gets stuck, you know what she can do and what she can't do, but her still being able to like slap you down almost, and say, 'I can do this myself'. Then you know there is an appropriate time to come in and an appropriate time to back off but having to accept that there are going to be times when she is going to kind of slap you around verbally and just be prepared to stand back and wait to be told when you can go in. She was quite assertive in telling me, you know, 'bugger off, I can do this myself'. Sometimes inside you were seething cos you're thinking, 'Oh, I've got so much to do I can't wait for this', but having to back off and say, 'that's OK. If you want me I'm standing here'.

Jan: Doing things at her pace.

Joyce: Yes. Having to, because it wouldn't help her otherwise and it helps her realise when she needs help herself and she'd tell you. It's finding that balance about how far do you go in and how far do you withdraw and that was about getting to know Susan and what mood she was in on a particular day, and about her being able to tell you herself. You could tell as soon as you met her off the bus you could get a good idea of where she was at. But then she could be in a smashing mood and it would take one thing, one rejection from somebody, a look from somebody was enough to completely turn her around from being in a happy jolly mood to feeling rejected. I remember it happening one day — she loves children, and she's got a tendency to be in the face of a child, and we'd been working with her to ask permission to talk to someone's child because a child is a precious thing and parents get a bit worried about anyone touching their child, anybody, not just because it is you. She had been doing very well and it had been working for her because she was getting to talk to lots of children and their parents were fine about it.

And then she did it with one woman and this woman said, 'fuck off', for no reason. Susan was very gentle, very kind — in my view it was because Susan was black — this woman was white and she was a horrible woman anyway but Susan took it very, very personally and she said, 'it's because I have got a learning disability, because I am black, I didn't do any harm, the world is not fair, if only this hadn't happened to me '. It's just awful to see that just one nasty person can trigger off a whole trail of emotions which you then have to listen to and work with and try and help Susan to understand what's happened to her in that moment in time, how it's triggered off, all sorts of feelings from old times. I personally think it's been very helpful for her to have that sort of level of support. You can get somebody coming in doing all the practical things but without having an idea of how to address her emotional needs, well it wouldn't work with Susan, it wouldn't work with her. It would work insofar as we'll get the rent done, get the shopping done, get this and that done, but you wouldn't actually be helping Susan to move on and Susan has actually reached the point now where she is cooking for herself and she's doing all sorts of other things on her own and it's because she is in a better emotional state.

Her flat, you can help her tidy it up one night and the next day it's like a bomb has hit it and her flat usually reflected how she was feeling emotionally, very jumbled and mixed up, then the flat reflected that. When she was feeling more organised and together then the flat tended to be organised and together. You could actually put that back to Susan: 'Your flat's looking very tidy today and you seem very organised, I wonder what's happening'. And you could ask her what was happening that made it so good and that would help you be able to push her up that little bit more, and move her up the next step and encourage her in that she was doing a good job and that she is doing it well and that she's trying really hard. Just the encouragement and the positive feedback about herself and basically knowing that somebody cared about her and somebody loves her that's how she took it, that's how she feels cared about and loved and in doing that in all sorts of ways, making sure that you listen to what she says, like she said:

'I play pool at the day centre and they don't have a decent pool cue and I'd like a pool cue for myself.'

' OK, we'll go and buy one then, if you've got the money.'

'Can I?'

'It's your money and you play pool and you enjoy it so you deserve to have nice things.'

Her flat, when I first started working with her — her flat was dark, dirty depressing, the furniture was old.

Jan: Had she always lived there?

Joyce: No, she's been at home, been in respite, been in other accommodation, in hospital, she's been in hospital quite a lot. Her flat reflected depression — the people who were working with her said that Susan needs to know she's a valuable person and this environment doesn't tell her that she is valuable. So we need to do something in a very practical way to let her know that and so we started working on doing the flat up, which made a tremendous difference. Her choosing nice furniture with nice bright colours, colours she wanted, and basically her flat looking nicer and that in itself gives you a bit of a lift. If your environment around you says that's all you deserve, it was giving her a very clear message that she was worth more than and her flat being nice was important because she was important. So it was almost like feeding it in at every angle if you looked at her life, like where did she need to have it, it needed to be a very holistic approach to her life. In my view a very person-centred holistic approach.

Jan: This makes me wonder whether you come into conflict with other people for whom the Person-Centred Approach is not their preferred way of working, their way of being?

Joyce: Yes, I have done at times. It's not just about being Person-Centred, just people's general attitude to people with learning disabilities. Where a lot of people are in a position of looking after other people, or working with other people, they seem to feel that the people they are working with should do as they are told, and either do what they are told or do things for them, or treat them like kids, look down on them, look at their behaviour as naughty behaviour. Whereas behaviour for me, anything that somebody does, is a communication of some description.

So you have got a lot of people with learning disabilities who haven't got any verbal communication but they have communication nonetheless, and I've worked with some good people, but I have also worked with some other people who will just judge you as soft because you are looking for a way to understand. I suppose their view was that I was wasting time. You don't spent half an hour talking to somebody about having a bath, you just tell them, 'you're having a bath', which I wouldn't like somebody to do that to me, because they may have a very good reason why they don't want to have a bath. They might prefer a shower for instance. They might have some fear or they might be watching something on TV. Just because somebody can't talk, doesn't mean they can't watch something on the TV.

So I would spend time finding ways of communicating to make sure that person . . . do they want a bath? Do they understand what you are saying in the first place? Trying to find ways of communicating in whatever way I can, whether it be actually taking the bubble bath and the soap, shampoo and towel to show them, or drawing it. Whatever. Whereas some people would say, 'bath, you're going for a bath', and because of the position I have been in, I would not be able to stand by and watch that.

I suppose being in a management position most people would listen because they felt what I had to say was important and anybody who knew me well enough would know that I wouldn't do it just to undermine what they were doing. But I have had occasion where people think that's what you're doing, and that has to be addressed at a different time. But a lot of people dealing with learning difficulties think you keep them clean, feed them and take them out occasionally whereas they don't see them as people who have got abilities, feelings, wishes, ambitions, dreams and the rest. The trouble is they haven't had the opportunities to have those looked at or listened to or met.

I am reminded of Kevin [a young man with learning disabilities whom Joyce saw for counselling sessions] and his desperate desire for a girlfriend. Perfectly reasonable, perfectly normal desire but somehow it just doesn't happen for him and somehow it's almost as if obstacles are put in his way rather than having the path cleared. He is almost dependent on having somebody else to open up the opportunities to allow him to get any way near to even get to know a woman and the opportunities are just not there. His life is controlled by other people.

Jan: So you're reflecting on the difference between controlling, managing, and allowing a developmental process to have the space to continue.

Joyce: Definitely. People can do some tremendous things if they feel somebody is there who is supporting them in doing that. Be allowing and enabling. At the same time if you have got the wrong person working with someone with a learning disability, not only are they going to stand still, but possibly go back a way. Not only in terms of losing skills, because the person who thinks they are doing good is actually encouraging that person to become more dependent on them. It might be for having a heart but having a wish to having a person grow — I suppose Scott Peck[2] comes to mind. Some of his stuff I've read, him saying, 'love is caring enough to let someone go', and I got this feeling of a butterfly. And if you put that into terms of someone with a learning disability, as like constantly providing an environment, and providing the resources, and the individuals with the skills to help them on their way to meet their dreams, and their ambitions, but also having the ability to cut the strings and let them go. Too many people hold on to

2. M. Scott Peck: *The Road Less Traveled*, 1988, Rider.

them, but they should know when to let go and let them move on in the world and make their moves in a better way. More enabling the environment that you can provide, and that's for me, it's where it's at.

It's just remembering — for some people love is a mushy sort of word but I would actually say for someone like Susan it's to watch that someone grow. Emotionally grow. It's just with her in particular it's been such a lovely experience to see that happen in front of my eyes, and feel for me that the Person-Centred approach is there and sort of almost feels as though it's become a whole part of who I am, my way of being rather than a technique or this or that — it's about me as a person, no matter who I'm working with I'd be working in a similar way. I've left Susan now and moved on to a different group of people and I can see myself doing exactly the same thing. I keep questioning myself and saying I can't get as involved with this group of people, but it's almost like there's an attraction to someone who listens to where they are coming from, and it's really hard to keep myself away.

Jan: They are attracted to you once they realise you are going to listen so it's almost like they involve you, not necessarily you involving yourself?

Joyce: Yes. Obviously, my job is to listen, to be there for them, and to appreciate the difficulties they might be having in the community. I can feel that sort of, there's something about the way that I am, it's the feeling that they are not being fully heard and I'm providing something that they haven't got, and I'm constantly having to look at myself to find what that's about. I think it's because I am a good listener and I listen at where they are at, not where I think they are at or . . . because I don't see any point of me being the one to tell somebody what to do because at the end of the day my job is enabling people to live by themselves as independently as they can.

Jan: And some of the people you support have quite severe and possibly profound learning difficulties?

Joyce: No, the majority of them are mild to moderate, so for me it's almost like a move up — like going through the whole learning disabilities continuum from one end of the scale to the other, from very mild to very severe. I hate those words. The people I am working with now in many ways are people who are expected to cope with very, very little support and they do cope under extremely difficult circumstances, living in accommodation that myself — well, I came home last night thinking I couldn't live there. I couldn't do the taking on a residents' group, and there are drug dealers in the block, and shootings going on and you name it, it's there. It amazes me the skills they have got for survival, really. But despite their ability to deal with some really shitty stuff it's like they are very vulnerable in strange little ways. Maybe it's their need to be heard about something that maybe may seem very minor, but to them, it feels like a big problem.

So it's about appreciating that that is a big problem to them and finding out what it is about, that particular thing, that makes it so worrying or so difficult for them to deal with. And the fact that somebody listens to them is half the battle. If somebody's heard it and sometimes given advice or give any direction of any description, because just by being heard and reflecting it back to them allows them to be able to go off and do it on their own. Sometimes I think to myself, 'that problem's gone but what happened to it?' And sometimes it's like, 'well, I must have done something right'.

Jan: It's actually therapy in action. We're coming back to therapy on the hoof rather than one-to-one, sit-down, let's focus on this — it's the actual moment-by-moment listening to what really is being communicated, and the evidence for you is they just go off and just do that thing.

Joyce: Yes. A lot of people have experienced things like messages they get about themselves that are so horrible and nasty. I had a tenant this week who has taken on something that really worries me in terms of what's going on in the block of flats — drug dealers, guys abusing women and all sorts of things going on. He has really bitten this off and is dealing with it, and I didn't want to frighten him but at the same time I was worried in case he wasn't aware of what the implications of what he was doing could have for himself and I was actually . . . it nearly brought tears to my eyes. He is somebody who talks about his learning disability quite a lot — 'I've got learning disability' — 'life with learning disability is about expecting horrible things to happen to me. Nothing could happen to me at this time that could be worse than anything that has already happened to me'. And it's the sudden realisation of, 'my God! I wouldn't have the courage to do what he is going to do'. But maybe I would if I had to live there — I don't know. I don't think I would, actually, but it's almost like, 'whatever you do with me now is never going to be any worse than has been done already', and it just made me realise just how difficult his life must have been for him to say that.

It's survival with people with learning disabilities and they haven't been treated like human beings basically. They haven't been treated with respect, haven't been given any idea from everything that's around them: from school services, from social services, everything around them tells them they are bad, nasty, thick, they are this they are that. What must that do to their self-esteem? So any work we are doing is about working out these damages that have been done and trying to address these damages that have been done. You can't put back what has been done, but try to help to build someone's self-esteem in a way that they can feel more valuable and have more self-worth.

Jan: I'm struck by how deeply your relationships with your clients affect you, how passionately you feel about your work with them. So with this group in particular, because they have mild to moderate learning difficulties, is there any sense of them as not able to live in the world of the learning disabled and they don't really live in the world of the so-called 'abled' — somehow or other they don't really fit anywhere, they are kind of almost a sub-class. Does that make any sense in the light of what you're saying?

Joyce: Yes — so many of them are very much about identifying with other people with learning disabilities, but then you get other groups of people who want to disassociate themselves altogether with people with learning disabilities. I've had some input from a training course where some research had been done and it was trying to explain why people with learning disabilities quite often will not want to be with other people with learning disabilities. Being 'normal' — pushing everything to do with learning disabilities aside — like being like other people so that they would fit in, and I would say that you can see that quite often.

Jan: And does it work?

Joyce: For some, it does to a certain extent on the outside but I would imagine it's quite hard if it's not really you. It's almost like putting on a false face, hiding behind it, and not being able to ask for help when you really need it because you were trying to be 'normal', coping.

Jan: As if normal means doing everything alone.

Joyce: Yes. I mean I find myself saying — when I first started in my job — I found the people I was there to work with were the people getting me around the place. They were giving me directions, they were telling me which buses, and I know it's a simple thing but for me it felt like . . . I think it was quite nice for them to see that they could help me because at some point in the future I am going to be the one they are going to be asking for help, so it feels more of a relationship which is built on a two-way thing. I don't want to be in a position where I am the big power over them. I'm there, it's my job and that's what I'm there for, but a little bit of sharing doesn't go far wrong and like there is one guy who is extremely good at computers and it's like he's taught me things, things I didn't know.

Again, it's like he is very focused on that type of thing and best on the computer and he is just dying to show me something that he can do and that in itself is like being on the hoof, 'I can do something you can't do, I can do something for you', and it's about building relationships that he will be able to take off and then use somewhere else. It's not just a one-way, me relating to him, it's a relationship based on a two-way thing. It feels to me that you are feeding things in, without even being aware you are feeding. You're feeding all the time. Giving messages in all sorts of strange little ways and I think the funny thing about being Person-Centred is you don't have to think about what you are doing — it's just there, it's natural, almost instinctive.

Jan: Like some kind of organic process that's going on between you and the other.

Joyce: Yes, it's a real thing. If somebody said to me, 'what are you actually doing?' It's sometimes quite hard to . . . you can look at things like and if you were looking at a theoretical way, you can reel them off. You can talk about all those different words but to actually do them in a way that doesn't sound like you are theorising . . .

Jan: Like if you can be yourself and *be*, and be with them, it ceases to be something that you are aware of in terms of, 'now I'm being empathic, now I'm being accepting, now I'm being genuine' — it's something you cease to be aware of because you're being involved in it in a relationship.

Joyce: I don't even think about all these concepts really — it's just part of who I am.

Jan: It strikes me that what you are saying then is actually, it's like you're bringing that set of qualities out into supported living or into the street, wherever you are at, you're bringing that place where growth may happen out there.

Joyce: I suppose so, yes. One of the things I'm told in my job is, 'you're not a counsellor in your job', which I am very much aware of, obviously, but I can't leave that part of me behind because that part is in me. So I am doing it wherever it happens and it happens because it's there. I can't lose it or put it on a shelf for a day, it's just there, it's a part of me. And I think sometimes it is quite hard to think, what has happened? What happened to make that happen? Sometimes you need to take it back to the theoretical to actually understand what has happened. What's happened in that relationship? And I think talking with you here about Susan has helped a little bit with that. I didn't always understand what happened and it helped to talk about it.

Jan: So that suggests then if you are allowing yourself to be fully engaged with people as opposed to doing to them or doing for them somehow, even though you are not counselling per se you still need, and benefit, from a space to talk with other people to try and really figure out what is actually going on here.

Joyce: And I don't necessarily — other people around me are not necessarily aware of that. Like you would understand the processes, but the role of my own management supervision would not necessarily — wouldn't have thought that would have been part of what my job would have been.

Jan: It's like they are not expecting, they've made that clear also, they are not expecting counselling from you, so they may not be expecting you to step back and figure out the relationships between yourself and other people.

Joyce: Because of the actual role I am in now, because I am a bit more distanced from the clients like, we've got a community worker who works for them directly, and my job is supposed to be supervising people who work for them, but I am expected to go in when that person is on holiday. So my view is that you can't just say, 'X is on holiday, I'll go in now', I need to know who these people are. I need to know what the relationships are. I need to do that because I'm going to be covering while they are on holiday. I want them to know who I am. I want them to know they have somebody they can come to if for any reason there's problems with their worker, and I want to be able to know I can provide the community workers with support by knowing the sorts of issues they are dealing with.

Sometimes you might get somebody having a problem and you think to yourself, 'well maybe I'm not approaching this quite right', and to make assessments of where people are at, where they are coming from and that's maybe helped by the way I relate and which allows me then to support the worker. So my direct job is still not thought of as necessarily important but my relationship is. We expect to have good relationships but the actual process wouldn't be something that would be thought of as something that would be looked at because I would be expected to have that, not that everybody does have it.

Jan: But there is something about the quality of it that you're picking up on, the quality of that relationship

Joyce: I'm so glad that I have done my counselling training and because it allows me to give so much more. The relationships develop so much more empathically than they would have a few years ago. I think the empathy has always been there, but it's something different. Something to do with communication, about things I am prepared to say which I would never have thought of saying before, pick up on feelings, put words to things.

Jan: Like you trust your empathy more than you did before and maybe that allows you to express it.

Joyce: Yes, that's probably true. Some people are quite quick to tell you when you have got it wrong anyway and that's something you need to be very careful with. The client group that I work with, sometimes they will just go along with what you say, but you can usually tell by keeping an eye on facial and body language and all the other things, but it does makes you very much aware of things and meaning than previously.

Jan: Because you worked with people with very severe learning difficulties and, as you say, came through a continuum to now currently people with mild to moderate learning difficulties, is there anything, if you were to be in their shoes knowing them as you do, about the voices of the voiceless, if they were given a voice is there anything you think they would say? What they would want people to know? I guess it would not be the same for all of them along that continuum . . .

Joyce: To be listened to in terms of their communication, whether that be verbal, facial expression. To be listened to in whatever shape or form that would take and for staff or whoever is around to make the effort to find a way of communicating. To be treated with respect and to be recognised as having the same needs as everyone else. Things like dreams, ambition, sexuality, the right to a job, the right to be in the cafe, the right to be around, the right to express themselves, the right to be everywhere and anywhere like everybody else. If they are able to go there that they should be able to be and have the same — I don't know what it comes down to — like you go along to a GP and there is always the assumption like a GP said the other day, 'oh I don't think she needs counselling'. It's almost like somebody with a learning disability can't use counselling. I suppose it encompasses all the things I have just said really, that they have the same needs as the rest of us. 'Give us a voice, a chance, allow us to show you what we are made of. We can do things — we can — give us a space to do this'.

The pace of life at the moment, people gets squashed anyway. I just hate to think that people with learning disabilities, because there is no time, people haven't got time for each other so how are they going to have time for people who may need more time than maybe someone else. There are things I have noticed like shopkeepers, everybody wants to do things quickly and don't have time to address — just an extra five minutes here, an extra two minutes there doesn't do anybody any harm and it can make such a difference to someone else's life in a way that they could never imagine. Somebody rushing Susan because she is talking to the woman behind the counter, if you could only realise what a difference it makes to her to have that little bit of rapport with somebody behind the counter I'm sure you could spare a couple of minutes. Yes, all of those things.

Jan: Thank you for your time.

Carpe diem — seizing the day: developing day opportunities for
people with profound and complex learning and other disabilities
by
Michael Farrell

*Michael Farrell has been working in social care for seventeen years with people who
have a variety of problems including learning disabilities, mental health issues, drug
and alcohol dependencies and homelessness. He has a diploma in Person-Centred
counselling and currently manages a day-opportunities service for people with learning
disabilities and others with mental health problems. He has a stepson with learning
difficulties, and is a trustee of a charity for families with disabled members.*

The community nurse closed his bulky file at the end of the meeting and said
with some considerable relief in his voice, 'I wish all my reviews were like
that!' Barbra is a young woman who has developed magnificently within the
day-opportunities service over the last two years. She has a number of mental
health and learning disability[1] labels and a history of becoming 'obsessional'
with staff and objects. In consequence we always that ensure the goal-focus of
the activity is the key to her programme and that the staff facilitating the activity
are rotated frequently. The emphasis is always on what she is achieving rather
than who she is working with or developing a relationship with. We also
realised that she is more likely to become stressed if she has unstructured gaps
in her week. The team have noticed that she thrives on a busy schedule which
includes some form of physical activity: a gym session or swimming or a ramble
every day. She has a lot of energy. It is not rocket science but her respite manager
commented that two years ago she was becoming fixated with the washing
machine at the respite unit. This was not the same bright and assertive woman
we were working with today.

　　We don't know exactly what was going on before, but she's never shown
that kind of interest in equipment if there have been any other alternatives.
Buoyed by the apparent success, the Day Opportunities Manager told the
meeting that Barbra has been studying on our employment training project to
nationally accredited standards with a view to moving on to employment.
Warming to his theme he began to wax lyrical about the integrity of the
programme and the learning outcomes. Everyone in the room felt inspired by
the possibilities of Barbra moving on. Her mum said, shakily, 'do you think
she could hold down a little job, then?' and the professionals nodded sagely.
Someone turned to Barbra and asked what she had learned on the programme.
She paused and said, 'I take the rubbish out in black bags'.

　　In this statement Barbra was asserting her personhood in a way that only
the day opportunities staff in the room would really understand. We knew
(and could produce evidence in certificates), that Barbra had learned all kinds of

1. The term learning disability is used here rather than the term learning difficulties, which
has a much broader definition within the education legislation. A definition may be found
in *Valuing People* (Department of Health, 2001, p. 21).

skills and disciplines with regard to holding down a job with a range of activities. We also knew that she would take any opportunity she could to take the black bags down to the refuse bins because Frank, one of our other employees with learning disabilities, would work around that area and they would have a squeeze and a kiss behind the bins. And in the scheme of things, having employment-related skills comes a second best to having a sex life. Herein is the challenge to a modern day-opportunities service. It's nice to know about money, travelling on buses and to have seen all the accessible sights in London. It's great to have a 'little job' or even a 'big job' which brings in some cash. But it's not a life. Most of us staff would not be content with just work and leisure and education activities. These are not ends in themselves, they are means for us to understand our environment and maximise our ability to enjoy ourselves, but also to take care of those we care about and be who we want to be which may include being sexual, glamorous, foxy, committed, a mother, etc.

So, Barbra was asserting her perspective on her situation. And my question is: how many of our clients are expressing rage and frustration about their difficulty in achieving the things that are really important to them? Secondly, are these the same things that we have identified on people's menus for services? In Barbra's case, as with so many other clients, she was dependent on us for any access to opportunities. It was therefore incumbent on us to understand her needs and facilitate them. It is not appropriate to be taking time out of work to have sexual encounters. But, hang on a minute, she seems to be saying, 'if I don't have any other chance to express myself what do you expect?' When we enabled Barbra to attend the Octopus Club[2] she was able to express her need for dancing and social contact and, yes, maybe even sexual contact.

> A person-centered approach is based on the premise that the human being is basically a trustworthy organism, capable of evaluating the outer and inner situation, understanding herself in its context, making constructive choices as to the next steps in life, and acting on those choices.
> A facilitative person can aid in releasing these capacities when relating as a real person to the other, owning and expressing her own feelings; when experiencing a non possessive caring and love for the other; and when acceptantly understanding the inner world of the other. When this approach is made to an individual or a group, it is discovered that, over time, the choices made, the directions pursued, the actions taken are increasingly constructive personally and tend toward a more realistic social harmony with others. (Rogers, in Kirschenbaum and Henderson, 1990, p. 382)

Barbra's development could be interpreted in other ways, for example it could be argued that her mental illness had gone into remission. We will return later to the challenges for services when clients seem to be outgrowing them. I would now like to consider an anecdote about a client who has almost no developed speech.

2. This is a dance club for people with learning difficulties]

Philippa is a young woman who has been in the day opportunities service for a number of years. We do not seem to have found the right interventions to enable her to develop her skills and abilities. She is a woman who has a dual diagnosis of mental health problems and learning difficulties. We decided to train the entire staff team as pre-NVQ assessors to enable ourselves to improve our ability to understand the impact of our interventions with clients. We wanted to get better at enabling people rather than doing things for them.

Philippa seemed very ready to participate in the training process. She joined the staff team for some of the training and seemed to be having a great time. We decided to try our hand at enabling her to improve her self-care skills. We were all energised by the idea. Looking back on this it seems hard to recall a potential pitfall that we didn't fall into.

Philippa sometimes forgets to take herself to the toilet and sometimes forgets to 'prepare herself for the outside world' after she has toileted. So we felt it would be an excellent intervention to help her work on her personal care in a systematic way. We brought our checklist in and began to prompt her through it; washing and drying hands — that went without a hitch except we didn't have a towel prepared. One of the team dashed off to find one. Applying hand cream — we found some. Brushing hair — we produced a brush. Nobody had noticed that Philippa's hair is braided. She must have wondered what was going on. She tried to brush her hair and looked a little confused when the brush got stuck. A staff member intervened and offered her own hair for brushing, as practice. Unfortunately, it was heavily waxed and when Philippa tried to get brush through it the hair began to stand up with static electricity. This was, of course, a lot more interesting than simply brushing hair. Eventually we had to intervene. Philippa had realised that by bouncing the brush on the staff member's head the hair took on a life of its own — tremendous. A quick scan down the checklist brought us to 'checking your appearance'. She was satisfied with her appearance but not necessarily from looking in a mirror. We realised a whole new bunch of learning outcomes would be required for her to become interested in mirrors. Whew. We had completed the process. All our checkpoints had been checked and we could begin the process of evaluating how we had done in empowering Philippa to develop her ability to care for herself. As we walked down the corridor chatting away about how good we had been at the exercise and carefully celebrating her own contribution and achievement, one of the staff suddenly stopped in her tracks, saying, 'Philippa, do you need the toilet?' There was a nod and a smart dash to the toilet. It was a comical situation where a significant part of the meaning of the activity, i.e., this is what I do when I have gone to the toilet, had been removed from the process. Whilst we had been busy trying to enable and empower her to take better self-care she had a growing need to go to the toilet. Learning must never be separated from personal meaning!

Rogers states six observations as to how the Person-Centred Approach may have relevance to the helping professions. It seems valuable to revisit those, when considering our experience in developing day opportunities.

1. A sensitive person, trying to be of help, becomes more person-centered, no matter what orientation she starts from . . .
2. When you are focused on the person, diagnostic labels become largely irrelevant.
3. The traditional medical model in psychotherapy is discovered to be largely in opposition to person-centeredness.
4. . . . those who can create an effective person-centered relationship do not necessarily come from the professionally trained group.
5. The more this person-centered approach is implemented and put into practice, the more it is found to challenge hierarchical models of 'treatment' and hierarchical methods of organization.
6. The very effectiveness of this unified person-centered approach constitutes a threat to professionals, administrators, and others, and steps are taken — consciously and unconsciously — to destroy it. It is too revolutionary.
(Kirschenbaum and Henderson, 1990, p. 393)

Here we are principally concerned with people with severe learning difficulties who present challenges to services or people with complex needs. The following definition, from Knowsley Social Services, may help to define the client group of concern:

People with learning disabilities who have one or more of the following additional support needs — physical, sensory or communication impairment, mental health needs or behaviour which challenges people and services — or any combination of these factors. Because of their multiple needs they may have been excluded or have had reduced opportunities for activities, roles and types of relationships which others enjoy and that would enhance their quality of life. (McIntosh and Whittaker, 2000, p. 55)

It is tremendously exciting to see the emphasis on person-centred practice in the recent government white paper (Department of Health, 2001). It is 30 years since a significant government statement was made about people with learning difficulties. The last paper tried to address the problem of institutional care — moving people from hospital to community. It seems like this paper is also addressing the same problem — helping people be a part of community. There is no single model of how the work should be done except to say that it should be driven by the needs of the person. The priorities will include: healthcare, supporting carers, enabling people to have control over their lives, housing choices and employment opportunities.

The principles on which developments are based will be:

• legal rights
• personal independence
• personal choice
• inclusion in the community. (Department of Health, 2001 p. 33).

The resources invested in this sector are significant. An estimated £3 billion was spent on services for people with learning disabilities in 1999–2000. Even so: 'some 20,000 people with Learning Disabilities, often with the most severe disabilities or Challenging Behaviour do not receive a day service.' (Department of Health, 2001, p. 32).

The antithesis of a person-centred approach is an 'institution-centred' approach, described by Goffman as:

A basic social arrangement in modern society is that the individual tends to sleep, play and work in different places, with different co-participants, under different authorities, and without an overall rational plan. The central feature of total institutions can be described as a breakdown of the barriers ordinarily separating these three spheres of life . . . the various enforced activities are brought together into a single rational plan purportedly designed to fulfil the official aims of the institution. (Goffman, 1961, p. 17)

Residential and day services have often been building-centred, staff-centred, resource-centred, institution-centred, rather than person-centred. Institutional care is characterised (at best) by an attitude of 'care'. This is essentially something that is done to the recipient, 'what I do to care for you'. The significant shift in attitude is to an attitude of support. This is characterised by an approach that seeks to identify what support this person needs to have as ordinary and meaningful a life as possible and access to all the things that lie therein.

These have been characterised in five 'service accomplishments'.

Accomplishments describe worthy consequence of service activities . . . Each accomplishment supports a vital dimension of human experience which common practice limits for people with severe learning disabilities. These interdependent qualities of experience include:
* *growing in relationships*
* *contributing*
* *making choices*
* *having the dignity of valued social roles*
* *sharing ordinary places and activities.* (O'Brien, 1989, p. 19)

Living within the community is more than a political stance. The Person-Centred Approach is relational. The first condition for constructive personality change to occur is that 'two persons are in psychological contact' (Rogers, 1957, p. 96). Segregating clients, even those with severe disabilities, within uniform disability environments reduces the possibilities of psychological contact. A person-centred approach will seek to identify the person's aspirations and community networks, including their personal and cultural interests, and facilitate those.

Jane lives in a secure unit. She was known as 'Hitler in a dress' to the staff. She would regularly defecate and spread her faeces over her bed and walls. Staff felt that she was doing it deliberately. She never went out because of her behaviour. When an activity staff member was allocated to take her out at a regular time to build her confidence in travelling to her local community her behaviour was transformed and she would wait expectantly for the staff member to arrive. She was only incontinent of faeces once in a year of work whilst she was out. Staff agreed it was a transformation. She now meets regularly with another service user and they appear to have developed a profound level of sympathy and communication which does not involve words.

> *Brian works in a restaurant cleaning the dining room . . . staff recognise that difficult behaviour, which led to his institutionalisation and has frustrated their efforts at behaviour management, happens less frequently since he has been working. His job coach notices that Brian seldom bites himself, swears loudly, or sucks his thumb at work and thinks it is mostly because of the influence of his co-workers and his interest in his job.* (O'Brien, 1989, p. 3)

When Rama first came to the service she was placed in a large room with the other clients. This was a noisy environment with people coming and going and a lot of shouting. She would throw herself off her chair and bite and spit. We realised she didn't like noise or being in groups of people she didn't know. She was stressed. She was insisting that we listened to her. For the periods she was in the centre we ensured that she had her own space amongst things that she liked and sounds she felt comfortable with. Her behaviour was radically transformed.

Our attitudes and expectations for people with even profound disabilities will reflect wider social attitudes and expectations. If we recognise that helping our clients with their *learning problems* is an essential part of enabling our clients then how are we doing with helping people to learn generally? Carl Rogers had a lot to say on this in 1975, but it has an uncannily familiar ring today:

> *I feel that conventional education from primary school through graduate school is probably the most out-dated, incompetent, and bureaucratic institution in our culture. It's also pretty much irrelevant to the interests of the students. It's really very disturbing to me . . . There have been such changes in religious institutions, in industry, in every institution you can mention, but education clings to the past like a leech. I think that perhaps it's because, unlike almost every other institution, educators get no feedback from their consumers. They listen to the alumni; they listen to board of education; they listen to the board of regents; they listen to politicians; but they do not bother to get feedback from their consumers. I think education has become quite out of touch with the modern world.* (Rogers, in Evans, 1975, p. 38)

It makes absolute sense that the consumers of a service should be the ones who dictate what service they receive. We would expect no less in our daily lives. The controversy enters the picture when we are the consumers of a service but not the direct purchasers. Who then is responsible? In the case of social care services the purchaser and the provider are always the two most important players, which is exactly the situation that Rogers has identified in 1975 with the education system. The potential of providing direct payments of benefits to service users to enable them to choose the services they wish to purchase offers an exciting future if a scary one for service providers. Believing in the right to choose and providing the tools to choose is an essential philosophical underpinning of a Person-Centred approach.

What else has Rogers got to say that is of interest? What is the purpose of social care work? is another one of the first principles which needs to be established. Speaking about the effectiveness of social welfare agencies Rogers says:

> ... *the only thing that really counts is whether you help to develop independence and self-understanding in people.* (Rogers, in Evans 1975, p. 80)

> *There is quite a bit of lip service given to helping people help themselves. When you come right down to it, there is very little in the way of technique that has been developed for helping persons achieve that independence.* (Ibid., p. 81)

Many social welfare institutions are not designed to develop the independence of their consumers. It is not in their interests to do so for the obvious reason that were they to do so their service users could graduate through the service and become weaned off from dependency. This would jeopardise the funding base of the institution and be a *failure* for the institution. Even if the income could be replaced by another service user or if the income is guaranteed through a block contract[4], development means change, which means disruption and disorientation for the staff team and client group and the institution, whereas stability offers familiarity, security and predictability.

The present challenges are to meet personal needs. That means staff need to embody the core conditions and be more fluid in their interventions. The role of staff members is to support rather than to care. This presents a problem for institutions. Contracts of employment are with the institution rather than with the person.

One worker describes an example of an approach based on empowerment:

> *The starting point is to ask one person what he or she really wants to do. Then go and make it happen for that one person. 'This is simplistic,' I hear you cry. Where is the flowchart and evidence from the USA?*
>
> *If someone expresses an interest in learning to make jewellery we often rush about looking for a class or we set up a new group. Six months later we end up with a segregated group meeting miles from people's homes, with perhaps just 5 percent of the class having any interest in the subject.*

---

4. A block contract is a contract for a level of service for a group of service users. It is not based on the particular individuals who may use the service.

Why not search out a jeweller running a small business in town and talk to him or her? Perhaps they could support someone for a few hours a week, working from a real shop or workshop, passing on skills. Perhaps the person can learn enough to sell their own work and earn some money. Perhaps we could buy a supply of stock in return. If the first jeweller says 'No' we go and ask another. Eventually one will say yes. Who knows what the possibilities are until we get out there.' (McIntosh and Whittaker, 2000, p. 63)

It is interesting how many of the challenges in the work with people with complex and profound disabilities are for us, the staff, who are supporting them. Rama is a young woman whose speech is limited to a few simple words in Urdu. She is cortically blind, wheelchair bound and doubly incontinent. When she is distressed she screams, spits and bites, otherwise she may spend lots of time huddled in a chair. Her only activity is being taken out for a walk in her wheelchair, she appears to like being on the move. Most staff do not like her or like working with her. Staff members request working with her for short periods so they do not get bored or feel the strain. She used to be taken swimming by two female staff members but they have both moved on and the consensus in the team is that she does not like swimming and anyway we haven't got the staff numbers to take her swimming. Effectively Rama has no friends or even meaningful contact with anyone other than staff in the day service: she has no meaningful leisure-time pursuits, learning inputs, and receives no culturally specific service. Imagine your life lived within these boundaries. Imagine you have no power to choose anything. Her quality of life is within our trust. What more precious entrusting could there be.

A small intervention in this cycle may sometimes have ripple effects that could never be anticipated. Nigel is a young man who has no use of his arms or legs and is completely wheelchair-bound. One day it was agreed with his support worker that we would try taking him home on the bus to see how he coped with it. By all accounts Nigel thoroughly enjoyed the experience. Furthermore, thankfully, there are increasing number of buses which offer a priority access space for people in wheelchairs so everybody was able to be comfortable. On arriving home, his mother exclaimed that Nigel had never been on a bus before. His teenage sister who was there said, 'It never occurred to me that Nigel could use the bus — maybe we could go out together occasionally. I've never been able to take him out because I don't drive.'

It is not too strong to say that from such a small intervention — to see beyond the special bus and special disability environment — new dimensions to Nigel's life have been added, as his sister has identified a way of them spending time doing new things together. By showing the way, the staff member has extended his social network and has not cost the taxpayer anything. It is not hard to imagine that if Nigel travelled regularly on the bus he might be recognised by the driver and other passengers who might take an interest in him and his life.

Often people say, 'what community is there to engage in?' But unless we use the facilities that are there and make our presence felt we are not giving service users the opportunity to develop relationships. Service providers will not adapt their premises or our needs, or adaptations may be withdrawn if they are not used. So the job begins to take on the challenge of helping to build a community.

> *Person-centred work challenges existing organisations, professional roles and personal lifestyles. It challenges workers to push back against the demands of the system to have the time, energy and heart available to respond to people.* (Mount, in McIntosh and Whittaker, 2000, p. 4)

> *Of course some people cannot communicate with words, but there is no reason to believe that their aspirations are any different. The challenge is to understand how they would like their life to be. Understanding someone's aspirations cannot be achieved by functional assessments or using checklists. It can only come about through sustained intense personal contact, friendship and understanding – and a willingness to make informed guesses, accepting that we all get it wrong at times.* (Wertheimer, 1996, p. 4)

With the right support we offer people the opportunity to aspire to their lives.

References

Department of Health (2001) *Valuing People. A New Strategy for Learning Disability for the 21st Century.* London: HMSO (the White Paper and a version for people with special needs is available at: www.doh.gov.uk/learningdisabilities/strategy)

Evans, R. I. (1975) *Carl Rogers, The Man and his Ideas: A Dialogue with Carl Rogers.* New York: Dutton

Goffman, E. (1961) *Asylums: Essays on the Social Situation of Mental Patients and Other Inmates.* London: Penguin

Kirschenbaum, H. and Henderson, V. (eds) (1990) *The Carl Rogers Reader.* London: Constable

McIntosh, B. and Whittaker, A. (eds) (1998) *Days of Change: A Practical Guide to Developing Better Day Opportunities with People with Learning Difficulties.* London: Kings Fund

McIntosh, B. and Whittaker, A. (eds) (2000) *Unlocking the Future: Developing New Lifestyles with People who have Complex Disabilities.* London: King's Fund

O'Brien, J. (1989) What's worth working for? In: Bradley, V. and Bersani, H. (eds) *Improving the Quality of Services for People with Developmental Disabilities: It's Everybody's Business.* Baltimore: Paul Brookes

Rogers, C. R. (1957) The necessary and sufficient conditions of therapeutic personality change. *Journal of Consulting Psychology,* 21(2): 95–103

Wertheimer, A. (ed.) (1996) *Changing Days: Developing New Day Opportunities with People who have Learning Difficulties.* London: King's Fund

The asexual myth

It has long been the notion that people with learning disabilities are asexual — they simply do not have sexual needs or desires — they are different from 'us'. On the other hand, there are those who feel that, given the opportunity, people with learning disabilities would be sexual all the time, and 'we' must do something to prevent 'them' from that, and especially the possibility of pregnancy. It is the latter notion that has provided the impetus for forced sterilisation of people with learning disabilities, and this has raised further dilemmas. If there is a fear of people with learning disabilities getting pregnant, for whatever reason, then this can lead to services denying that people actually have sexual needs, or denying them the possibility of fulfilling them.

The eugenics movement of the late nineteenth and early twentieth centuries saw to it that the passing on of 'defective' genes was prevented either by separation of sexes in institutional care or by sterilising women 'defectives'. Sterilisation of 'undesirables' was widely practised, especially in the USA, during the early twentieth century.

This practice was refined as a model that the Nazis used as part of their programme of sterilising people with disabilities. The thinking of eugenicists lay behind the extermination or mutilation of people with learning disabilities throughout the Holocaust. By 1941, 100,000 people with disabilities had been murdered. Forced sterilisation of people in institutions continued till the 1970s in many areas of the world. David King (1998) quotes a study conducted by Wertz and Fletcher (1994–95), who found that in 37 countries outside northern Europe the vast majority of genetic counsellors direct their patients in their decision-making from their own overtly held eugenic views. Though the laws are now more clearly valuing people with disabilities, and working towards positive discrimination, there seems to be a separation between what is available for those with physical disabilities, and those who have learning disabilities. Wertz and King have shown that there are professional advisors whose attitudes and behaviours are still belying eugenic principles. These issues may need to be discussed fully wherever there may be the desire to offer people with learning and/or physical disabilities services that allow them to choose to have (or not have) sexual relationships.

It has to be said that to assume that all people with learning disabilities want a sexual relationship is as dangerous as assuming that all people with learning disabilities are asexual. The crucial factor is what the person themselves is telling us, through their communicative behaviours. Supposing the person does want a sexual relationship: how would they know about the variety of issues involved, like relating in general, contraception, pregnancy, HIV, STD? Education in Britain was neither compulsory, nor widely available, for children with learning disabilities until the 1970s, and there was no question of sex education being included in the curriculum. There are two probable reasons for this: 'They won't need it because they won't be sexual' and; 'They would start being sexual if they had information on how'. Fortunately, more recently, sex education is offered in learning settings to children and some adults who have learning difficulties, but it is by no means common practice.

Partly as a result of having no access to sex education, but more importantly, little access to opportunities to develop 'no' skills, people with learning disabilities of all ages are vulnerable to abuse. If, in the name of care, choices and decision-making opportunities are reduced to the minimum, how can a person exercise a choice about who touches them or how they are touched? There is evidence that very large numbers of people with learning disabilities have been abused, compared with the numbers of those abused who do not have disabilities (Brown and Craft, 1992; Watson, 1989). Sexual abuse of people with learning disabilities has relatively recently been discussed, with action programmes and training for care staff being introduced (Brown and Craft, 1992).

People who have learning disabilities, however severe, have sexual feelings and needs in the same way as those without learning disabilities do. However, these feelings and needs may be different. First, for some, their sexual awareness develops later than usual due to developmental delay. Second, without access to sex education there can be more confusion and insecurity for some with learning disabilities. Third, because of their learning disability and restricted social developmental opportunities, people with learning disabilities often have less awareness of the societal norm of privacy around sexual expression.

Some of the clients who have been referred to me have been creating difficulties and embarrassment for their support workers due to inappropriate sexual expression. This takes many forms, from publicly masturbating to sexual touching of others. Some enlightened workers refer clients to me as they sense that sexual frustration may be an issue for the individual.

In these circumstances I am required to, at least initially, focus on a particular agenda. This does not sit comfortably with my Person-Centred approach and the inherent desire to allow the client to self-direct. The contracts in these referral situations are in reality with the referral agency rather than the client. It's as if I have to create a double-decker contract. The initial one is concerned with frequency, number of sessions and payment as well as an affirmation of confidentiality between myself and the client. The second and most important level is between the client and me — how they would like to use the sessions we have to look at the referred issue is explored between us. We can work in an empowered way within the boundaries set by the referral.

In circumstances where an agenda has been set out I will usually begin by explaining what counselling is and working together on the above decisions. Then I will say something like, 'I have been asked to work with you on something that seems to be causing you difficulties'. I then relay in clear, simple terms, what I have been told and invite the client to let me know their feelings about that. I then let the person know that, although I have been given this agenda, the space is theirs and what they want to bring to the space is acceptable, whatever that is.

For most of the clients with severe learning disabilities whose referral is due to 'inappropriate sexual behaviour', there have been communication restrictions which require me to find ways to meet each individual in their own particular communication system, whether that be sign, pidgin sign, pictures, restricted language or severe speech impediment. Whichever, it is my task to learn the other's language as quickly as I can.

For the educational and informational aspects of the work, I use line drawings and photographs created for this purpose by Dixon and Craft (see footnote p. 90) and begin by trying to understand whether my client is clear about the difference between public and private. Secondly, I need to know if my client can sense whether another likes or dislikes something. Line drawings and photographs help with this. Rather than being a one-to-one teaching session, I am concerned to share my empathic understanding of my clients' responses at all times, as well as to be free in offering my own genuine response if I am touched in a way I dislike, or is in any way inappropriate. I am also endeavouring to communicate my acceptance of my client as a person, whilst clearly demonstrating that certain behaviours are not OK with me. This is never easy to convey, but I must always try.

It feels essential to me to demonstrate my acceptance that my client's sexuality and desire for sexual fulfilment (in whatever terms that may be with the exception of abusing another) is healthy and perfectly fine, as so many have been punished for expressing their sexuality. The intended message from workers may have been that the expression of sexuality (in masturbation) was not OK in public, but the individual can generalise the rebuke to mean it is never OK, if there is no follow-up to explore what is acceptable.

Some of the clients with whom I've worked on sexual issues have needed to learn and understand the basic idea of private versus public. When that has been understood it is as if the inappropriate behaviour just stops as the individual has learned that private means being alone in places like a bedroom or bathroom, which are acceptable places for masturbation.

One of the issues I was asked to work on with Ian was on his continual touching of women's breasts, which, it had been assumed, was sexual in nature. In fact I doubt if Ian's interest in women's breasts had anything to do with sex or arousal. In the course of our work I learned that he associated breasts with his mother, who had had one breast and then the other removed due to cancer.

Though not an appropriate behaviour and potentially embarrassing for workers when they were out in the community, Ian was not being sexual, he was testing, it seemed, for prostheses and making contact through an intimacy he had shared with his mother. He needed to learn to restrain himself, even though there was more understanding of his intentions. It was important to explore with him his curiosity about breasts. For him it was interesting to test for those that were real, and those that were not. Had his interest in breasts included a sexual charge, he might have been diverted from touching any passing woman by applying the radical idea of allowing him access to erotic material. This would have allowed exploration again of the importance of knowing whether another person does or does not want or like a particular touch. Of course, one would need to set aside any of one's own feelings about the existence of erotic material, and might include important discussions about the difference between what might be erotic and what might be pornographic. It might have led to giving Ian the opportunity that other men have, of freely choosing to view erotic material in private. With Ian, I was not challenged to suggest such a potentially contentious strategy to his support workers, as it was clear that he was not actually sexually inclined towards breasts. It was important in his case to clarify and understand what his particular feelings were and address those, in order to help him understand that, though mum let him touch her prosthetic breasts, other women did not like it.

For other clients there is a need to learn the simple technique of masturbating successfully, because their attempts, whilst inappropriate and obvious, were also obviously unfulfilling, and frustration and outbursts would often occur instead. I know of some therapists who risk prosecution (Brown and Craft, 1992) for hands-on teaching, something I have not felt able to do. However, the use of line drawings (Dixon and Craft, see footnote p. 90) specifically designed for this purpose can help the individual to learn the technique to autoerotic fulfilment.

The world of consensual sexual activity is often unavailable to people who have severe learning disabilities and yet some do want that, including the fullness of intercourse. This begs the question for me: is the desire for intercourse innate or socially learned? For some of my clients it is utterly clear why intercourse and only that will do, and why consensuality is irrelevant. This is because they have experienced sex against their will, though nevertheless finding it arousing and enjoyable. One of the most confusing issues arising from sexual abuse of children, vulnerable adults, and those who have been raped, is that arousal, and sometimes orgasm, can occur even though the individual may have been frightened, distressed or, against their own will, quietly compliant (Sanderson, 1995). The body is made to respond to stimulation, so that no matter what the emotional response, there may be physical stimulation to the point of orgasm. Where abuse is part of the person's experience, then that needs to be addressed as part of the work. To ignore that, and move straight to attempting to encourage responsible sexual behaviour, is likely to be doomed to failure.

For those people with learning disabilities who do want intercourse, and act on sexual impulses with any passing person, inappropriately touching or thrusting against them, the first part of the work is to focus on how we know another person likes or dislikes something. The basic idea that intercourse (I have not been called upon to work on the other myriad of sexual possibilities by my clients with severe learning disabilities) needs to be consensual is a difficult one to get across. The extreme difficulties of finding anyone of the opposite sex (apart from support workers, who should resist the idea) is fraught with difficulties since care systems tend still to put obstacles in the way. It is interesting to note that the myth that says that people with severe learning disabilities are asexual extends to the mistaken notion that if they were interested in sex at all, it would be of a heterosexual nature. This is not necessarily true .

In my experience, most inappropriate sexual expression has become habit due to lack of confidence on the part of family or support workers to challenge and channel it. It is much harder to support an individual to change a behaviour they've been doing for fifteen years than one they have been doing for fifteen minutes.

It is never easy, especially in public, to manage inappropriate sexual expression. As I write, I am in Greece. Yesterday, in the swimming pool, I saw two women passionately kissing and fondling as children played about them. Later a man and a woman did the same. Is that inappropriate? Am I a prude? Somehow it felt to me unhealthy for men and women to be expressing their sexuality publicly, especially with children present. Each culture will have its own norms which will include what is and is not appropriate sexual behaviour. Sometimes I've heard parents or workers saying they couldn't challenge their son/daughter/client when being sexual in public because

• they wouldn't understand anyway
• it's too embarrassing to acknowledge it, so best ignore it
• they wouldn't know what to do to challenge it
• the son/daughter/client might become violent if challenged.

Training volunteers for Kith and Kids (see p. 122 ff.) on sexual and affectional needs, I encourage them to consider first what they feel comfortable with. There have been times when I know one of our members is going through a phase of self-arousal wherever they are. At other times there may be no members doing that, but if volunteers feel they would just be too embarrassed to challenge it, they need not be assigned to support a person we know is currently doing that.

However, it is possible that an individual with severe learning disabilities may, that very day, in that very situation, find that their genitals are the most exciting new objects of interest in a long time. It is in that crucial phase that so much can be achieved by sensitive, yet firm, challenge — 'not here, people are about and you need to be private, I'll take you to (named place) so you can be alone'. The first message associated with the feeling of arousal is then, 'it's fine and needs to be private'. Few people go from the first stirring of genital interest and arousal immediately to orgasm, there are usually several exploratory experiences along the way. If this individual is in the early exploratory phase, there is less likely to be a feeling of urgency or deprivation if stopped at that point. If the individual is not verbal or has very limited understanding, diversionary tactics whilst in the supermarket, with the message, 'it's fine in private', can work so that the public expression is not allowed to take root as a habit.

Having said all this, most clients referred to me for therapy have been through many failed attempts at behaviour modification via various psychologists for inappropriate sexual expression. If we could realistically offer some appropriate opportunities for sexual expression these behaviours would not be needed. We are a long way from that.

One man who was wheelchair-bound, blind, and severely affected with cerebral palsy and a variety of other medical conditions, was desperate to have a sexual partner. He talked of his sexual frustration, and desire for a life partner, someone who would look past his physical impairments and find him attractive, someone who would want to have a sexual relationship with him. For him, intercourse was all — it would show him he was a man. Yet this had never happened for him, and, though in his late forties, it remained his sole ambition. If he could not have that, he said, why couldn't someone just help him: he could not even masturbate. He talked of his idea for 'enablers' or prostitutes. In some countries (but not in the UK) these services exist for anyone like him who needs help for all his basic needs. Here, there were no such possibilities for my client, who was dependent upon support workers to even make enquiries about such possibilities. It is easy to see why no-one so far had taken the risk, and yet my heart went out to this man. Were he freed from his range of disabilities, or even from just a few of them, he would have had the opportunity and ability to seek sexual fulfilment in some form. He had a healthy sexual appetite with absolutely no way of fulfilling his needs nor of finding relationships with others where he might experience being desired, he felt. All I could offer him was my heartfelt understanding.

Whenever a client was referred to me for work on sexual issues I refused to begin until and unless I worked with the team caring for them. To support an individual to make changes, there must be a consistent approach in their home environment, to support the learning and development of healthy and appropriate sexual fulfilment. Unless carers have opportunities to explore and examine their own attitudes, whatever work we may achieve in the therapy room will be undermined or confused if there is not a consistent approach in the home.

Even the most profoundly learning and physically disabled person may have sexual needs and may find ways of pleasuring themselves if given space. For some their fulfilment comes through other means, for example massage. This can be worrying for the giver if they do not understand that possible sensual fulfilment may have a sexual component too. To deny a person massage because they seem 'blissed out' (this happened to a man with severe learning disabilities I was working with) and might be sexually aroused seems cruel to me. After all, men and women who do not have learning disabilities may also become aroused during massage, but perhaps be better at diverting their own thoughts, or hiding the evidence! Feeling sexually aroused need not be a problem. It is the inappropriate or inconsiderate acting upon sexual arousal that is problematic. It may be for some that meeting needs for physical contact *is* fulfilment, where full sexual contact is unavailable, denied or simply not needed by that individual.

'I want a sexual relationship'
Nora's story

I worked with Nora for a period of about six months some years ago. Like so many others I mention in this book, to call her to mind brings her presence to me as if I were talking of only yesterday. I can only call her to mind because she remains present there, her experience so confining and unnecessary.

The first aspect of Nora's confinement was simply due to her entry into the world, which left her with a severe physical disability. Confined to a wheelchair, and confined within her body, Nora's only controllable movement was of her right arm. These movements took enormous concentration and effort, and were frequently thwarted by the predictably unpredictable spasms which affected her whole body, either completely or in isolated muscle groups.

Speech was completely impossible for Nora and no-one was very clear about her learning disability, or whether she had simply suffered from lack of relevant education. She could spell and used a very simple computerised board to spell out her messages. It could take ten minutes to type 'I want to talk to you', and this message might have to be re-written several times as each letter, painstakingly typed, could then be confused by the random several letters accidentally typed in during a spasm. When this happened, Nora would patiently delete each letter, as painstakingly as she had typed them in, and begin again. I have never met a more patient woman.

Many times I felt frustrated on her behalf about the primitive nature of her communication tool — with technology as advanced as it is, how could she still be using this method of communicating? Her acceptance, without complaint, meant that other, more sophisticated, resources did not come her way.

I saw Nora for counselling sessions as had been suggested by her tutor at her college, where she took part in a course for people with learning disabilities. She was very upset on that first meeting. Our sessions were extremely slow — I have a video tape of one she allowed me to record for supervision purposes. She was pleased to watch herself on video, and happy for me to keep the tape to always remember her by. Watching the recorded session reminded me of the intensity of the work, the enormous effort on her part to communicate, and the total focus on my part, watching her and her words as each appeared on the screen — sometimes for as long as twenty minutes or more, for a short sentence or two. As she typed, the words appeared on a single-line screen, big enough to hold four or five small words at any one time, and they would disappear as more were typed. It took enormous concentration on my part to capture the whole of what she had to say, especially if the spasms had interrupted proceedings. Two big issues were the main focus of our work, both relating to Nora as a woman with emotional and sexual needs which she did not have met.

The first of these involved her love for a key worker at her home. Living in residential care with very high personal care needs, Nora was continually in contact with people performing the most intimate of personal hygiene tasks — and these contacts were almost her whole experience of being touched. The key worker, here named Vicky, would give Nora a hug at bedtime. Nora valued this enormously and saw it as a part of being cared for and loved by Vicky. Nora was hurt and confused in her session with me — why had Vicky suddenly stopped being her key worker? Why wouldn't Vicky talk to her? She wanted to know what she had done wrong.

The following session was very painful for Nora. She had learned that Vicky would be leaving in six months. She had been told it would be easier if she and Vicky did not spend time together, then Nora would not be upset when her loved key worker left. This was Nora's understanding of what was happening. She was frustrated and upset. The only way she could talk with Vicky was if Vicky came to her, or someone took Nora to Vicky — and then Vicky would have to wait while Nora typed into her board what she was feeling and what she wanted to know. For many weeks Nora shared her sadness and frustration — 'people always go' — and I felt myself how tragic it is that, so often in the 'caring' professions, the client is not given the space or support necessary to demonstrate that it does actually matter to them when someone they have cared for, and felt cared for by, leaves.

Whatever was considered the degree of her learning disability, it was absolutely clear during her sessions that Nora possessed a high level of emotional intelligence (Goleman, 1996). She was clear about what she was feeling and able, to some extent, to make guesses about what the other was feeling.

Nora's confinement meant that others could keep distances and avoid her with no risk of confrontation by her because she needed physical help to even begin.

We explored other losses Nora had experienced and this led to her talking of her need to be cuddled and desire for romance.

One day, she arrived for her session in an extremely agitated state and without her communication board. It was even more important, it seemed to me, to meet with her, though it had been suggested by the person who brought her that it may not be any use without the board. I wondered if others were more reliant on the board than Nora was.

I told Nora I wanted to be with her, I could see she was upset and I wondered if we might find a way to understanding even though we hadn't got the board. She nodded vigorously. Nora's body was always a good indicator of whether I really had understood her, or whether I simply thought I had. Like people whose bodies are fully or even reasonably fully functioning, empathy was met first by a physical response. In Nora's case, if I really connected in understanding how it was for her, she would move excitedly and nod. For responses that were nearly right she'd move a little and nod — when I was wrong she looked confused. So there was no problem there in letting me know if I was on the ball.

In that session we somehow found a way to communicate. I would guess at a feeling and she would let me know if I was right. From our previous conversations, having established if this was a new issue or one we'd discussed before, I was able to review our previous discussions until Nora let me know which issue was on her mind.

It was not a session of earth-shattering consequence as far as the content went. But Nora and I moved to a different level that day. Again, it reminded me that the difficulties in communication that Nora had were less about her, and more about people around her. It was necessary to listen to the whole of her, her movements, facial expressions, eyes, the sensing of emotion in the space between us — and importantly recognising what is our own emotion and what is coming from the client. Nora's communication skills were highly developed, way beyond the confines of her disability. I felt in awe, after the session, of this wonderful, pure spirit, trapped as it was within a body that could not be relied upon in ways that most of us simply take for granted.

Loss, and especially loss of potential for sexual fulfilment, were the major focus in our work from then on. Soon, though, Nora happily informed me that she had a boyfriend who wanted a sexual relationship with her. Listening, I felt protective and concerned, knowing how physically vulnerable she was and how needy. It was not appropriate to share this with her and I endeavoured to openly listen whilst acknowledging my concern within myself and with my supervisor.

In the next session Nora wanted to talk about sex and we explored that — she needed to know about getting pregnant, she said. After answering the questions she brought to that session, I encouraged her to ask to see her GP and she happily said she would.

Over the next few sessions Nora described how she and her boyfriend relied on staff to bring them close to each other, he too being severely affected by physical disability. She said she had been put on the Pill. She and her boyfriend wanted to be together.

I was concerned when she told me, in a later session, that staff at their home had said her boyfriend would need to use condoms as well as her being on the Pill. As Nora had already told me that neither of them had experienced sex before I wondered why this had been insisted upon. Nora had just accepted the view of the staff and asked who would help her boyfriend with the condom.

As she relayed this to me I could picture the scene of unrest and even disgust which I had experienced with some care workers on workshops I had facilitated about sex and people with disabilities.

Nora disappeared, as far as her sessions and college attendance were concerned, quite suddenly for a while. I wondered what had happened and why the sudden unplanned trip.

When I next saw her she was thrown back into loss, her hopes dashed. After her trip a staff member had told Nora that her boyfriend 'has been kissing someone else'. Nora was beside herself. She had thought he loved her and now this and, she said, he was lying to her — he said it hadn't happened. Nora was lost in the pain of betrayal. Meanwhile I was wondering what motive lay behind telling her this, even if it were true. The next week she told me she now believed her boyfriend and all was well again. They wanted to be together, and they wanted to be sexual with each other.

In the next session Nora was devastated. Her boyfriend had, quite suddenly, been moved to a different care home. She had come close to a loving, sexual relationship — something she had wanted all her adult life — and now she felt she had lost everything.

Not long after this Nora was moved to a different residential home — an unplanned move as far as she was concerned. She had now lost her home, familiar people and her counselling.

Nora never spoke of, or gave any sense of understanding, the obstacles that were continually put in her way. Nor was she angry — because she did not see — about how her disability was made a handicap, not by herself but by those around her. She was a person wanting to love and to be loved — surely not too much to ask.

What was so sad in this situation was that staff clearly had not thought through the reality of the issue. Even if Nora and her boyfriend had been put in the same bed and even if it was thought essential to use condoms despite no previous sexual history, it was a physical impossibility for Nora and her boyfriend to have intercourse.

But, with less panic among those who cared for them, it would have been possible for them to share a room and a bed. They could then have worked out between themselves their own sexual and loving expression. They could have cuddled and touched — they could simply have been together and shared their loving. That would have fulfilled Nora's greatest ambition, to be a loving woman, and show her love in the way she perceived other women did.

Was that so much to ask for?

'He's behaving inappropriately': the importance of the shed
Simon's story

I introduced Simon (p. 6 ff.) when discussing dilemmas in the work which are particular to people with severe learning disabilities, in this case a middle-aged man referred because of his inappropriate sexual behaviours. He had very severe learning disabilities and extremely limited speech that was difficult to understand. Initially Simon could only manage about twenty minutes in session and let me know that it was time to finish by taking himself to the front door and ignoring me. I had agreed with the support worker who escorted Simon to and from sessions to phone him on his mobile phone to collect Simon whenever he was ready, to give him some power and choice about the work. So when he upped and went to the front door I would say: 'I see you are ready to leave, I'll phone Gary and he will come and collect you'. Over the months Simon gradually increased his time with me to forty minutes and I felt honoured since his attention span was so limited.

The team who referred Simon were ahead of their time in recognising the potential benefits of counselling for their day centre users with severe learning disabilities. Because of that recognition, and their commitment to supporting the work in terms of transporting to and from sessions and sharing relevant information, the clients I worked with referred by them had the opportunity to explore some long-term painful issues which had never previously been addressed.

The first word I recognised that Simon uttered was 'shed' and that was a word he repeated frequently throughout our work. I asked the support worker if 'shed' had any significance and he informed me that they always ignored him when he said it, as it was a meaningless repetitive word for him. I wasn't so sure.

Simon's inappropriate sexual behaviour was to go up behind women and thrust himself against them, which was not only uncomfortable for staff in his day centre and home, but also socially extremely difficult when it happened in Sainsbury's with a stranger. No amount of effort on the part of the staff had convinced Simon that this was not a good thing to do.

All the people I worked with with severe learning disabilities were referred to me because of their challenging behaviours, and because they had exhausted psychiatric and psychological routes to change or manage the behaviour.

It is almost impossible to address challenging behaviour unless one is confronted by it. I worked with Simon for eighteen months before being confronted by his attempt to thrust himself against me. And I lost the moment! I was shocked and responded with 'No' rather than being able to quickly follow through with an alternative for him — to help him understand when people don't or do like things, as well as concepts of private and public. He was beginning to show interest in the masturbation line drawings[1] I had been using

---

1. LDA 669. Hilary Dixon, Ann Craft and Nottingham County Council, *Picture Yourself*

in our work, along with efforts to teach him where his sexual expression was fine (in private), to empower him to fulfil his own sexual needs. He expressed some fear that he was wrong for being interested and I wondered if he had been admonished for his own attempts.

My plan had been that if I sensed that he was becoming aroused, I would show him to the bathroom, tell him he could be private and alone, and leave him to figure out whether he wanted to follow through with his sexual arousal, or lose interest.

Something I say on all training courses about challenging behaviours that can be of a violent or sexual nature when extreme, is 'never turn your back, always be aware of the potential for impulse'. But this is what did I do eighteen months into my work with Simon — and there had been absolutely no sign of the behaviour for which he'd been referred in all that time — I turned my back to open the door and he was upon me. In my shock I raised my voice when saying 'No!' and I think this shocked him too.

It was in that session that we confronted his sexual needs and his frustration that they were not being met generally, and that I certainly would not meet them then. The direct confrontation actually took us to a different level in our work. Getting over to Simon, who had very limited understanding, that I was not angry or sending him away because of what he'd done, was not easy and needed several repetitions. I needed to be clear that I did not like or want what he had done, but that I did want to work with him.

The eighteen months of regular sessions which led to that pivotal point had been characterised by Simon leading the sessions, and he, like most of my other clients with severe learning disabilities, developed a routine for them. He saw my guitar at his first session, and always liked to sing as I played for him. Many of our most connected moments came when I recognised and joined him in a few repeated lines of one of his favourite songs.

Simon would talk often of mummy and daddy and of course the repeated 'shed'. I attempted to track his utterances closely, always hoping that he would say a little more about whatever he raised. It was slow work.

'Shed' seemed terribly important and he would repeat it over and over. I would often respond, 'you're telling me about shed — it seems important, can you say more?' but he seemed happy simply to hear me say the word and I felt more frustrated than he appeared to be.

In desperation I asked his support worker to bring photographs of any sheds around Simon's home, day centre — anywhere so that I might help him express what its significance was.

The support worker duly supplied the photographs and Simon and I looked through them in a few sessions. For Simon this seemed OK, but we didn't relate at all to his shed — he still repeated the word in the same way after looking through the pictures.

I was reduced to cutting pictures of sheds out of catalogues and DIY brochures. Simon was not impressed. Whenever he mentioned 'shed' I tried to maintain my interest and attention although I was beginning to believe, despite my gut feelings, that the information I had been given at the beginning — that it was a simple meaningless repetitive word for Simon — was true.

One day, around the time of the session where Simon pinned me against the door, I was feeling frustrated. I really wanted to understand what Simon was trying to tell me. I resorted to grabbing a sheet of paper and drawing a primitive square. I said, 'it's your shed, Simon' and he was very interested. I asked, 'are the doors open or closed?' — 'closed' said he. I drew two lines and said, 'is there anything in the shed Simon?' 'A hat', he responded. I drew a wool hat and said, 'your shed has closed doors and a hat inside'. He was transfixed, showing more interest than he had shown in anything. 'Tree' he announced. I couldn't believe a tree was in the shed, so I drew it by the side and repeated the whole again — 'your shed has closed doors and a hat inside, and a tree outside'. 'Window' says Simon. 'You see a tree from the window in the shed?', I asked tentatively. He nods vigorously, 'And what else?' Simon responds, 'Simon shed'. I ask, 'Simon's in the shed?' and he nods again, so I draw a stick figure and repeat the story again, 'your shed has closed doors, and a hat inside, you are inside too and you can see a tree through the window', Simon is riveted. I ask, 'anything else?' 'Uncle Ken', says he and his arousal becomes clear as he begins to move his hand to his genitals. His mind is otherwise occupied now, so I suggest he have some time alone in the bathroom.

After this session, and our work on our own relationship after he had pinned me against the door and thrust himself against me, he gradually talked too of the sexual activity with his father. Simon knew that Uncle Ken was 'in heaven', so that what he was showing me actually explained why he approached women always from behind, though he was also clearly expressing his own sexual preference. The way he had been sexualised by his uncle had taught him that he should approach from behind when feeling aroused. His object of preference, when aroused, was women, not men. When he spoke of sexual activity with his father and his mother, I had a dilemma. I was unsure if he was saying something about what had happened or what he would like to have happened. Supervision sessions provided the essential space to clarify again the confidentiality policy agreed between myself and Simon, as well as between myself and the referring organisation. My concern centred on not simply dismissing Simon's vague references to his parents at the same time as not leaping to action on the basis of such vague and unclear utterances.

Simon's 'shed' had been part of his verbal repertoire for many years as it transpired but it had always been assumed to be meaningless. It was important to have the two parts of the equation before any change might be possible. That is, until there was an understanding of why Simon chose that particular way to express his sexuality, there could be little change. Simon had experienced sexual activity with others and enjoyed it. Though, as a vulnerable adult, what had happened to him would be considered abusive, to Simon it had been enjoyable and he wanted more of that.

Carrying the dilemma was not easy — I don't know what the *most* right action would have been. He never did communicate a clear connection between his parents and his sexual arousal, and I never did breach confidentiality. I worked with Simon to recognise that sexual activity is certainly fine in private. I encouraged him too in learning the difference between someone wanting and liking sexual activity with him and not liking it. That work will be ongoing, I imagine. However, Simon stopped throwing women against the wall and thrusting himself against them.

It was a slow — a very slow — process and the real work in terms of shift happened after eighteen months. It took that long to find a way into Simon's world and for him to take me into it — eighteen months of relationship-building and trial and error.

I only hope that Simon does find someone who wants a sexual relationship with him, and that they receive sensitive support in learning about each other, and learning that sex needs to be mutual. I hope that for him, but I know the reality is that Simon is likely to be thwarted in his desire for sex. I am aware, too, that it is this kind of complicated dilemma that can prevent people from really listening to those like Simon, who can quite easily have their repetitive utterances ignored, or be quickly disempowered by the actions of the authorities in their attempts to protect from abuse.

A Person-Centred challenge to 'challenging behaviour'

The term 'challenging behaviour' is an uncomfortable one which, whilst it is accepted parlance in the field of learning disabilities, begs a number of questions. Firstly, whose behaviour, and what exactly is challenging about it? The term is not used to include those who may have provoked or goaded an individual, since they may be staff members, but it is used about those who are being supported. Vic Forrest (see p. 33 ff.) prefers a more humane term, 'challenging needs', to describe those whose difficulties are such that they require highly skilled support to enable them to live socially with others, and without causing harm to themselves, others or their environments. Perhaps the field of learning disability will adopt this term in time.

Over the past eight years I have been invited by various staff teams of residential care homes to give training workshops on 'challenging' behaviour.

I always invite teams to begin by defining what they mean by 'challenging behaviour' and there is always some shock at my invitation. Then just as commonly, people recognise the assumptions, especially pejorative, about the term. Through brainstorming and discussion, the general definition that emerges is that some behaviour or action exhibited by one person causes some difficulty for another person or persons. What may be challenging for one person may not be challenging for another. We explore the myriad of behaviours that the team finds challenging, along the way learning more about self and others. We move on to something seen as wildly radical then, which is to recognise and explore the behaviours of each person, that challenges people they care about or work with. Through personal insight I am encouraging team members to consider which of their behaviours challenge the clients they work with.

The teams with whom I have worked support people with severe learning disabilities and have become disillusioned with behavioural programmes devised to manage challenging behaviours, but which rarely worked. Some members in every team I've worked with have admitted that they had so little faith in the programme or psychologist who devised it that they never bothered with it, and dealt with the behaviour in their own way. Many times there are expressions of discouragement, frustration and a feeling of having given up on the person they are supposed to be supporting.

The general approach to challenging behaviour is to observe and explicitly define the challenging behaviour; get a base line data on frequency and duration; devise a programme for modification or management; implement the programme; and evaluate by gathering data on the effectiveness of the programme in terms of frequency and duration. In practice, as team members tell me whenever I give this training, the programme is difficult to manage as staff members — those who do try to keep it up — have different styles of implementing it, so that some have more success than others. One of the key issues is that the person all this attention (or not) is directed at has no say in the process. Indeed, some behaviourists argue against informing and including the persons in discussion about the behaviour problem and the devised programme as it is deemed unnecessary for the treatment's success (see Lovett, 1996).

From when I began as a lowly classroom assistant, with no knowledge of psychology, it seemed to me to be madness to assume that only the person displaying the challenging behaviour was actually involved in it. What about the interaction between that person and others? For example, why did certain behaviours only happen with certain people and not with others? Also there was often no consideration given to what the person is communicating through their behaviour. In addition the person themselves may actually be happy with that behaviour: that it may serve them well, either in getting what they need, or in surviving their lives.

People with learning disabilities are less able to recognise the impact of their behaviour on others, especially those within the autistic spectrum (Howlin *et al.*, 1999). Of course, that statement can be true of any of us if we defend ourselves against awareness of our impact on others. However, people with learning disabilities are less likely to be defending and more likely to be missing the cognitive abilities for such awareness.

It seemed to me then, and still does now, deeply disrespectful to reduce a person to measurements of behaviours that others disliked without considering their meaning and to devise a programme to change, divert or eliminate that behaviour. I felt then, as I do now, that there must be some other, more humane, and hopefully more successful method of encouraging people with learning disabilities to develop their social awareness and I felt and feel passionately that this had to begin by understanding the significance of the behaviour.

It is much harder to change habits than to understand what is being communicated in new behaviours (see p. 132 ff.). Understanding at that stage may help prevent the habitual stage developing when the habit can reinforce itself, so that the message is lost.

If this is to be possible, then parents, teachers, carers, psychologists — all who have a role in supporting people with learning disabilities — could play a part in preventing 'challenging behaviours' developing in the first place by endeavouring to recognise, understand and communicate that understanding to the person. This can be done without the addition of any judgement, with acceptance of the person and with a genuine expression from themselves.

For example, Angela is repeatedly picking her nose and examining what she finds there — one way of responding (and I've seen this response to children and to people with learning disabilities) might be, 'Stop that, it's [by implication you are] disgusting'. One alternative might be, 'I see your nose is bothering you, yet what you find is quite interesting. I don't like seeing you do that, here is a tissue, perhaps you'd like to clear your nose'. This is a rather rehearsed and unflowing possibility, but I hope it offers some sense of relationship, which a behavioural programme would not. *Programme*: When Angela picks her nose, hand her a tissue and tell her to blow.

One hideous programme I was required to carry out involved sitting with Peter, a young man who regurgitated and chewed frequently after each meal, and getting him to spit the contents of his regurgitation into a paper bag I had to carry for that purpose. I was to say nothing but 'spit it out Peter'. It felt inhumane. It did not ever stop the behaviour and it totally ignored Peter's need for more to eat (he'd been placed on a diet for some reason that made little obvious sense as he was not visibly overweight) or to occasionally chew — perhaps a more successful response might have been to offer chewing gum.

Plenty of people without learning disabilities have the choice and power to ask for, or get for themselves a snack, or bigger meal if they need, or want, it. The mind boggles at the reaction we might receive if we dared hover around with a bag and say, 'spit it out'.

My efforts as an unqualified classroom assistant to voice my views about these matters were thwarted mostly by my own lack of confidence. However, when I did feel really strongly and verbalised my views, I was at best offered some slightly interested response or at worst ignored. My team leaders were great at listening and encouraging and even trying out some ideas. But if the psychologists were involved it was behaviourism full stop. I once had an argument with a psychologist who insisted that when I speak to the young people I must only use simple instructions because 'they don't understand anything else'. I was horrified at the idea of offering such sterile relationships to the young people I supported in the classroom, and refused to follow that instruction. Of course at times of crisis it would be important to reduce speech to a minimum and clearly give an instruction, especially if tempers were fraying. But communicating generally with the students was important to them and to me, and I knew if they didn't understand every word, they did understand that I valued them as people, and as a result of developing relationships there was progress. There were those who could manage their behaviour quite well when receiving an understanding approach, someone talking with them and responding to their communications. So many times I'd go for a break and come back to find Elspeth in isolation for having punched someone, and I could see that the probable reason was there was a visitor on the unit and no-one would have thought to reassure her.

When I went to study psychology, I wondered if somehow I'd find I'd been wrong all along and that behavioural management was really the best way for people with learning disabilities. But having studied the psychology and application of behavioural techniques I was more convinced than ever that it was against everything I believed people were worthy of.

Having said that, I have, in various settings (including in supporting my own son to manage his own behaviour), modified the behavioural techniques I learned about and had worked with in the school. If a student or later a client wanted to manage their behaviour in different ways — or if I had a problem with a student in the classroom — I would explore with them what the behaviour meant for them, what they needed and if they could see a way that would help them do something different.

I preferred this process to be initiated by the individual and often it was, because they didn't like responses they had from others for whatever the particular behaviour was. But sometimes I had a problem and I needed to let the student know that. For example, Sarah, a young woman in a group with learning disabilities and 'emotional difficulties' would repeatedly interrupt any other student, and especially any interactions I had with anyone but herself. She was not a popular young woman, and her behaviour did not endear her to her peers. After class I asked her if we could talk, and told her I was finding it difficult and uncomfortable being interrupted. I wondered if she was needing more of my attention. She talked then of her frequent moves from foster home to foster home, and the imminent move to a hostel — 'no-one has time for me, no-one likes me'. We thought through how we might both feel better — her getting some time with me to talk and me being able to talk with others in the group without interruption. She said she wasn't sure she could stop herself — 'it just happens'. Together, we devised a plan that allowed her to check her own behaviours. We talked about how she might interrupt without aggression and how she might reward herself when she knew she had resisted an interruption. We made time to talk when she needed it.

This behaviour programme felt respectful and encouraged Sarah to develop her self-control and her ability to express her needs in a way more likely to get them met. Behaviour programmes with people with learning disabilities, especially with severe learning disabilities, by their nature are done to the person and can only develop external control. I simply find that inhumane, based as it is on judgement and denial of relationship, both at the level of initiation of the behaviour and in attempts to manage it. That approach nearly always avoids recognition of the impact of ourselves on the person with learning disabilities and their behaviours.

A Person-Centred approach to challenging behaviour will naturally focus on the relationship in which the behaviour occurs, and attempt to understand what the behaviour is actually communicating. And rarely it may be necessary to implement some behavioural programme when all else has failed, in order to protect the individuals or others from harm. Even in these circumstances, a person-centred approach would include communicating an understanding of what may be happening for the individual along with a firm and congruent statement of intent to prevent the harm. For example a recommendation for encouraging Rachael (see p. 118 ff.) not to attack other residents was to recognise what she was communicating first — 'I see you are angry Rachael, and you want to hurt Jane: I want you to stop and tell me what you could do instead'. This approach was supported in Rachael's individual therapy where her frustrations and anger were allowed expression, and she had time to think about what upset her, and the consequences.

In training workshops with teams of residential care workers, having explored the myriad of possibilities of challenging with our behaviours, I invite participants to spend time alone reflecting on their own first experience of being confronted because of their behaviour. Materials are available for creative imagery. Participants are told that after the time for silent individual reflection, during which they can choose to represent their experience in whatever way feels right to them — image, words, silence, objects or private reflection — they will have the opportunity to share with the group, if they wish to, what they have learned about themselves and what it felt like to be powerless in the face of adult (so powerful) confrontation about their behaviour.

This is always a moving part of the training workshop, when people share feelings of embarrassment, humiliation, confusion, powerlessness, defencelessness, and often the inability at the time of the incident to really understand why what they had done had caused such clear messages that they were not OK.

From this place in the training it feels appropriate to focus then on the particular difficulties participants are having with the people they are supporting and their challenging behaviours.

Prior to the trainings I send analysis sheets for focusing on particular challenging behaviours. These ask participants to reflect on:

- The behaviour you find challenging (please be as specific as possible).
- Focusing on that behaviour — who or what is it directed at?
- What were you feeling prior to the incident?
- What was your response to the behaviour? (Be as specific as you can.)
- How did X respond to your response?
- How did other residents respond to the incident?
- How did other team members respond to the incident?
- How did you feel after the incident?
- How did you respond to the resident after the incident?
- How did other residents and staff respond to the client after the incident?
- Can you guess at what the resident was feeling before, during and after the incident?
- Was there any build-up — could the incident have been anticipated in any way?
- Is there any pattern in the behaviour (include times of day, people present, routine or changes of routine, people absent, epileptic activity, before, during or after the incident)?

These analyses sometimes shift the thinking even before the training, as they focus on relationships and feelings as well as behaviours.

The rest of the workshop allows participants to consider what the real message may be behind their residents' behaviours: some find it helpful to role-play, whilst others prefer discussion and sharing ideas. The team are encouraged to think of ways of approaching the people behind the behaviour in ways that communicate understanding and choice — choose the old destructive behaviour or the new positive one.

I have felt greatly encouraged when working with teams who, to a person, really want to support their clients to change. And for change to happen it feels to me that there must be a commitment from all to consistently support each other in supporting their clients.

Sadly though, sometimes attitudes in caring professions are anything but caring. Some people genuinely believe that 'they won't learn if they're not punished for it'. Some people entered the caring professions desiring to care, but with unresolved problems of their own. In particular in the field of learning disabilities, it is easy to feel powerful and superior to, as by definition, people with learning disabilities, especially those with severe learning disabilities, as they tend to be powerless and limited in their cognitive abilities. I have come across carers, support workers, teachers and psychologists who displayed a degree of cruelty that elsewhere would be deemed unacceptable, or more likely to be found in oppressive groups rather than in the caring professions.

It is sometimes sadly the case that a person with learning disabilities is labelled as challenging, due not only to the innocent mistake of not understanding their real message, but due to mishandling, misunderstanding and sometimes even wilful goading. It is essential in working on challenging behaviours to support workers/carers in recognising their own part in triggering or escalating challenging behaviours. Incident records are nearly always about what the person with learning disabilities did or said — and they can't usually challenge that — the reporter of the incident is at liberty either to not recognise their own part in the incident or to sanitize their part. A Person-Centred approach would include understanding workers, carers and the individual displaying the challenging behaviour.

Amanda, a young woman with autism which included no discernable verbal ability, would hit out at anyone in close proximity, especially if they were people she did not know. This was regularly happening on her transport into the day centre. Most of the time the others sharing her transport were known to her, but sometimes there were changes. Sometimes the driver or escort changed. This was clearly creating enormous anxiety for Amanda. My feeling was that the solution lay in recognising the difficulty Amanda was communicating through her behaviour, and reduce the changes as far as would be possible. This might mean Amanda having her own taxi to the day centre, with a regular escort who would be trained in recognising Amanda's anxiety, and talking her calmly through it, whilst physically sitting as far away as possible in the taxi, so that Amanda would not feel crowded. In fact the solution that was used was to use a leather harness which strapped Amanda's hands to her sides, and this was used on her daily. The effect was that no matter how anxious or frustrated she became, Amanda could not lash out at anybody travelling with her. This was the alternative to listening to her communication — I weep whenever I think of it.

Challenging behaviour is, by implication, unacceptable. How does this fit within the Person-Centred Approach and its emphasis on acceptance? It is most important here to communicate the acceptance of the person as well as the non-acceptance of certain behaviours.

No Person-Centred practitioner would say that biting another person is acceptable. However, they would seek to communicate that the behaviour is not OK and dangerous at the same time as accepting the individual — sometimes in 'practice' this acceptance is communicated by *not* saying something like 'it's naughty, you're a bad boy'.

What has been missing in the field of challenging behaviour is the recognition that we cannot change anyone's behaviour but our own. Attempts to get another to change their behaviour are doomed unless the other actually *wants* to change. If there is an investment, reward and meaning in a behaviour, why would the individual want to change it? Yet when we take responsibility for changing our own behaviour — and here I'm advocating attempting to understand the meaning first — then change tends to occur in the other as a result.

If we can really understand what is being communicated, and find a way of letting the individual receive our understanding, there may be an opportunity for growth to occur, and less need for control and management. It requires an investment of time, resources, and every ounce of patience that can be summoned up to meet a person whose behaviour challenges us, and together to find ways of communicating needs, wants and dislikes without resorting to destructive behaviours. My final thought on this particular issue is that I have many behaviours that I find challenge me, and may challenge others as well. I would resist with every pore of my being any attempt to impose some programme to change my behaviours, and would embrace any attempt to support me in understanding them for myself so that I can change them myself. It is from that perspective that I approach challenging behaviours. Perhaps a prerequisite learning experience for those working in the field of learning disability would be an exploration of their own challenging behaviours, and considerations for growth and development such that that particular behaviour might be reduced or replaced by some other more positive behaviour.

Interview with Sara Watson:
Supporting clients with challenging needs

Sara Watson worked for social services for eleven years supporting people with learning difficulties of a variety of age groups and needs, firstly as a support worker, then as deputy manager. Subsequently she transferred to the voluntary sector as deputy manager of a house for people who challenged services. More recently, Sara works as co-ordinator of a supported living project for people who have challenging needs. She has based her approach to the people she supports on an intuitive philosophy that places the individual at the centre of services.

Jan: Perhaps we could start by talking about what you feel about a person-centred approach, and what attracted you to that, rather than anything else in your work.

Sara: I think I've always had a belief, that individuals are — just that: individuals. To have a general care regime that everybody works along doesn't fulfil people. I've tried it several different ways. I have tried other approaches and I've found that they tend to meet staff members' needs, rather than the people that we're meant to be supporting and enabling. So I've always been moving more towards a person-centred approach, particularly with profound disabilities — that's the field that I've been working in mostly. Although I've worked across many different care fields including dual diagnosis, elderly, adolescent . . . many different fields. I think as an approach, you can work in any care field with adolescents, with children, with people with varying disabilities: it works because you're identifying something that supports the person themselves, holistically.

    I think the starting point is that all forms of behaviour are a form of communication. If people can understand that when they first go into the care field, and that can be underlined with them, then a person-centred approach can be developed naturally.

Jan: Do you mean if you're really listening to the behaviour as a form of communication, then you can't help but try and understand?

Sara: Yes, and move on from that as a starting point. OK, so, maybe that person is displaying that behaviour because of . . . not because they're trying to get at you, or it's not for 'attention-seeking'. All forms of behaviour are communication. Somehow acting as a detective is part of the role, to find out exactly what's gone on in the person's history, because we're all defined as individuals by what has gone on in our lives. That's often extremely difficult, particularly with people with profound learning disabilities, in my experience, and particularly for people who come from large institutions, ages have been lost, identities have been lost. There's just been a number on a file, and 'that person's always done that' — I ask, 'Why?' You know, people have moved on, the messages have got lost, and the original behaviour was probably far less extreme, but probably not listened to, not recognised, and it's gradually grown into something that's not manageable. So, I think finding out the person's history is really important.

Jan: I see. Can you just say a bit about what you understand profound disability to be, as there seems to be some confusion in the field about the continuum from mild learning difficulty through to profound learning disability.

Sara: I would place profound learning disability as non-verbal, probably within the autistic spectrum. But again, it's difficult for me to define, because when you start getting into definitions, then you start taking away the individuality again. It's very difficult. What I might see as profound, you might not see as profound, and it's something that we come across all the time in care work. Social services have got one identification system, the health authority have another, the speech therapist may have another, and then of course, all these cross-references lose the person. I struggle with definition, because it's open to interpretation. I feel what's important is to understand the person's history, if you can, as far back as possible, and look at the factors. Some people's behaviours are brought on because of change of routine: if you've been brought up in an institution and your routines are set in a particular way, and then somebody comes in and changes that routine without any rhyme or reason, then that may initiate a behaviour that is later labelled 'challenging'. All those issues, particularly about standards, including how families have interacted with the individual. I think we as professionals tend to ignore that: 'Oh, they're mere carers, they've always done it that way, and we think we have a better way', and again it's easy to lose the individual preference within that.

I've found, particularly with profound disability, we need to look at the person in depth. Again I resist the professional term 'assessment', though I know that is what it is — I want to really, really look at that person, look at the odd hum, here there and everywhere — why does that person hum when s/he comes into the kitchen? Is it a good sign? Is it a bad sign? Is it something they're requesting? Is it because they're too hot or too cold? Really spending a lot of time looking at that person in depth, so that you get a profile of that person . . .

Jan: Gain an understanding of that person . . .

Sara: Yes, and their individuality, their details, their intricacies, the things that are important to them. That can take a long time, in my experience. I worked with a chap who was placed in the autistic spectrum, non-verbal, was extremely aggressive to himself, not particularly to others, but he would self-mutilate, would head-butt kitchen units, to the point where he had a big callus in the middle of his head, and big calluses, bite marks on the backs of his hands, big bruised areas on his knees where he would just butt himself all the time, with no apparent reason, as far as the staff team could see. So we spent a lot of time looking at him in depth, when these occasions occurred, and it became blatantly obvious that it was usually out of his frustrations. He would butt his head on the kitchen unit because, (a) it was right there, it was nice and convenient, (b) it would have an instant effect, because the staff would either ignore him and walk out, so he could help himself to the kitchen or they would start running around trying to hold things up to him, trying to identify what he wanted.

Jan: So either way, it got some action.

Sara: Yes. So we started to work on that particular behaviour and said to ourselves, 'OK, what is it we think this chap is trying to achieve?' And eventually, after much trial and error, we tried every time he did it offering food: it was very hit and miss. Sometimes he would take a bite out of an apple, and throw it on the floor; sometimes he would just ignore it, or push it away, and butt even more. We tried various different things to see what stimulated him, but after a process of elimination we found out that he was actually asking for a cup of tea.

Jan: Ah, that's what he wanted.

Sara: Yes. Because the cups were actually in the cupboard that he was butting.

Jan: Right, so by really, really listening you found the answer.

Sara: Yes. By thinking about it, breaking it down and discussion has to be the key word — communication amongst the staff team, and talking about the real nitty gritty. It can drive staff teams mad, you know, like — why are we concentrating on this stupid area...? When I got to this particular project they'd spent two years trying to teach this chap to put his T-shirt on. I was saying to them . . . 'why?' . . . 'Because that's what we're doing, it's his care plan, and we know that he can do it'. And I said, 'Yes, but he hasn't got the motivation to do it'. I mean, if he's going to get three meals a day and be dressed and bathed and everything else, why is he going to suddenly start thinking, this is a good idea putting a T-shirt on? All you're doing is creating more friction.

Jan: It's not relevant for him . . .

Sara: No. So we worked considerably on this head-butting, and it took us five years, but we got to the point where this chap could go into the kitchen — we stopped locking the kitchen door, as had been the previous regime — he could go into the kitchen, we taught him to open the cupboard instead of head-butting it, and take a cup out of the cupboard and put it in front of the kettle.

Jan: Right. So you knew it was cup of tea time.

Sara: Yes. And the empowerment that that gave him was absolutely amazing. We reduced the behaviour considerably: once we got to that point of understanding what he meant, after five years, he started to have less time when he was locked in his own world, and less self-mutilation. He stopped pulling his hair out, he'd had huge bald places where he been pulling it out before, and stopped all of that. We followed up with some aromatherapy work as well, so that when there were times when he would get frustrated because we couldn't read his language, we would put the burner on — we learnt that he liked the flower smells after a lot of trial and error again. It would be help him to chill out, and calm down and then we would start the process again, and say, 'Well OK, we understood that we weren't understanding you that time, you've calmed down a little bit now, we're all chilled out, we all feel a bit better, let's try again'. We would then guide him round the house to suggest things to look at to find what was frustrating him.

Again, they used to bath him twice a day before I came. I asked why . . . 'Because that's what we've always done'. It used to be confrontation issue in the bathroom, not a particularly big space, fully tiled, and this poor chap squeaking resistance, and the staff would be standing there insisting he get in the bath. It was absolutely ludicrous. So we spent a lot of time talking in the staff team about things like, what time of the day is it better for this particular chap, is it in the mornings, is it the night times — do we have more success at midday? Let's try all different times, so we did, and found that he was more co-operative in the evenings, when he seemed to be more chilled out. We started using the aromatherapy oils in the bath, to encourage him into the bath. We started picking really nice bubble baths and oils, to make him feel nice and relaxed, and eventually we stopped the confrontation there as well. Again it took several years, a process of elimination — to me that's the essence of person-centred work.

Jan: A willingness to stay with the process.

Sara: Yes.

Jan: As I understand it the behavioural approach is still the dominant one for people with learning disabilities in your care field . . .

Sara: Very much so.

Jan: And what you're offering in contrast takes a long time, but actually allows the individual to grow.

Sara: Yes, and take more control in their own lives. Because continually what we as professionals are trying to do is make decisions, and think this or that is best for the person, and it's not necessarily so. I did a training course once where part of the course was to look at our morning routine — we all wrote down our morning routine in lots of detail, passed them round to each other, and had to looked at the next person's routine. Just a small example was how people brush their teeth. Some people use hot water, some use cold, each had a preference for a certain toothpaste, and we're all grimacing at how people could do things that would be abhorrent to us. But the chap I was talking about could have any one of fourteen members of staff walk in and do his teeth, or any other thing for that matter, in a different way, because it suited them. And then, everyone is upset because he's 'throwing his weight around' as they termed it. Well, I would be as well! That exercise worked particularly well to highlight what that must feel like for people with learning disabilities.

Currently I've used a person-centred approach with regards to encouraging empowerment with profound learning disabilities. So looking at day services in particular. Looking at how we can encourage a person to make more choices about where they wish to go, and what they wish to be involved in, and move away from the more domineering type of model, and focus more on 'We'll go when you are ready to go'. Again the biggest struggle is staff time. Obviously you have to have a certain amount of, and abundance of care hours, and staffing ratios, particularly with profound learning disabilities in the community. A lot of the places I worked at have been based in local communities so it's incredibly difficult to have a choice-based activity programme when the local community is quite resistant to having people running around the neighbourhood as they would see it, making bizarre noises and kicking and so on. There has been a lot of resistance in those situations. Also using objects of reference — this is a speech and language type process, where people with profound learning disabilities can actually use objects of reference to identify their choice. This can also reduce difficult situations when out in the community.

Jan: Do you mean like, I'm thinking of somebody I worked with where a particular orange juice carton was her orange juice. So we cut up a carton, so she could keep the picture to show us when she wanted juice. No other orange juice carton or picture would work, only that particular one.

Sara: Yes. Another chap that I worked with, he came from a large institution and would actively seek out cigarette butts from the ground and eat them. He again was autistic, and extremely demanding when he was in one of his 'paddies' as they termed it. So, consequently when he got to us, he had a complete addiction, to the point where he would jump out of first floor windows to get a cigarette butt. So we worked on objects of reference, setting up a routine for him. So rather than having a resistance to taking him out, because we'd have him scrabbling on the floor for cigarette butts, we set up a routine for him. He came from an institution, and was familiar with routines, and identified with that type of thing. So we used a twig to signify actually going outside to the park. We started with offering him the twig and saying, 'It's nine o clock', pointing to the clock, 'we're going to go out for a walk', and giving him the twig to fiddle with, and then we'd go out for our walk. And slowly, over time again, we built up a box, so that he had particular objects of reference, and he would take the things out of the box and bring it to a staff member to signify when he wanted to go out, or for this or that, so I think that worked really well. Extremely well, and again, it empowered him so much.

Jan: And they were his objects of reference, that seemed important.

Sara: Yes. He was in control. And it reduced the cigarette butt craving markedly. We had been told it was physical, and we'd never be able to reduce it, and we'd have to use medication and so on. Also we would have to restrict his walks because more than fifteen butts was toxic and so on. But because he was taking control and he felt more empowered, he didn't need it so much. It wasn't a sticking point any more.

 I also use the person-centred approach in sensory work: looking at somebody's emotional needs is something we quite often overlook on a professional basis. So I've used a lot of massage techniques, foot massage in particular, aromatherapy oils, sensory rooms, using sensory stories, encouraging people into sensory rooms and using the sensory story to build their experience, and that's helped people considerably as well. And, allowing people to be angry, allowing times to be able to say, 'OK you're really peed off at the moment, let's go and bounce around in to sensory room, punch a few bags and so on', and that's fine, there's not a problem with that.

Jan: So rather than actually trying to suppress the anger, and label and judge it, you're seeking to make space for them to experience it and accepting it, it's OK.

Sara: Yes. I worked with another lady who used to swear a lot, and she had a profound learning disability label on her head, although I would doubt that, but I think she just had years and years of being a square peg being pushed into a round hole, and she had a lot of learned behaviours. A lot of family pressures too. She'd been pushed to the point where she didn't recognise negatives. So, for example, if you asked her to draw a happy face and a sad face, she could always draw a happy face, but she couldn't bring herself to do a sad one. When asking her if she was OK, she'd say, 'Yes, yes, I'm alright', then she'd be walking off talking and huffing under her breath, using all the obscenities she could think of. It was like turning that around, and recognising that when I shut my own front door, if I've been caught up in traffic etc., I might swear, or scream and jump up and down, and it's perfectly acceptable.

Jan: It seems that people who have a learning disability have to be more than the rest of us, because we are always ready to 'work' on their behaviours.

Sara: Yes. Well, we tried to encourage this lady by using art therapy to help her develop a happy sense that was real, and again it took many years to encourage her to have an understanding that her negativity was OK, and just accepting that there are certain places that you can go with that, and certain ways without attracting too much attention. Ultimately she moved into a supported living project, and she's in her own flat, so she's gone through the whole process. But that person-centred approach to her environment, and her, saying to her, 'yes, you're an individual, and you've got every right to be happy sad, indifferent, sexual' — let her know over that long time, that she was acceptable.

The difficulty is getting staff teams to sign up! The overall staff team, getting them to sign up for the whole philosophy, because I think a lot of people go into care work to fulfil their own needs. It can get to the point that they're there because they want to be seen as a caring individual. And you can still be a caring individual, but you don't have to be in control. You're there to support.

Jan: Not to punish.

Sara: Exactly. It's incredibly difficult to get, especially larger staff teams, and unfortunately quite often people with profound disabilities and associated challenging behaviour have huge support. Large staff teams that aren't doing anything in particular, other than controlling really. They're also making sure that when people go out in the community, they are not in danger. OK, fine. I haven't got a problem with that, but do it hand in hand with empowerment and choice, and moving forward for somebody to actually have an aim and focus.

Jan: It sounds like the difference between a developmental model and a control and management model. That there is some kind of balance there.

Sara: Yes, and it is very, very difficult to move away from the control because then you're talking about risk as well. And risk is a huge no-no, in lots of care sectors, especially in recent years, where litigation and the media are very much to the forefront. Registration is also very limiting I found, working in many registered care homes. I've found registration extremely limiting unless you've got a care plan that's full of consistent details with a clear direction: 'Oh yes, you're teaching this person to put their T-shirt on, how wonderful.' It's not looking at 'How does this person communicate?' I've found the attitudes within registration extremely constricting in many respects, because they're looking at the environment, they're not particularly looking at residents' individual needs. Or how the staff team are supporting those people to identifying their own needs, and move that forward.

For the chap that I was talking about before, we identified as part of his person-centred planning, as part of his long-term development process, an ultimate dream of his to be living in a rose-covered cottage, because he likes rosy flower smells of aromatherapy, in a big open expanse where he's got a lot of open space around him so he can wander along in his own space in his own time, without busy roads, and without others controlling, and have several female members of staff supporting him when he needs support. To encourage him, and pick up on the skills he wants to develop, and to encourage him to take more control, at the speed and motivation levels that he chooses. Not saying, 'You conform, this is what we offer, these are our care fields'. Rather than trying to fit him into a situation where the routines and regimes are set and have nothing to do with him, so that he ends up in a challenging behaviour unit all his life, I want to provide an environment where he can develop as far as he is able.

Jan: I know that's something you're quite involved in, running a challenging behaviour unit, so some of the things you've said already about staffing and so on, come into it. But I suppose I'm hearing the criticisms which came within my own background in an environment which was entirely steeped in behaviour modification, when I was an unqualified care/teaching assistant — the argument essentially was that certain behaviour must be stopped or modified, that 'appropriate' behaviour must be increased, the argument being a lot about how the other people in the environment were protected. I suppose I'm wondering how you approach those issues in an environment where everybody exhibits challenging behaviours.

Sara: I think the people themselves sort it out. We're all human beings, and I know for a fact that the more controls that are put on me the more I'll retaliate. If I feel that somebody else is getting uptight with me because of what I'm doing, then I'll think that's their problem, not my problem. I'll move towards who's around me to feel secure. And nine times out of ten I've found that's what the residents do in the environments I've worked in — they will move towards another resident. Although it can still result in clashes of behaviour at times, they might attack other residents at times, but ultimately again, we live in our own home environments. I'm not saying that somebody's got a right, if they've got a lesser challenge than that person, to come and beat them up completely, but I'm saying they've got a right to work out their own wrongs within a group, with us waiting on the sidelines ready to jump if necessary — but who are we to say that? I'll look at ways round it. Say, this person's going to scratch, then keep his nails short and file them, and look at diffusion techniques before it gets to the point where there's going to be an attack. Look at the environment. Maybe you can make that better. Maybe there's something in the environment that's problematic.

I worked with a chap with tunnel vision. Nobody knew he had tunnel vision, they just assumed it was just his behaviour. We changed the whole decor of the house to emphasise different sections of the house, so he could identify where he was and his behaviour's reduced. I think, because we so concentrated on 'oh, it's too risky, ooh it's dangerous', we stopped seeing the wider picture. And people will work out their own roles within the living situation. If only we would stop intervening constantly, they will work out their own roles. And they will work out who's dangerous, who's not dangerous, not matter how profound their learning disability is. Time and time again I've had that proved to me. They will work out who to attack, who not to attack, who to go to for comfort. Definitely with non-verbal profound learning disabilities, an understanding of facial expression, body language is there. It's so subtle, their reading of it of every subtle little movement, is way beyond ours. We wouldn't even notice it, a blink of an eye, a twitch, whatever, but people with profound learning disabilities will know that. They're not stupid! They won't go and sit next to someone who's scratched them before; they'll avoid that corner of the room.

Jan: So if they are allowed to, then they are empowered to make those decisions.

Sara: Yes. And they can go to their room if somebody's in there screaming and shouting and jumping up and down and having a difficult time then they can choose to go off and go to their room. Or they can choose to go and sit next to them. Maybe they're feeling that they can comfort that person, but we're not privy to that language, but we make ourselves privy to that language. We think we know, or we decide that we know. The six people that I work with the most, they all came from large institutions and probably knew each other before they ever came anywhere near me. They have their own roles and relationships and their own ways of reading situations. And then we come crashing in say, 'no, it's not that way — risk, risk', and I think in many ways we encourage these behaviours, we compound it, via the environment we put people in, and via the approach, and how we deal with situations.

Jan: Somehow, what you seem to be saying is, if you steam in you teach the person not to trust themselves to deal with it themselves, and therefore that escalates matters.

Sara: And we make that person very selfish, very self-focused. And we take away all of those skills about group living and group interaction, because what happens then is they go straight into an 'attention-seeking' model. 'If

I do this behaviour, then somebody's going to come steaming in and spend time with me.' It should be the other way round. We should be spending time with that person, because it's positive time, and we want to spend time with them and encourage them, not ultimately wait until there's a situation. People pick up very selfish behaviours. Working in support living now it's become very clear to me, the other end of the scale. People have come into that environment from institutions totally narrow, self, self, self, self, focused on 'Well, I'm doing the cooking', they don't care about anybody else, that's it. 'I've got to learn my skills, stuff everybody else.' The hardest part of the supported living project has been to get people to gel as a group. To learn to identify facial expressions, and understand something about each other. Why was that person laughing, why was that one looking sad, what was the meaning of that subtle touch of the hand? Actually working with people to have an understanding of other people. I think we've become too protective. We go completely too far the other way.

Jan: And somehow prevent any kind of social interaction, which escalates the handicap in a sense. Things stop being a difficulty or disability and begin to be a handicap because we've imposed it.

Sara: Many times yes. Ultimately we've really got to look at a person-centred approach, then you've got to look at that individual, and look at all of them holistically. Their emotional needs, their sexual needs, their skills, their development, their approach to life, their favourites, their likes and dislikes the whole holistic area and then empower. Look at that person very, very closely they will give you cues of how they want to develop and where they want to develop. That chap I mentioned, for example. He was obviously doing that, giving cues. He'd been doing that for five years before myself and a new staff team arrived, and we started saying, 'there must be something' — he was quite clearly identifying his developmental need. He was quite clearly saying, 'I want my needs met'.

Jan: But nobody had actually understood it, or listened.

Sara: No. And when we did understand, he moved it on from there. Once he felt he had achieved something there he went on to, 'I'm not particularly happy around my bath times' because he was jumping up and down and showing behaviours there, so we said, 'OK, we'll look at that then next', and then he identified cigarette-butt addiction. So he's chosen the direction of the work, he directed the whole process. And it doesn't matter how profound the learning disability, as long as you've got the time and the energy and the commitment to actually look at it in such minute detail — it can take a year, five years, ten years. And I think that's where we struggle as professionals, particularly with registration. They want to see little bits of immediate progress. They want to see that that person has made an improvement in that particular area. They might have made an improvement in their toileting for example but they might have taken several steps back in another area.

Jan: It's like the practical skills, and eagerness about independence at the expense of social interaction, and social and emotional development. If they can iron their clothes, fantastic, but the fact that they throw the iron at another resident . . .

Sara: Yes. And we keep refocusing it to what we think the goals are. We measure by our priorities in life, but we haven't had their background. We haven't had their experiences, how can we then decide that this is the focus that we should follow? We've got no right to do that really. OK, yes we do have obligation of care. We can't just throw it all up ion the air, but we've got no right to impose what we think is the right development on somebody. Going back to that chap for example, if it was his wish for the rest of his life to decide when he wants a cup of tea, then that is fine. If he felt empowered by doing that, then that's fine. There are people in the so called 'normal' world that spend their lives wandering around the streets and their only developmental goal in life is to be socially accepted or the local friend of a lot of people: may do a lot of good work in the local community, but nobody questions that. We come to impose it, I think, and we can't see the wood for the trees a lot of the time.

Jan: Like living in a goldfish bowl.

Sara: Very much so.

Jan: In my experience, there have been times when the Person-Centred Approach poses a threat to the usual order, and certainly in the care field, where psychiatric diagnosis and treatment, psychological assessments and treatments mostly using a cognitive behavioural, or most likely a strictly behaviour approach still tend to be the main approaches to people with learning disabilities. What is your experience of offering your person-centred approach among other professionals?

Sara: I think that people who actually work with me for a length of time actually feel the benefits, ultimately for themselves, but particularly for the residents. But yes, I have met several brick walls, particularly with other professionals especially in the health sector. Obviously, because all the literature and that sort of stuff comes from eminent people who have all sorts of qualifications, and I'm just a mere person who works with the residents on the other end of things. The only thing that's ever really worked for me all the way through is actually turning it around on its head and asking people how it would be for them if they were in that situation — by the Grace of

God we are not. As I said, what right have we got to say this is right, wrong or indifferent? God forbid we step out tomorrow, we could be hit by a bus, and we could be in a residential unit with no voice, no abilities, and how would we like to be treated? When I start feeling that I'm bashing my head a against a brick wall, I will say that to staff teams, and to other professionals.

Social workers and review systems I've struggled with for many years. I feel it's incredibly intrusive and invasive to actually have a group of professionals sitting around the table talking about the intricacies of somebody's life. Sometimes these professionals are on the very edges of people's lives, say a speech and language therapist for example. I've actually experienced a professional talking about a resident in front of them who had probably profound learning disabilities, was verbal but had limited understanding of the situation, talking about her sexual behaviours with other people, at a review. I found this incredibly uncomfortable and stopped the meeting and said, 'No, I'm not prepared to continue with this', and left the room. As far as I know they carried on the meeting. After much discussion with a resident advocacy group, where we were talking about reviews and how we could make the situation better, bouncing ideas around, most of the ideas were about banning reviews altogether, but because of the protocols we couldn't do that.

So we came up with an idea on a special 'try it' week[1] to go through to social services and discuss with them their review system. So we set up a training day and pulled in lots of different professionals, not just social workers, as part of the advocacy group and spoke about the review system in particular, and said how uncomfortable we felt. Social services said they understood but reviews had to happen. So we turned it round and we said, 'OK, we'll go off and research some details about a couple of members of this group' — we took names and addresses and that sort of stuff — 'and we'll come back and hold a review for you guys'. And the residents were incredibly intimidating. They actually went and gathered various rumours that had been floating around the organisation with regards to certain members of staff, so they came to the review with these various rumours about relationships and so on. One particular social worker squirmed and practically disappeared under the table while they were talking about 'and they said this, and they said that, and she's been knocking this person off', and it was really empowering to the residents. It was empowering for me too, it taught me so much, it was just a suggestion, a one-off, completely spontaneous, we hadn't really identified the risk, which was considerable, but it was incredibly empowering for the residents, for me, and ultimately for the other professionals, although I think they felt we were just being a bit too candid about it all. They did get the gist of what we were saying.

---

1. A week at the day centre where lots of different activities were on offer for people to try out

Jan: That whole squirmy feeling of having all those professionals sitting around talking about what the person has done and what targets they're setting without the person themselves actually being able to participate, it can feel quite inhumane…

Sara: Well I've been in reviews where the person hasn't even been there, because it's been deemed that they're too challenging to be there. Then why hold it? What's the importance? What are we going to be saying that the person couldn't identify for themselves if only we could understand their language, but we haven't taken the time to learn their language, so why are we all sitting here discussing it?

Jan: Of course, the argument is that we must have reviews to justify the money. What would you recommend?

Sara: Again, the issue is how we interpret justification of the money. I was continually being asked in my supervision in my previous organisations what I was achieving with the residents, when we were actually spending five years teaching him to open the cupboard door, to show us he wanted a cup of tea. And I said, 'we're not really achieving anything, but if you want something quantifiable, his life is empowered, so as far as I'm concerned we're achieving everything we set out to achieve, and his behaviours are lessening'. The other thing is to monitor behaviours incredibly in depth with individually designed forms, so that you can look at the behaviour precisely. It's very time-consuming and it needs a lot of commitment from the staff team. You can clearly see — it might not be leaps and bounds, but over a period of time you can see little bits of the behaviour begin to ebb away. I've seen it physically ebb away with people. The chap I mentioned, the big callus on his head began to fade and now it's not there, he stopped pulling his hair out. He stood out like a sore thumb in the community anyway; he had huge bald patches where he'd pulled his hair out. That all grew back and he had a lovely shiny head of hair. And he used to love the various shampoos we used to get him. He started to take pride in himself. We encouraged him to be part of our shopping trips — he'd be all over the shop, and squeaking, and all that sort of stuff, but we discovered through all this that he quite liked orange so we used to buy a lot of orange stuff, and we wouldn't have any behaviours at all for those three hours, because he had his orange T-shirt on. So if you're looking for quantifiable, you have to really know the person, from manager downwards, and know them so well that you can communicate for them on their behalf when necessary, to others who hold the purse strings.

Jan: I'm getting a picture of an awful lot of work being done on your side, in developing continually your relationship with your residents. Do you find within those relationships that clients begin to respond?

Sara: Yes, very much. Respond particularly to the individuals that are working with them. Moving back to this chap again he was quite far into the autistic spectrum on the severe side and he was extremely locked in his own world. He would only really come out of that world when he wanted his needs met: the rest of the time he was trolling around eyes up in his head, looking at the ceiling, fiddling with bits, and physical contact was extremely limited. He wouldn't hold eye contact, and everything we had involvement with him often involved confrontation, even down to giving him his medication. We had to wait till he was spooning his food in his mouth and I found that extremely objectionable that we'd have to shove tablets into his mouth while he was spooning his food in. But he had quite severe epilepsy so we really had to work out a system and that was the only one we could work. But when we started turning things around, and empowering him, he started to spoon his food and then stop, and actually look up. So we started to say 'thank you' and give him a smile, respond to him, and move on from that. Eventually it got to the point where he would come into the kitchen and we could give him water instead of the food, instead of waiting for him to spoon frantically, because he knew we weren't going to abuse him. We were actually respecting him and saying, 'thank you very much' and sometimes giving a rub on the back or a small touch on the back of the hand just to let him know that.

   Later we gave him foot massage. At the beginning, the aromatherapist could get thirty seconds with him. For over a year and a half she was coming in three times a week, she'd touch his big toe and then he'd squeak and be off. As a team we spent a lot of time supporting the aromatherapist, encouraging her to keeping trying, and keep experimenting with different oils and so on, and at least ten to fifteen minutes after every session was spent talking about how she felt, how it went encouraging her to keep on trying. After a year and a half, one day she just came in, he sat down on the sofa and put his foot up. And now, he still dictates it. Sometimes she comes in, and he puts his hand up and walks away, so she'll just go and give to someone else.

Jan: He gets to choose. And massage again is a different way of listening; he gets to direct his own needs in that space.

Sara: He quite clearly identified the floral oils were better for him than the spicy ones, and he particularly likes rose, but he identified that for himself by the length of time he will allow her to massage him for. We looked at it over a period of six months, and whenever she used the spicy smells, she would only have five to ten minutes with him, but when she used the rose smells, she would have twenty to thirty minutes. It's just about reading the language. It's putting yourself into that person's position, leaving your own hangups and power at the door step, so that they can say, 'I'm coming in here to support you', support being the most important word. Not control, not move, not push — but support, and to go with the flow. Sometimes I'll have a terrible shift and feel like I haven't achieved anything, everything's all upside down, and what the bloody hell am I doing? Now when I go back to that house I walk in and say, 'hello', calling out his name, and he'll come walking up the hall and I'll say, 'give us a hug', and put my arms around him, and he'll respond, and there's a new group of staff there now, and they'll say, 'I've never seen that before'. Our relationship is still there, and I go and visit regularly and spend time, and if I go to a sensory workshop, and bring something back and we'll have a game and use the sensory room, so that we've still got that relationship. And the aromatherapist has got an extremely good relationship now, and he loves her, you can see it in his face when she comes, it's not just a smile, but his eyes light up. His whole posture changes, usually he's crouched up, humming, but his whole posture changes.

Jan: I'm wondering what your position is on force-feeding. I am bothered by some of the situations I hear about where it seems clear that the individual is communicating, 'don't feed me, don't give me tablets, I've had enough, just leave me alone'. And these people end up in hospital being tube fed, sometimes in restraint, or being sat on and forced to take their tablets. It disturbs me that somehow these people whose quality of life is sometimes really dire, are having their only possibly choice taken away. I'm assuming you will have had to manage situations like these, and wondering how you do that in a person-centred way.

Sara: It's something I've struggled with too. I've worked with many people with dual diagnosis[2], who hover between learning disabilities and mental illness and obviously when the mental health side comes in they can be extremely suicidal. I feel like a broken record, but we're not reading the language. Nobody wants to die, but what they're saying is, 'please stop controlling me, leave me alone'. Whether that's right or wrong, if we start making it a sticking point, a confrontation, it just becomes worse.

If you've got nothing in your life, and you're sitting in living room for eight hours a day staring at a television with limited activities, limited stimulation and the only time in that eight hours that you've actually got staff contact or you feel that you're actually getting attended to is three times a day when staff come in and give you your tablets, what are you going to do? You're going to fight it, so you make it that much longer. Or you're going to feel that you're going to be abused. Somebody's coming towards you, they haven't paid you any attention for the rest of the time and suddenly it's all businesslike and brisk, and then we're surprised when people start resisting. Stop making that confrontational. Maybe that particular time is likely to lead to confrontation. OK, so maybe for the hour

2. See Michael Farrell's chapter, pp. 70 ff.

before, spend some time, talking, having fun, let's go to the room and play records, whatever is a good thing for that particular person, something they like — then do that for the hour before you have to give the medication. It might take a long time, but it has to be worth trying.

Jan: That makes a lot of sense. I can't imagine being willing to take tablets from somebody who hasn't spoken to me all day, and then sits on me and tries to force them down my throat.

Sara: Or from somebody who had ignored you all day. And suddenly wants to be your best buddy so they can get your tablets down your throat. Or they're offering you a nice glass of orange juice that you could well have done with an hour ago, but it just comes to get you to take your tablets. No thank you!

Jan: *'It's not tea time yet . . .'*

Sara: Yes, all that sort of thing — we've thrown that up in the air. People will establish their own routine if their allowed to.

Jan: That is your bottom line, isn't it? I think you said earlier how systems and protocols and all of that actually are there not to suit the person who they're meant to be supporting but to fit it with the regime, and be as cost-effective as it can be.

Sara: And meet registration standards, and the parent's needs, a hundred and one other people are considered, but rarely the person we're meant to be supporting, particularly in residential. I think supported living is the new direction, and the new care standards for 2002 with the White Paper[3] and the draft and the Valuing People[4] document are incredibly empowering. So there's a step in the right direction, underlining no matter what your disability, you've got rights. But the other thing with supported living, the hardest part in my job is saying to the tenants, 'Yes you've got rights, but you've got responsibilities too. If you want to be living independently in the community, you want to live your life the way you want to, then you have pay your rent on time, you have to be at least conducive to your neighbours and those around you. I'm not saying you have to like everyone, but you have to make sure that you do the work you're meant to be doing, filling forms in for your benefits. You can't just chuck it up in the air and say, "I've got rights as a disabled person", you've got responsibilities'. It's about teaching people about responsibilities, because when they've come from family settings, or institutions, they've been extremely closeted and become extremely selfish. Everything's been done for them most of their

3 and 4. Available from HMSO

lives, and they now want to take control, and that's fine, but they must take responsibility too.

Jan: It feels like you really have been giving a voice to the voiceless in all you've been talking about. If you could encapsulate what you understand from your experiences of the people you work with, in a sentence or two, what do you think they would be saying to us?

Sara: Spend time listening to my language and stop corralling me, and putting me into labelled categories, because it meets your needs, not mine. We can't keep shoving round pegs in square holes, and that's what we do. We can't just say, 'Oh, that person displayed challenging behaviour when he was five, so that's a challenging behaviour label for the rest of their lives, let's push them in that direction'. Or if that person has been labelled profound learning disability because they didn't talk till they were thirty, or that person is in the autistic spectrum, we're going to put them in a home with lots of other people who are autistic. So . . . understand my language, spend time to listen to my language and don't put your own interpretation on it.

Jan: Thank you.

'Her outbursts are a danger to others'
Rachael's story

Rachael was referred to me by the manager of the group home where she lived. There were problems with her behaviour, and things had got to the point where she may have to be moved for the sake of the other residents.

Rachael was forty-five when I began seeing her, and we worked together for about two years. Her speech was relatively easy to understand yet her frequent lapses into silence, sometimes mid-sentence, meant that our sessions were often quite fragmented.

Rachael would lapse, in the main, because she had very severe epilepsy. I had been informed that she 'only' suffered with tonic-clonic seizures[5], and that her pattern was to have these in the mornings. We made appointments for the afternoons to give her the best chance of being well enough to attend. I knew too that Rachael's mother was dead, but she did have some irregular contact with other members of her family; that she had experienced rape; and that she had lived for many years in a long-stay hospital and had been living in the community in her current home for only a year or so, having been moved because of her behaviour a few times.

The behaviour causing concern was that Rachael would attack other residents and sometimes staff members, biting, scratching and hair pulling. Even when she was at her most agitated from time to time in our sessions, she never attempted to attack me, and so I never witnessed this behaviour first hand.

Though I had been asked to address this worrying behaviour in our sessions, Rachael's referring manager understood that I would be working in a Person-Centred way, and be establishing a relationship of trust, where I hoped Rachael herself would raise the issue. I explained in the first few sessions what the counselling was about, inviting her to use it to talk about anything she wanted to. Rachael, however, had formed the idea fairly early on that she had to bring 'problems', and when she couldn't think of any, was sometimes silent for lengthy periods.

I learned that staff in her home were referring to her counselling in that way, and I became known by Rachael as 'Jadice, the problem lady!' I never quite understood why my name had been elongated in this way — but Jadice I remained throughout our work. It took many, many months before Rachael understood that she could talk about anything. The issue of 'problems' was an interesting one. Rachael did not tend to think in terms of 'problems' unless she was told something was a problem: she either thought about it or didn't, but not under that heading.

Our early sessions then were characterised by lengthy silences, anything up to half an hour long, then sudden utterances, which I would endeavour to catch and encourage expansion upon. On one occasion, Rachael began to talk

---

5. These are generalised seizures of a convulsive nature, sometimes also knows as *grand mal*.

about a seizure she had had, which had caused another injury to her face. She was grappling to tell me what her fit had felt like and couldn't get the words out at all. I had, as usual, paper, pens and other material, and Rachael began drawing on a large sheet of paper. She became totally absorbed in her creation and I observed her, joining her silence as she worked on a large black circle with a long black protuberance. I was amazed by her concentration and her patient effort in creating her image. I, witnessing what I assumed was the black hole of unconsciousness, was amazed by Rachael's ability to represent in image, but not in words, how her seizures felt for her. I learned a humbling lesson that day. When she had finished, I invited her to tell me about her picture — to which she responded, 'it's a frying pan!' Well, of course it was, and I could see it clearly now. Somehow in the time it had taken her to create the image, its original purpose had been lost and drawing for its own sake took over. Rachael was delighted with her frying pan and pleased that I had recognised it and her pleasure in it. We returned many more times to the issue of her epilepsy and over the time we worked together, Rachael was able to express her frustration and anger about how it stopped her doing things. Her seizures prevented her attending at all at times, and at others, though there in body, she was not completely there in mind.

Rachael was fortunate to have around her a staff team who really wanted to help her make her placement work. They all seemed committed to giving her a quality of life and to building her self-esteem. She always looked well-groomed and enjoyed showing me when her nails had been painted or her hair had been cut and styled. The team saw beyond her challenging behaviour, to her generally sweet nature and caring qualities. Yet there were still times when staff as well as residents were frightened of Rachael, because her outbursts were very violent.

In one session about three months into our work, Rachael commented in a surly way that she'd been in trouble. This was the first time she had mentioned the outbursts — but she was not actually talking about the outburst. It was as if she didn't know why people were angry with her, and she certainly didn't like it. I knew, as I had been informed, what had happened the day before when she had attacked a very vulnerable resident. But for Rachael, she felt that suddenly, out of nowhere, people were angry. Her whole sense of the situation was of being attacked, not attacking.

This view of her world led me to wonder if her epilepsy was playing any part in her outbursts. It is known, for example, that some people can become aggressive due to anti-epileptic drugs, underlying brain abnormalities or the confused (postictal) state after some seizures (Devinsky, 1994). Others have quite severe mood swings associated with inter-ictal [6] activity and/or the side-effects of anti-convulsant drugs. I encouraged her carers to have this checked out, but they were frustrated and despairing about the doctors who cared for Rachael. Everything, it seemed, was put down to learning disabilities and no further investigations were deemed necessary.

---

6. Abnormal neuronal activity between seizures.

Rachael was certainly having epileptic activity in sessions, though never a convulsive seizure. She would lapse into frequent absences and have periods of complete confusion. These subtle states are very familiar to me, not only because of my experiences with students and clients with epilepsy, but also having been sensitised to the subtle manifestations of it through living with a son who has the condition.

It was important to recognise the disruptions in Rachael's cognitive processing and I tried to meet her wherever she was when she returned from a lapse — and that might be somewhere entirely different from what she'd been talking about before the lapse. The rhythm of our sessions was dictated by Rachael's epilepsy first and foremost.

After many months I risked challenging her about an attack on another resident, when she was talking about being in trouble. I said that I wondered if she might be worried that I wouldn't like her any more if she were to tell me that she'd hurt someone else. I risked this, as the quality of this particular disclosure seemed different from those when she had genuinely seemed not to know what had happened. I got the sense this time that she did know, but was embarrassed. She had said she was in trouble whilst looking away and covering her eyes — not her usual searching way of communicating. In response to my challenge, Rachael visibly stiffened until I said, 'Rachael, good people do hurtful things sometimes, and if you have hurt someone, it won't stop me liking you'. She visibly released. That was the shifting session.

There always were examples of her not grasping why she was in trouble, and yet from then on, there were times when she was able to admit, with embarrassment, that she had pulled someone's hair or bitten someone. We were able then to explore what she might do instead and it became clear that Rachael had no way of recognising or expressing anger, even though evidently she felt it and acted on it. She was calmer always after her sessions, staff reported, and yet there were still — though less often — outbursts.

We played around with stamping and shouting 'I'm angry' and Rachael thought this was utterly hilarious. She initially thought it was very naughty, but liked the game. In different ways we focused on other feelings — naming them through my empathic responses to her mood, facial and physical expressions and her vague utterances in grappling to say what was happening for her.

Rachael was learning a language for her emotions which she had previously been without. Because of her verbal ability, it may well have escaped attention throughout her life that some of her outbursts may well have been avoided if she'd been able to say how she was feeling, and have time with someone to talk that through.

So many like Rachael get labelled, and then through fear avoided, or through a need to punish, ignored. Of course these actions exacerbate both the need for one-to-one attentive listening and the frustration and heightened arousal when it is missing.

Over the months Rachael learned to recognise what she was feeling and to ask for someone to talk with her. Her outbursts had stopped before we finished our work together, due to the sensitivity and commitment of the staff team in her home responding positively to the changes she was making.

Rachael was a woman whose life had been determined by her epilepsy and restrictions of her learning disabilities as well as by continuous losses and upheavals as, over the years, carers she learned to trust would come and go, usually without a goodbye. Family members had died and she'd not attended funerals, and others disappeared altogether for her, whilst some would visit when they could. Rachael had no power herself in any of these relationships. Without the support of her staff team, and encouragement to say what she was feeling as well as ask for time to talk, I would expect Rachael to go back to her outbursts. Her message would be, as it had been before, 'I'm bursting out of myself with feelings — I have to show you how bad I'm feeling and this is the only power I have'.

During our two-year relationship, we focused on other matters too. She never did want to talk about the rape I'd been informed of, though she did talk about a relationship with another resident where he was touching her sexually and she was very clear about not wanting that. We worked through her complicated feelings — she did want him to be her boyfriend but definitely didn't want sex in any way, shape or form. We worked on how she might stop unwanted touch, and how she might get help if he didn't listen. I encouraged her to think about what she'd like to do with her boyfriend which was a revelation to her — she had no idea. I knew Rachael's boyfriend was vulnerable too, and they would both need help in negotiating their relationship. Again I was aware of how much hope I had for Rachael, knowing the staff team supporting her. It is rare to find such commitment.

After about two years, Rachael made it clear that she was ready to move on to other things. She was relating in a very different way and her ability to let me know she didn't need to come any more was evidence of that.

I always felt a connection with Rachael that went beyond words. I often felt moved being with her in our lengthy silences, as if at some level we were communicating wordlessly. I was picking up feelings and waves of energies as she gazed silently, far away — often in the realm of epileptic disturbance. My sense of her was of a caring, loving woman who had no other way of expressing her feelings than hurting someone else, and making them scream for her. She didn't want to be like that, and it embarrassed her. When another option was presented in our explorations, she chose to go for it.

Interview with Carol Schaffer:
The Person-Centred Approach with a family support group, for those with family members who have learning and/or physical disabilities

Carol has spent the past thirty years working for Kith & Kids *(for address see p. 131), a family support group for families who include members who have learning and/or physical disabilities. During that time she also trained as a Person-Centred therapist, and applies the Person-Centred Approach throughout her work. She also has a small private practice.*

Jan: Perhaps we could start with how you have applied the Person-Centred Approach within your work?

Carol: I'm involved with people with learning and physical disabilities: they range from currently 7/8 years to 47/48 years so it's a wide range of people with a wide range of disabilities. I have major involvement with them on our projects, which are projects where we are supporting people to develop essentially socially, but in any other area that we may be able to be supportive — we being myself and colleagues. I also do a lot of advocacy support work with members. And actually sometimes with their siblings so that's briefly the kind of work I do.

Jan: Why the Person-Centred Approach?

Carol: Because so much of the learning disability field is about management and control; it is about directing people all the time; it is about not allowing people to be — certainly not allowing to experience themselves emotionally. For those very reasons I try to work with a person-centred approach in order to allow people to begin to experience themselves, hopefully with adequate support, to try and offer a safe environment for that to happen. To try to support people to feel as though they are being held in order to be able to explore themselves. But that's what I am hoping is what I and the people I work with are offering our members with a disability, and I will stick my neck out and say it is very, very rare that they get that anywhere else. Which reinforces to me that this has to be. So much so, that when I go into their homes and situations, that is what I am trying to do to change attitudes of other staff and people who work with them in their daily lives.

Jan: Do you mean in their residential homes?

Carol: Residential situations and day care situations. It's not easy and people feel quite threatened by it, I have to say, and it's so slow. I often feel as though I am going round in circles.

Jan: So it's attitude change that you are trying to promote amongst all these different homes and different day care centres, but you still find in those services that there tends to be that sort of management and control approach.

Carol: Absolutely, but why do people end up with challenging behaviour? My theory is challenging behaviour is all about people not being listened to. If you are not listened to what else are you going to do? I'd also pick a bloody chair up and throw it through a window, believe you me. In fact I have sometimes felt like it myself when I am faced with this rigid bureaucracy that is often practised today. So, yes, it is about trying to change attitudes and trying to support people to understanding what is going on, what I believe to be going on.

Jan: That's from your understanding of what the members are saying either verbally or those who don't speak, from other cues?

Carol: I'm doing it in a myriad of different ways. Through their body language, expressions in their bodies, tenseness of bodies, expression in their faces, physically and otherwise; yes, absolutely, and I see it on the project as well. Somebody gets a little bit aggressive at the project and we have to ask ourselves why — we then need to be gently trying to explore and if people have never had that on offer its like, 'what the hell are we talking about? What are we trying to do here?' So it's about feeling our way in. It's hit and miss all the time.

Jan: I've just come from a project today and one of the things that struck me was there was a young person I have never met before who had, on their first project, become quite aggressive and dangerous and I could picture the scene elsewhere where he/she would not have been welcomed back but I was talking to the project worker who was saying when this person was welcomed back with open arms things seemed to shift and there was something about that welcome and that acceptance of the person that there was room for that person to have been aggressive or whatever and there was room for it possibly to have been because it was a new environment, new people etc. So this person didn't suddenly get a label and I found that very refreshing.

Carol: I had a phone call from a parent about half an hour ago whose child is on the project — not a child, she is an adult actually — who's having a very difficult time, and I was just talking to her and supporting her actually and she said to me that no other project would keep her. But you don't get rid of people because they are having difficulties. In fact, on the contrary, it's why you do say to people, 'no we want you and you are going to stay unless you yourself don't want to be here of course', that's a whole different ball game but the recognition is that she does, actually.

Jan: So maybe what would be useful is to talk a little about how the projects are set up: its almost like, OK, we are saying this is a person-centred approach, but how does it come over to the members and the volunteers and the families? How would you describe that building of community?

Carol: We have three training days prior to any project — three Sundays — and they will be ten till four each one of them, and our whole premise for those training days are to support the volunteers with an outline understanding of being involved with people, and I actually do mean people because at the end of the day that is who we are talking about. So we offer workshops around communication, around epilepsy, because many of our members have epilepsy in various ways, in how to support somebody in lifting them and how to support people with being approached in a dignified way, in a respected way. Anything we are asking our volunteers to do for our members we are actually saying to our volunteers we expect all of us to be treated in the same way. We are also saying the major thing about the project is fun and support so if we feel well supported our members are going to be well supported. Support means we have to value each other. We need to have some understanding when any of us feels things are a bit difficult and we can't cope. When any of us feel we are being asked to do something that we either feel uncomfortable with or we just don't have the confidence to do it or we make a mistake. We all make mistakes, let's own it and we can do something about it. If we can put all those things in place for each other, if we can get that message across, then that is what is handed down to our members. And our members do respond and our members are going to be expected eventually as they understand these concepts, they are going to be expected to be involved with us in this way as well. So that is the premise we put across throughout the three days together. We also play games together. We get a bit childish and silly together but what the hell, that's what team building is all about. Everything is explained, why we do what we do and how our members engage and get involved. I have to laugh sometimes because one or two of the parents find that quite difficult because they have a difficulty in being childish. For most of us there is a kid in us somewhere that comes out but play, being childish, needs to be supported where and when it's appropriate, and we need to support volunteers to understand the importance of our members knowing and understanding appropriate play.

Jan: So there is encouragement to be themselves and to own what's difficult and what needs help with and for that to be OK and not a failure.

Carol: Yes, that is a major thing in our society, success and failure and supporting volunteers to recognise that things are positive and things are negative but if you look at the negative you can find the positive in it and turn it round. We have a de-brief everyday with the volunteers, we get together with a couple of team leaders for an hour at the end of each day to look at how the day has gone, to be able to tease out what's happened. What's been the joys of the day and what's been the difficulties and to be able to turn those difficulties around. It's important we all need to feel, we all need to feel that we have achieved and that goes for all of us, not just the volunteers, the staff, everybody. I have to say it's incredible, it's quite magic and people come onto the project, I know the majority of the volunteers haven't done it before and they are quite nervous. Three days later they are in there, they are going there and they walk off the project thinking, 'my God, I did it!' — it's very magical.

Jan: There is that time to encounter each other and the staff share their difficulties also?

Carol: Yes, we share some of our difficulties. After that get together there is a get together of workshop facilitators and staff where we also share what has gone on. At the end of each day the workshoppers and the staff for Kith & Kids will get together and go through each individual member and look at what happened that day and where they need to be going the following day and also look at how we may need to support one or two of the volunteers with some extra help. Throughout the week I will have sat down with various volunteers and just looked at what's going on, recognising things they are encountering that are not so easy to overcome, it's not the norm. I think it's a project where if it's going to work for volunteers and our members it is inevitable that a lot of volunteers will be confronted with themselves in ways that normally they wouldn't be. There is something quite beautiful, quite cherishing, in the way they allow that to happen and the way in which they will even open up to me and there is something special. It's quite a gift because I know that it is the experience of the '2:1'[7] that is doing it, being involved with our members. Recognising how open and trusting many of our members are themselves. OK, they might be knotted up emotionally but they are so out there with their honesty. I can't think of any of our members with a disability who would have the mindset to be that devious.

Jan: No attempts at impression management . . .

---

7. 2:1 projects run three times a year, with an additional camp. 2:1 means two volunteers support one person with learning disabilities to access a range of activities within the one- or two-week project.

Carol: And our members with learning disabilities, they can't be that calculated, even if they try, five minutes later they trip themselves up and I sometimes want to weep about it, because it leaves them so vulnerable, prey to people who have a need to abuse their power.

Jan: For me it's like they are the most congruent of people, which is why I enjoy and feel safe around them because they are so straight up, there is no side.

Carol: Absolutely, I continue and continue to learn. I am not meant to do 'Two-to-One's any more but I missed it because the projects bring me back to the ground, they centre me, remind me of some of the important points of life, this is where it is, I love it.

Jan: You were saying before about the projects, volunteers, the members, and touched on families, but one of the things that has always struck me as tricky in your position is that you are attempting to facilitate sometimes interactions between volunteers, parents, sometimes siblings as well and members with learning disabilities and that facilitation process and how that happens . . .

Carol: It isn't always easy; sometimes it's easier than others. Sometimes when I'm involved in a situation whereby we are looking to support the needs of the person with the learning disability we may need to meet with Social Services and the parents are always involved with me. Rarely do I do anything without the parents being there — it's not my place to make decisions, it's my place to support parents so very rarely will I be involved in a review meeting without the parents being there and quite often the person with the learning disability would also be involved. Where I am aware that I might find myself in very tricky waters I get a colleague to come along and he would be involved with the person with the learning disability and I would be involved with the parents but I have on many occasions over the years been facilitating between the two.

Jan: You mean if there's a conflicting situation you have the advocacy person for the person with the learning disability, that frees you up to be there for the parent?

Carol: Yes, and it means that afterwards with we can have a four-way involvement and look at areas where there are things to be sorted out. On the whole if we are aware that there may be some conflicting things we will talk beforehand. I also need to say that on the whole over the years I haven't come up with major conflict in respect of the children and the parents. Usually I have been involved with the parents in a growing process so we are talking and exploring our way up to this point of 18/19 years when their son or daughter is going to be going and doing whatever so one of the big issues is leaving home, but it has been quite a process in Kith & Kids. It started quite early, we were talking about it, where I started talking about it with parents and children when they were 14/15 years old, and we can slowly build the process because it is a sensitive process for all concerned.

Jan: So there is something there about the relationship, it's not just about doing for or supporting in practical ways or coming in when there is a crisis and leaving when there isn't, it's about a relationship in which the joys as well as the trials and tribulations are shared.

Carol: Yes. You see, I was involved right from the beginning with Kith & Kids because I started off as a volunteer for eight odd years and then I started as the first paid worker. The whole process for me has been a unique one in that I worked for and with a group of parents. Not many people can understand this. Most people seem to say to me, 'Carol, how does it work?' I was valued by Kith & Kids, I was paid by Kith & Kids, but I was valued by Kith & Kids, and I hope I have offered that valuing back, and it has been very much a two-way process. The actual process of your bosses, which it was, I mean 50 odd families in Kith & Kids are my bosses, all of them are my bosses, but I still had this relationship of valuing on both sides. I quite often had to pinch myself and say, 'God, I'm being paid to do this!' because I loved it and it's been so varied through supporting families, through advocacy. I was training and supporting volunteers setting up projects doing many things over the years.

Jan: So over the years you identified, from what the members were letting you hear about, what the needs were . . .

Carol: It always has been client-led — we started off with an idea for young people, the first project, and 31 years ago, the group set up, 29 years ago, the first project, which was a one-to-one.

Jan: What did a one-to-one mean back then?

Carol: One volunteer was linked in with one member so that each member had their volunteer, the same volunteer, for the two-week project, five days per week, Monday to Friday each week, and the same volunteer went through the project. The volunteer would have been offered a profile of the person that they were going to be involved with, and would then have sat down with, in those days, one of the staff members, and we would have gone through our understanding of the person they were going to be involved with. When I say our understanding, I am a little bit careful about that, bearing in mind that my picture and my knowledge and the way a member operates with me, you need to understand may, subtly, operate differently with somebody else. The volunteer also will sit down with parents and gain understanding from them about their daughter/son. It's particularly around specific things like if somebody does have epilepsy the best way in which to work with that or if somebody does have a real dislike of specific things again an understanding is important. And then supporting the volunteer and the member by having some workshops, by offering time to go out into the community and get various things. Say somebody is doing cooking in the project so they need to go out themselves to get all the ingredients etc., and come back and cook and share it with the community, the project being a community.

Jan: It has evolved from real needs.

Carol: Yes, and in the same way at the end of each day each person is assessed individually. A couple of weeks after the project we get together with the workshop people and we will assess each individual to look at how we should go forward for the next project. We have to bear in mind between each project people are out doing their things, etc., and they are going to come back to us with I don't know what developments. Changes happen not just on the projects but also at various education and training centres that our members attend during term time and we need to be prepared to adapt accordingly. The lovely thing is that the members know me and I know them and it's beautiful. I said earlier I wasn't meant to be on this project this time my hours have recently changed. I have to say to you, one of the members said to me on my last training day, 'you're not on the project, are you?' and I said, 'actually, I'm going to be on it now', and she just looked at me and said 'good, goody goody'. I love it, I felt so valued, and if that wasn't enough, I've got some siblings on the project and they are in a difficult phase in their lives and one in particular on the first day we talked a few things through. I came in the next day and as I came in she looked at me and said, 'I need a morning hug, Carol', and I felt a very special acceptance. Its things like that are important.

Jan: It's the relationship again.

Carol: Another thing I like, which for me is personal and my kind of culture, is that we are looking at whole family involvement. My children are grown up and have their own lives and friends, but I am always accepted, they've shared friends, they are not afraid to have friends home and even today I go out with them and their friends, for me that's a norm and that feels right to me. In Kith & Kids it feels like we are a whole family that we are sharing and passing information between all these different generations of experts and we all have a relationship and something to offer.

Jan: So it's not putting obstacles in the way, it's clearing the path.

Carol: Yes, that's right and really important. On the whole my experience is that the parents recognise where to come in and where to stand back. On the whole I think that's true. OK, there are exceptions to every rule, and that's where other parents are there to support each other and parents come in daily and help where needed on the projects, but importantly it is an opportunity for parents to chat and support each other.

Jan: That sort of physical — 'oh, they know what I'm talking about'. So one of the unique parts of your work is relating to the sisters and brothers and certainly in all of the other services that exist to support people with learning difficulties, particularly people with severe learning difficulties — there tends to be nothing for the siblings so the relationships between the two are not fostered but Kith & Kids actually does foster that relationship.

Carol: Yes we foster it by having the siblings on projects in their young years, provided we have got the volunteers, and they would come on and be supported with volunteers. They have a real need of being part of a special family, they have needs as well to be seen and heard a lot of the time and as they grow up and become more independent, many become volunteers themselves if that's what they want to do. Some people don't — some people just want to get away from it, understandably, and some people go away from it and then come back. So whatever way, because of my involvement with families over the years and getting to know them I am in touch with people who are not involved in the group any more, but are part of the group for the very fact of being a sibling.

Jan: This book is about voices of the voiceless and I think siblings, though they have got speech and the ability to speak, where is their voice?

Carol: Because you have the ability to speak doesn't mean to say you have a voice.

Jan: What I am wondering is, from your experience, were you to put a voice to the kinds of things they say to you over the years, what would they be, what would be the siblings be wanting understood about growing up with a person with a learning, physical or sensory disability?

Carol: Quite often they have a major sense of responsibility, that there's a need to be looking out for their sister and/or brother. A recognition that the parent/s are under massive stress with their brother/sister and some of them feel that they have to achieve where their brother/sister hasn't for their parent. The guilt which comes in a variety of different ways, a sense of being lucky, a fear for their own possibility of having children of their own with a disability. And I say a fear, there's a fear that it might happen but there is an acceptance that if it does that's OK, they will cope with it. I only know of one sib who told me that if they were expecting a child with a disability they would seriously consider abortion — others have said to us that they would go ahead and would cope with it. And a sense that they need to be strong and some have a need for rebelling and that may be done in a rather overt way but can be quite often is done in quite a covert way. This awful fear that they can't speak up — that they mustn't say what they really feel — 'I hate my brother/sister' — all brothers and sisters love and hate each other but of course if you have a brother or sister with a disability then you must not say anything. But similarly parents turn round and say, 'Oh God! I wish I could have a day without', but to say that about your child with a disability and when parents meet each other and they dare voice it to each other — it's like a relief.

Jan: Do you find that because the volunteers, many of them, are of a similar age to both the younger members and the siblings so when they are going through that turbulent time — what impact does it have being around young people who haven't grown up with disability?

Carol: For the siblings themselves, to be together gradually offers them the possibility to voice this to each other because that's safe. To voice that to other volunteers who haven't had that involvement, that's a whole different story and I think that takes longer, if at all. I think they would have to build to a good relationship and feel trust to be able to do that. What the other volunteers offer them is freedom to get out there, to go to the pub together, to have a drink with people who,, because of their experience on the project, are sensitive to disability. The volunteers, through their involvement on the project, gain a sense of what disability is, they can't know what it would be like to live with it, they find themselves in a peopling situation where they are starting to become open, they're meeting people that they don't usually meet in everyday life. One of the siblings was saying to me the other day that over the years she had made so many really good friends from being involved in the projects with Kith & Kids. They have been the people she has built her important friendships with through the years.

Jan: As a person-centred therapist because you have a practice outside of Kith & Kids, do you work with people with learning difficulties there? And are there differences?

Carol: I haven't done for ages and I have not done it in any big way. I had one client a few years back in 1980, an older lady, but I don't have a big practice anyway. I work with people with such diversity and that's how I perceive Kith & Kids. At my practice I am also working with people who are diverse, coming because they are having a major struggle. In Kith & Kids they are having a major struggle all the time — I should have to think about that more because its interesting — it doesn't feel that way to me.

Jan: You talked about diversity there, how do you facilitate that?

Carol: We don't have any difficulties around cultures. It's not anything that I've ever been particularly tripped up with. We happen to have a young man on the project this time, who himself has been quite racist — this is a member — and our sense is that he doesn't actually understand what he's saying, other than it's bringing a reaction. There's been so much built up around it in the way people have — people outside Kith & Kids — people have kept on and on at him to stop, that in itself could be a reason why he's doing it. So, what I needed to do was talk with the volunteers — talk with them privately about our perception of what's happening and how we would like them to — if it's possible — to just ignore it, and not make a big deal out of it, and if anybody did have difficulties around it, to just come to us and talk about it. Because, you know, some people might, they just can't take it — I don't know what people's backgrounds are all about. So — but that hasn't occurred for years — once before, one of our other members was enjoying the fact that he could say these remarks and get a response, but no, it's not a major problem. Certainly with the volunteers, I've never had any big issues around it.

Jan: That's interesting, and quite an achievement within the current climate in our society. We're coming to the end of our time now, just reflecting on the title of this book — Voices of the Voiceless — I'm wondering if there are voices that need to be heard that are not, in the whole of the time that you've been involved with Kith & Kids, from your understanding of those people you've supported, what would they be saying if they could find their own voices?

Carol: Treat me equally; give me choices; let me be part of society; make society work for me as well; listen to me; hear me; negotiate with me; and let me have something of a life, a quality of life.

Jan: Thank you very much.

Kith & Kids
c/o The Haringey Irish Centre
Pretoria Road
LONDON
N17 9DA
020 8801 7432

'Attention-seeking': how to avoid really listening

In all the training I have ever done around learning disabilities, and abuse issues too, the phrase I dislike more than any other is 'attention-seeking'. Even writing the words evokes irritation at how easily communications, which may be extremely important, are ignored. Worse than ignored: the implication is that the person doing the 'attention-seeking' is consciously demanding what they *should not* have. Or an even more insidious dismissal — that they are unconsciously 'acting out' and demanding attention and should be ignored.

It is not just children's behaviours that are dismissed in this way: people with learning difficulties are continually treated with a lack of respect based on the assumption that behaviour which demands notice or attention is inherently unworthy of consideration. This communicates to the individual that they are not worthy of attention or, at the very least, attention is *conditional* upon behaving in ways that another person ordains as acceptable.

The dominant mode of treatment and management for people with learning disabilities in care and educational systems remains within the behavioural tradition. Sadly the possibilities within that tradition are often reduced to the following practice: behaviour which is desired is 'reinforced' by positive attention or rewards, whilst undesirable behaviour is ignored at best or punished at worst. For many, being ignored is being punished and actually reinforces the need for attention.

I had four years' experience of working within a behavioural regime at the beginning of my career. It was what led me to study for my degree in psychology and to my counselling training that I did alongside. A few examples might serve to elaborate why I chose to broaden my understanding beyond the behavioural. I found it to be one-dimensional, at best and often inhuman, at worst. My desire was always to understand the meaning of behaviours for individuals, not simply to modify or manage behaviours.

Raheena was a teenager with severe learning disabilities. Though she could walk unaided, she required physical prompts for everything she did and continual physical and verbal prompts to continue through an activity. She seemed to understand very little and needed guiding throughout each day. Her one spontaneous expression was simultaneous heel walking and hand flapping whilst opening and closing her mouth. I had learned from being in her presence over time that she only ever did this when she was either happy or frightened. This seemed important to me and I would respond with whichever seemed relevant — 'oh Raheena's happy' or 'Raheena is frightened?' to let her know I wanted to understand. As a classroom assistant my views did not count for much, but I regarded Raheena's communication as a success in that I managed to argue the psychologist out of creating a 'programme' to stop Raheena's 'socially unacceptable behaviour'.

A young boy who had moderate learning difficulties spent most of his time in a special unit which focused on a token economy. Tokens were earned for staying on task, sitting on their chairs etc. Sammy had begun soiling himself

— a new behaviour for him. The psychologist devised a programme of rewards for clean days. The reward scheme had little effect and a couple of months went by with Sammy managing some days to stay clean and on others he missed out on his reward by soiling again. Even then, before my studies, it struck me that not getting the reward was like a punishment, carrying with it the assumption that:

• Sammy was 'attention-seeking' by soiling
• he had control over this embarrassing problem: his evident embarrassment did nothing to dispel the assumptions.

It was after I had left to study for my degree that I learned that the truth behind his behaviour had emerged. Sammy had been moved to a new foster family where he told of his previous foster father's sexual abuse. Sammy couldn't control his bowels, it was found, because of tears and damage from anal abuse. My outrage centres on the total disregard for what his behaviour might be communicating. During the months he was being abused, and his wounds were found to be significant, he was also being implicitly told he could control his soiling.

Though behaviour modification programmes have their place in supporting change, it seems to me the first and most important step is to try to understand what is being communicated. In his case it would also have been prudent to have medical reports before assuming this was just more 'attention-seeking'.

Carl's story (see p. 150 ff) shows the ingenuity and symbolism behind his 'disruptive' attention-seeking behaviour. He was communicating something important, and when that was attended to, he didn't need to do it.

Pat had a history of sexual abuse. As a middle-aged woman with a severe learning disability, she lived in a residential setting. A psychologists had made written recommendations that when she cried or talked about her abuse, she should be ignored, because she was 'only attention-seeking'. How will it ever be possible for Pat to heal those wounds if no-one will listen?

Danny's impacted wisdom teeth (see p. 1 ff.), and his new biting behaviour, were assumed to be attempts to get attention, and demand his special toy. His example shows how a behavioural approach, without thorough consideration of what may be the real communication, simply reinforces the difficulties it seeks to alleviate.

I have found Alfred Adler's (1870–1937) individual psychology approach helpful whenever I am asked to work with 'attention-seeking' behaviour. If, by listening, I am unable to get some kind of handle on what is being communicated, I consider the Adlerian school's four mistaken goals of behaviour as a way of meeting my client part way. Often this is the approach I offer when training volunteers and care staff, if only to begin to broaden their ideas on attention-seeking. Essentially four types of 'erroneous' behaviours are considered. This means behaviours that take the individual further away from their basic needs for connection, belonging and acceptance (see Adler, 1963; Dreikurs and Cassell, 1972).

The four types of behaviour are:

Power	I need power over you at all times
Revenge	I want to hurt you like I've been hurt
Assumed disability	I am so discouraged I need you to do things for me all the time
Attention-seeking	Any attention will do for me — I do not feel OK unless you are attending to me.

This model is a good start to shaking the idea that all demanding, challenging or disliked behaviour is about 'attention-seeking'. However, the danger in offering this model is that assumptions are made that the person must be communicating one of those rather than continuing to listen to the individual and really trying to understand.

If all behaviours stem from a need, the more we ignore the need, the more the need will grow. Needs which are met tend to stop being needs. If ignoring 'attention-seeking' behaviour worked, it would be a relatively simple matter to eradicate the behaviour since ignoring it can be so much easier than attending to it.

As a Person-Centred practitioner I seek to offer all of my clients my empathy, unconditional positive regard and congruence. These core attitudinal qualities are in complete opposition to making assumptions that a certain behaviour is just 'attention-seeking' — there is no empathy there. It is possible to seek first to understand — really seek. The assumption that a behaviour is *'only attention-seeking'* has to be a last resort rather than the first unconsidered dismissal of what might be an important communication. It is possible to meet continual demands for attention with empathy and acceptance whilst expressing genuine frustration. It is possible, too, to accept that a particular behaviour may just possibly *not* be occurring as an effort to gain attention from anyone else, but as a communication of attending to self — others just happen to be about, and find the behaviour irritating. This may be self-stimulation, self-comforting or some other autonomous behaviour. When we begin to really consider the myriad of possible meanings for behaviour, it seems incredible that only one assumption gains so much of the attention.

Sadly, much behaviour labelled 'attention-seeking' has never diminished with numerous behaviour management techniques, and become habits. Habits are so much more difficult to change and to understand since the nature of habit is repetition and loss of insight as to the original cause.

The best we can sometimes offer is, 'I know you've been doing that for a very long time, and I wish I understood why'. It may even occasionally be helpful to own that, 'I don't like it when you do that, so you can choose to stop and talk with me or I will go to the quiet (or other space) room till you are ready to try again'.

I do not have the answers to the problems of disruptive and 'attention-seeking' behaviours but I do have these questions:

- What would it cost to *really listen* to the message behind the behaviour?
- How would it feel to have our own behaviours labelled in any way, or dismissed as attempts to get attention?
- Is it necessarily wrong to want attention or to be noticed?
- How difficult is it to respond to attention-seeking behaviour by saying, 'I see that you need my attention'?
- What might we have to change about ourselves, if we were to abandon the dismissive judgement, *'s/he's only attention-seeking'*?
- What might we need to tolerate if we really listened to behaviour as communication?
- Why does the notion that 'attention-seeking' needs to be ignored persist, when all the evidence shows that behaviour does not stop by using that method?

Loss and bereavement

'There's no need to take them to the funerals, they don't understand anyway'

So often people with learning disabilities, especially those with the more severe forms, or those without speech or identifiable language systems, are assumed to have no capacity for anything but transient feelings. Because they are seen as not having the capacity to understand, they are either not told of the death of a loved one, or if they are, not given the opportunity to attend funerals or otherwise make real their loss. Despite assumptions about lack of awareness or understanding, it is my experience that many people with learning disabilities are caught in prolonged grief, but it is simply not recognised as such.

Let us consider how children's experiences of death are handled in our current British culture. Because adults want to protect children, and often express the feeling that children are less affected than adults because they are more adaptable, it is still, sadly, rare to include children in funerals. Adults with learning disabilities are in many respects infantilised and matters of death and loss are one of the clearest examples of this.

I recall being very young — around three — when an uncle, who I do not remember, died. Though I have no memory of the uncle, I was told that he had 'just gone to sleep and didn't wake up'. Subsequently I feared going to sleep in case I wouldn't wake up either.

The way we explain death to children and adults with learning disabilities includes some well-meaning but rather odd ideas:

- 'He's gone to heaven' — this can be very confusing if there is no concept of heaven. Carl (see p. 150 ff.) showed this most clearly. For him heaven was a bedroom in his sister's house. For years he had searched for his parents, and become distressed and disruptive on visits to his sister's home and it was because he thought he would find his mother there. Christopher (see p. 172 ff.), too, knew that heaven was associated with his mother, but had no idea what or where heaven was or that one had to be dead to go there.

- 'Only the good die young' — when this is the phrase used around children and adults with learning disabilities it can set up an odd fear: if I am good, I will die and I know that must be bad because everyone is upset. Well, I won't be good, then it won't happen to me. Parents and carers who become angry about bad behaviour like this at home have sometimes used the 'good die young' phrase and not realised the impact it has had. So 'bad behaviour' is not connected with the loss or consequent fear.
- 'She's passed on/over' — this phrase can lead to all sorts of confusion for those with limited cognitive processing and developmental delay. Where has she passed on to? What does passing on mean? When will she be passing back this way? It is difficult to comprehend the full reality of the situation unless words that clearly explain the reality are used.

For children the reality is easier to understand if they have had pets who have died, and been allowed to create a funeral of their own. Children with learning disabilities, are often denied these learning opportunities, and grow to be adults with learning disabilities who are chronically emotionally undernourished, having been 'protected' from everyday experiences, where, given adequate support, they could have learned to accept and cope with death and loss in healthy ways.

Many of the adults with severe learning disabilities that I have worked with in therapy have lived in long-stay mental institutions all their lives. Pets are a rarity in such settings. For those mentioned in this book, their experiences of death were of death of parents — other family deaths may never have been mentioned to them. My clients who were 'dispersed' to community residential homes had no language for their feelings in general, and no conceptual understanding of death and loss because it had never been deemed necessary to give them opportunities to develop them.

There are several possible reasons for this:

- the assumption that it won't affect them
- the assumption that they wouldn't understand
- the fear that it might upset them
- difficulties in actually communicating the facts in a meaningful way for the individual
- personal difficulties of carers around death and loss issues, impeding their abilities in that area anyway
- fear that they might behave inappropriately at the funeral.

I have worked with many people with severe learning disabilities who search for years for family members who have died (see p. 142 ff., 150 ff., and p. 172 ff.) who had no language to speak of what had happened and no language to help them understand.

One-to-one therapy is only one way of providing the space and support for understanding to develop, but it is very rare for people with learning disabilities and severe learning disabilities especially, to be offered therapy. It is, anyway, harder to convey new concepts and ideas at times of confusion and distress.

In training workshops for teams of residential care and social workers, I invite the groups to begin by focusing on their own earliest experience of death, and we explore how they each made sense of it. Fear is often expressed, both in terms of the first experience and also in the here and now, from those who so far had not suffered the bereavement of a close family member. From these personal insights we move to exploring how grief has affected them, with space for individual reflection and sharing. From there we explore models of grieving (e.g. Worden, 1983) and as we look at those, I invite group members to reflect upon the residents they are supporting to see if they recognise any behaviours or expressions of feeling which may indicate grieving rather than simply difficult behaviour. There is nearly always a eureka moment of recognition in any group I am working with.

It is very difficult to expect care workers to be able to support their residents in coming to terms with the death of an important loved one when they have not experienced this themselves, may have their own complicated or unresolved grief, and have had no training on the issue of how to support.

I encourage all teams I am invited to work with to develop an approach to dealing with death and loss within the day-to-day environment for residents, building in opportunities to observe and explore the life–death–life cycle. Using the real words with clear signs or symbols for those who use different modes of communication, residents can experience life and death in real and concrete ways.

This can be achieved through long-term projects like sowing seeds, watching them grow and live, and watching too as they die and offer their seeds for the next cycle. Small pets offer shorter-term possibilities, for example goldfish, hamsters, gerbils, guinea pigs and rabbits. None of these has a very lengthy life span, so that an occasional death is very likely. Those residents who cared for the pet and are interested can then be allowed to see and touch (if they want to) the dead creature, and the genuine responses of care workers will help model the expression of feelings. Residents can help with the funeral and throughout the whole process they can be offered a language for the living and dying, for the caring and missing, the happiness and sadness. How much easier would it then be to explain the death of someone close?

It is important that people with learning disabilities are allowed to truly experience the illness and death of loved ones, with space and explanation in language, including sign, symbol or whatever mode is used by the individual, so that they are not excluded from the process. However severely learning difficulties affect the person, if they are capable of showing a reaction to their loved ones, they are capable of experiencing the loss of them and grieving. The grief is all the more complicated when there is no conceptual understanding, as it can feel like they are no longer loved or wanted and that their loved one is actually hiding away or staying away from them, not that the person cannot visit because he/she is dead.

Being able to attend the funeral, with the explanations of process, again allows the person to begin grieving — they have that right.

All of my clients with learning disabilities have, at various times during our work, talked about members of staff they had been close to, who have simply disappeared. It is particularly likely with people with severe learning disabilities and no or limited language. Key workers, or others where attachments have been made, will suddenly be replaced, and there is no awareness of the possibility for grieving in those circumstances.

Some people with learning disabilities indeed seem to respond to other people almost as tools or resources, rather than developing relationships that include feelings of loss. For some, this may be an adaptive response to continually being moved from ward to ward or home to home, with their practical needs catered for but little or no recognition of emotional needs. For others it may be an indication of their cognitive development stage, or lack of any significant early attachment (Bowlby, 1969). If the person with limited cognitive ability and developmental delay is treated as an object, then they learn to relate to others as objects. Even in those cases, it seems important to explain and say goodbye, as over time being treated with respect as an emotional human being may enable the person to develop within relationships.

Nora's story (see p. 86 ff.) gave an example of withdrawal and later sudden departure of a loved key worker. Nora was well able to understand the situation, but also was capable of expressing her sadness. This may have been too difficult for her key worker to cope with so she avoided it altogether.

One team I worked with had developed the ritual of giving a farewell party to anyone, staff member or resident, who was leaving and that allowed everyone to share in the goodbye. Clients would refer to these in their sessions and seemed to find the parties a very useful marker of goodbyes and moving on. The fact that cakes were usually part of the proceedings was always fully described, and seemed to add to the ceremony of parting. That is a wonderful, though sadly unusual, example as in residential care work there can be a high turnover of staff and reliance on agency staff to maintain the necessary level of cover for safety.

In exploring what might work for a particular team in training workshops, we explore what team members would feel comfortable about doing, and endeavour to identify team members' strengths and vulnerabilities in supporting clients (and each other) when upset or distressed. One team agreed to have photographs of all team members and to try to keep up with photos of regular agency staff, as well as photos of residents. These photographs provided residents with something tangible to show a member of staff when they needed the explanation again, or to mention the person who had left or say 'I miss her'.

Several of the clients I have mentioned in this book were removed from their long-stay hospitals with little or no preparation. May's experience (see p. 8 ff.) of having her possessions — the contents of her bedside locker — packed in a case and being taken to a minibus is an example. She often mentioned missing the nurse she cared about. Hope's sadness (see p. 11 ff.) and continual desire to know where her sister was, whom she'd last seen when they were both in a long-stay hospital, is another. Hope had no idea, since leaving hospital, where her mother was either, and she too missed some of the nurses. May and Hope gave all the compliant outward signs of adjustment to their new homes, but in their sessions, both expressed confusion and bewilderment about their homes (wards), and who was in them now, and people who had cared for them.

People with learning disabilities experience loss in every day of their lives — loss of people to whom they have become attached, loss of identity (due to lost notes, so no birth date or family details), loss of familiar surroundings and familiar people, loss of opportunities for meaningful work (see Hope's story, p. 11 ff. and James's story, see p. 25 ff.), loss of ability to fit in, loss of family relationships, loss through death. As people who experience probably the most frequent losses they are also the least likely to have their loss and grief reactions recognised.

It is essential that people with learning disabilities have opportunities to understand the reality of the life–death–life, cycle in preparation for the inevitable losses they will experience. It is also essential to support the support workers in recognising and getting space for their own loss issues so that they are empowered in their work with their clients.

Bereavement counselling may be important too, and for that reason people with severe learning disabilities are in need of more therapists who feel able to work firstly to learn their own language and then able to provide space and empathic understanding for how this particular person feels about their loss.

It is worth mentioning here that parents of a son or daughter with learning disabilities have their own grief around the impact of the learning disabilities on their offspring. Where there is also a medical condition, there is often chronic grief — the grief with no resolution. Given this additional grief, and little or no recognition or help for it, it is little wonder that there are difficulties in supporting the family member with learning disabilities to understand death or loss.

When training volunteers for Kith & Kids (see p. 125 ff.) on emotional and sexual needs, it is always important to emphasise that many of our members form attachments quickly and some will refer to their volunteers as boyfriend or girlfriend. In the name of kindness and because volunteers sometimes think that our members with learning disabilities don't really understand, they play along. The intensity of the projects often creates strong attachments on both sides, and at the end promises are made about visits and phone calls. But when the project ends and the demands of their lives are back, volunteers find that they cannot actually fulfil these promises.

Many's the person with learning disabilities, nose pressed against the window pane for months afterwards, looking for the boy/girlfriend. We encourage volunteers to be clear about the time they and their Kith & Kids member have together, and to include the ending whenever relevant in conversations. I am reminded of Person-Centred cross-cultural workshops where the time limit and intense experience has often led to very deep connections being made. These are not less important for being limited in time. There is something in the knowledge of the limited contact which actually can facilitate the meeting at depth.

This is true too of Kith & Kids 2:1 (see footnote p. 125) projects. Being willing and able to share the joys, frustrations, lows and highs of a project with their partner and then willing and able to say goodbye and share tears if they are around — this gives our members the opportunity to experience relationship and loss in a supported way, which helps them in other areas.

It is to ourselves that we must look in changing the behaviours of people with learning disabilities. If we are able to relate at depth and experience in awareness sadness and loss as well as grief, then we will be more able to reach out to people with learning disabilities in our relationships with them in everyday life. Loss and death may then be included in discussion, but most importantly, there may be earlier recognition of the individual with learning disabilities who is lost in grief.

'She won't get out of bed at all'
Keeley's story

Keeley was forty-five when we first met, yet with the aspect and curiosity of a very young child. Her favourite phrase was 'osh at?', which she would say when pointing at any objects she hadn't seen before. 'Osh your name?' was another favourite question, and after we had got to know each other she would laugh mischievously when I responded, 'you know me, Keeley'. These were important games to her, and were always repeated with pleasure.

Our work spanned about eighteen months and was interrupted whenever Keeley could not be enticed from her bed. There were many problems that Keeley presented to the team supporting her. Refusing to move from her bed was only one of them — in the smooth running of a residential home, it is never easy or acceptable, it seems, for residents to simply decide for themselves if and when they will get up each day. There are of course logistical problems with staff being responsible for several people, many of whom are vulnerable or might have seizures, or might simply wander out of the front door without supervision. If staff are with residents downstairs, there may not be sufficient staff to cover bedrooms as well. Yet sadly, the logistical problems do mean that people living in residential care cannot simply choose to lie in in the morning, or have an 'off' day and decide to lounge in their beds. This does sometimes set up power struggles between residents and staff, it being one of very few areas where the resident can take power. I always wondered what Keeley's feelings were when she didn't want to move from her bed, and sensed that a mixture of many things may be playing a part. I'll return to this issue later.

The background information I had on Keeley explained a lot of her problems. She had been sexually abused as a child, and placed in a long-stay mental institution from an early age due to severe developmental delay. In the mental institution she was sexually abused as a young teenager (it was not clear if this was by another patient or a member of staff), became pregnant and was given an abortion. This was followed with breast reduction surgery aimed at making her 'less attractive sexually for her own protection'. She had been moved into her community residential home two years earlier during the 'dispersal' programme that gave us 'care in the community'.

Keeley would, at different times, attack other residents, especially those less physically able than herself; have screaming 'tantrums' where she would be out of control destroying furniture; scream and throw herself on the floor curled up in a foetal position and staff would have to physically move her; refuse to get on or off the minibus, creating all kinds of mayhem with other residents using that transport; and she would have periods of refusing to eat.

With a history such as the one Keeley had endured, with absolutely no input of a therapeutic nature (as previously she was deemed unable to benefit from that) it was small wonder to me that she presented her world with so many disruptive behaviours.

As a woman who had experienced such terrible abuse, she was prevented from receiving any healing opportunities because of her learning disabilities. There are women and men survivors of abuse with whom I have worked, who have not got to manage with severe learning disabilities, who struggle with variations of those same destructive behavioural tendencies due to triggers in their lives now that cause them to flash back or defend themselves by destructive behaviour towards self, others or objects (Sanderson, 1995).

I asked Keeley's staff team to try to see if there was a pattern in her behaviours — if there were any possible triggering events in her environment or whether particular staff members were around (or not) when they happened. I also asked for photographs of her homes, family, favourite things and the hospital, to facilitate our work. It took some time to get photographs together, but some did arrive with Keeley one day.

In the meantime, we spent our sessions getting to know each other. In all the time I was seeing her, Keeley never displayed her destructive behaviours. This confirmed to me once more that if people are met with respect and acceptance, and there is an attempt to understand and willingness to be real, then there is actually no need for a person to lose control.

Keeley liked to use colouring pencils and delighted in squiggling lines on the paper, which always represented something she wanted to convey. Her attention span was only seconds long and she would flit, both in activity and in topics interspersed with 'osh at?' She occasionally tested me by banging her hand on the piano to see if I'd be angry: 'bad girl?' she'd gleefully ask. I would encourage her to play the piano, but said I didn't want her to bang because it might break the keys. This, of course, meant that I had to drag off all the things on the top of the piano so that Keeley could see the strings that might break if she banged it!

She talked a lot about 'Mummy Kathryn' and more so when we had the photographs to explore. She talked too of her brothers and sisters. Keeley had regular contact with her mother and one of her brothers and clearly felt part of her family. She talked too of 'daddy' and there was confusion in her voice always. She continually asked where he was, and occasionally answered herself 'in heaven'.

I learned from her support worker that her father had died some time before, but Keeley had not been taken to the funeral because her family felt it would be too upsetting for her.

Sometimes Keeley would begin to say something, for example, 'bad girl Keeley', but then stray into 'osh at?' sessions or pick up and put down pens. It was hard to follow her flow as it was very disjointed.

One day when she had said, 'Keeley cry', I drew a stick figure with exaggerated sad face and lots of tears and wrote, 'Keeley is crying'. She was intrigued. I'm always amazed at the power and effectiveness of my limited ability in drawing. Keeley wanted me to draw more. I said, 'Keeley's crying, why is Keeley crying?' Gradually she described a situation in which she had been 'told off' for hitting Robert, another resident in her home. I drew each detail and relayed the story as it unfolded. She wanted me to write too, so I wrote her words. Keeley could not read or write at all, but she took some paper and 'wrote' words – her squiggles now tiny hieroglyphic symbols conveying her desire to do as I was.

We often drew, and I was instructed to write, in our sessions from then on. Sometimes she took her papers home; other times she left them with me. Of those she took, I would jot down the content after she had left, to keep some sense of her world, it being so fragmented.

I encouraged her to express her feelings when we were engaged in our drawings – she had had no language for them, but quickly learned about happy and sad. Angry came later – happy and sad were what Keeley felt most. We'd been working together for about six months – her attention had improved and she would engage with her photographs and our drawings for several minutes at a time – when I had a call from her key worker. Keeley's mother had died suddenly; she wanted advice about how to tell Keeley.

We talked about how hard it would be for Keeley, whose regular visits to mum were so important. As advice was requested, I gave it. One of the first issues to be faced in the grieving process is making the loss real (Worden, 1983), and my experience was that people with learning disabilities were generally not allowed to do this in the name of protection. It was also my experience that they would search and yearn and suffer for years because they could not comprehend the absence in any real sense.

I asked if the key worker thought Keeley's family would be able to allow her to attend the funeral and also to see her mother before it. A coffin and funeral are still unclear if there is not a real understanding that a person has died and is in the coffin, unable to move, breath, live. I made myself available to go with Keeley to see her mother at the hospital if, after consideration, her key worker felt unable to manage it. She called later to let me know the family had agreed and she was taking Keeley to the hospital that day and to the funeral the following week. I asked if it were possible sensitively to get some pictures of the funeral flowers, to use in our work – I have general pictures of funerals to work with.

Keeley was able to see her mother, touch her and understand, with her key worker's help, that her body could not work any more. Keeley saw and touched for herself. She managed this and the funeral and came to me for her session the day she had been to see her mother buried.

Keeley began with 'Mummy dead', and I drew her with a prostrate stick-figure Mummy. She decided we should put Mummy in the box and I drew and wrote for her. I checked her understanding and reinforced that 'Mummy can't come back now'. We had previously done some work with photos of a staff member Keeley was attached to and was leaving and she'd learned about 'missing'. She was quiet and unusually attentive in this session.

She then decided to do letters for her brothers and sister. She dictated each one and had me draw the coffin and flowers and cars on each. The first one said, 'Dear Jane, Mummy is dead', then 'Dear Stanley, Mummy dead,

Keeley sad', then 'Dear Andrew, Mummy dead, no coming back, miss Mummy'. She folded each carefully and held all three tightly. She then said, 'Daddy dead'. Keeley had made her own connection and now knew what had happened to her father.

When a death occurs, shock and grief can create difficulties in considering the long-term implications of our actions (Worden, 1983). There is pressure to deal with the funeral arrangements and, in our British culture, a tendency to stiff upper lips and reserve in expressing our emotions. Keeley was fortunate that her key worker was able to advocate on her behalf so that she could understand what had happened. For many with learning disabilities that does not happen, and in the name of protection, they are excluded.

For many months after her mother's death, Keeley wanted to talk through the funeral, and look at the pictures of the flowers. Gradually as the frequency diminished, the urgency decreased too. Keeley seemed to feel in command of that particular issue. We drew her upsets and gradually she admitted more of her destructive behaviours. It felt to me that Keeley needed therapeutic intervention when the outbursts occurred — that if she could be met with understanding when she began to become agitated or upset, that she may not need to explode.

I suggested some interventions, especially for when she was crying on the floor, screaming and sobbing. I suggested that her key worker, or support worker on duty, went on the floor with her, naming the feelings and behaviours, i.e. 'Keeley, I see you are crying (screaming), you want to lay here and cry, I am here too'. Even if only done as an experiment it might bring different results than trying to cajole or be firm or physically moving her. The staff did not feel able to try this intervention — again logistically, with responsibility for many, not just one — and lacked confidence in staying with the process.

Keeley's outbursts lessened, but were never absent. It struck me again that Keeley was quite naturally taking to her bed, as any of us might, when things become too much. Her needs for healing from her abuse were complicated by bereavement and her limited capacity for understanding. Her withdrawal to her room, and her preference for staying within the safety of her house, demonstrated clearly that she had a degree of containment for her confusion and frustration if she stayed within the confines of her own home. This frustrated her care team, who wanted to give her access to her community, and opportunities for development. The transition from long-stay institution into the community might seem to some like a wonderful opportunity that people would be keen to explore. For this particular person, however, the world was a very frightening place, and so far she had not been able to find a reliable sense of safety beyond her bed. This was Keeley choosing and communicating her needs, though her needs were in conflict with the needs of the home and staff team within it. It felt important to me that when she took to her bed, she might be allowed the peace to do so, whilst also being offered opportunities to leave her bed for meals and so on. If her need to remain quiet in her bed was met, it might, at other times, be possible to encourage her to move beyond it.

Engaging in power struggles to get her moving, or cajoling, or firm instructions, would never address her communication of need to stay put quietly. As time moved on, it became clear that Keeley was not willing to leave the house, and this prevented her attending altogether eventually, and so our work ended.

I always felt that Keeley needed an intensive therapeutic setting where her healing as a survivor of abuse might be the focus, rather than her disruptive behaviour. Though in the last twenty years there have been changes in awareness of the legacy of childhood abuse (Finkelhor, 1984; Bass and Davis, 1988; Sanderson, 1995), people who do not have learning disabilities still struggle to access therapeutic services that are capable of supporting their healing. There are some limited resources for people with learning disabilities who have been recently abused (i.e. RESPOND[1]).

There is little or no recognition of the long-term effects of abuse which occurred during childhood for people with learning disabilities, many of whom came out of long-stay institutions without records. So Keeley, and others like her, continue to show their distress through their behaviour, yet it's meaning is rarely recognised.

---

1. An organisation that exists to challenge vulnerability and sexual abuse in the lives of people with learning disabilities — 3rd floor, 24–32 Stephenson Way. London, NW1 2HD.

Learning new languages

Opening up to each new communication style

Essentially there is absolutely no difference between working with people who have learning disabilities — even of the most severe kinds — and working with people who do not. With every new client I must listen carefully to their own particular language and style of communicating. Early in my counselling work, I found it difficult to use certain words a client might use in my responses, and instead inserted my own words. So, 'You're really fed up' sanitised the more powerful, 'I'm fucking pissed off!'

The importance of learning our clients' own particular personal language is essential for expressing the core values of counselling was emphasised by Mearns and Thorne (1988). If I am truly to be attempting to walk with my client, and view the world from his/her own perspective rather than my own, I must enter his/her language world too. Because I can speak, this is somewhat easier with those who also speak, than with people who do not. With speech I am already in known territory and I can learn my client's language and style of communicating relatively quickly.

Working with clients whose first language is British Sign Language (BSL), I initially assumed there would be some degree of practice making, if not perfect, then gradual ease of learning. It turns out that, in addition to individual language or communication styles, there are dialects in BSL, and not everyone using BSL actually uses it with the grammar and syntactical structure with which it is imbibed. Some people with profound deafness are able to speak too and so may use what is known as 'sign-supported English' (SSE), which means to speak and create sentences in the way of spoken and written English, and use signs for almost every word. The structure of BSL is more like French in that instead of saying, 'my name is Jan', in BSL I would say/sign 'name me Jan'. Though many can lip-read well, a great deal is lost even among those whose lip-reading is excellent — they might be able to distinguish only 40% of spoken communication (Corker, 1994). Additionally, those who rely on lip-reading miss out on the vocal inflections and stresses which add meaning to words (Roe and Roe, 1991). I have found though that clients whose lip reading is excellent, really find communication with me is facilitated by me signing as well as speaking. Sadly, many people who are both deaf, and having learning disabilities, have missed out on opportunities to develop their signing abilities, and rarely live in environments where sign is being used around them.

I love BSL — it is a beautiful and complex language. If children were taught BSL as part of their primary curriculum, it would serve to enable all people to communicate at any time with people who are deaf. It would also serve to enhance the development of the neglected right brain, especially of spatial awareness (Sacks, 2000). Were we to include sign language into the language curriculum, perhaps more people would be more confident, and use sign more naturally. In residential and educational settings where people have learning disabilities as well as being deaf, they are denied access to everyday discourse if only certain support-workers can sign.

Many people who were deaf from childhood were assumed to have learning disabilities as well, simply because they had no shared communication system. And further, without being given a language, many were delayed in developing cognitive abilities, not because of congenital or organic abnormalities, but because they had no system of representing ideas and feelings. Many deaf children for years were denied the opportunity to learn BSL because of insistence that they learn to speak. Some had their hands tied so they could not use signs they developed between themselves — speech was seen as the only acceptable way of communicating (Sacks, 2000).

So people who are bright, articulate, and full of ideas have been denied opportunities to communicate, not because they themselves are limited, but because so few hearing people learn BSL, forcing deaf people to limit their interactions in the hearing world or rely on expensive interpreters.

It seems an awful prospect to me that anyone needing therapy or counselling might have to struggle with difficult issues and feelings with a third person present, whose role is to translate, because so few therapists can offer BSL. It's a beautiful language, and I encourage anyone who wants to offer counselling to all, to learn it.

Despite the differences in communication styles, working with deaf people is no different than with hearing people in that the world of ideas, feelings, and issues and generally the expression of these is one I share. It has been important to learn and understand particular cultural issues for deaf people and BSL courses include basics on these. I would recommend Mairian Corker's book (1994) for deeper insights into the deaf culture. People who are deaf and who also have learning disabilities particularly need counsellors available who are skilled in signing.

People with learning difficulties may have speech, and varying complexities with it, or they may have no speech at all. Some use Makaton, which is a simplified version of BSL, especially devised for people with learning difficulties. Not only is it important to learn the client's language and style of communication, but it is sometimes necessary to suspend reality entirely and enter into unusual and sometimes seemingly surreal worlds the person inhabits. In my experience there is always a meaning, a logic and a purpose in whatever is being communicated.

Some people I have worked with who have severe learning disabilities do use speech, yet the struggle to produce it results in distortions that I must bring every ounce of concentration to, in order to tune in and understand. One client, with very severe speech impediment, yet not learning-disabled, told me that when I asked her to repeat something she really knew I was listening. She could tell sometimes that people would nod blankly, pretending to understand, but she knew they couldn't. She also told me that she felt able to work with me because I did not attempt to finish her sentences for her, no matter how hard she was struggling to get them out. This feedback helped me when working with people with learning disabilities who were not able to tell me those things, but yet seemed to realise that my intention was always to understand them.

Simon (see p. 90 ff.) used very few words, mostly repetitive, and the endlessly repeated word 'shed', which his care workers told me was meaningless. For Simon it was by no means meaningless, but it took me a very long time to understand why.

Marie Cradock (see p. 156 ff.) describes her work with a youngster with learning difficulties, who she could only meet by entering his world through discussions of reptiles. All their work, and it was important, was facilitated because she was willing to enter fully into his world.

I recall a student of mine with autism, who was able to speak and was also utterly brilliant at drawing trains, yet incapable of relating socially. There was no other way in. All our communications took place in railway parlance — a language of rolling stock and signals that I had to learn quickly to enable him to develop within that learning environment.

Some people communicate only via a single controllable muscle, an eyelid movement, a facial expression. Whatever the mode of communication, if we are willing to really attend and learn that client's language, we can offer a space for whatever is causing distress.

With some people, with the most severe learning disabilities and restricted communication difficulties, we are called upon to listen even more carefully to our own responses and intuition. Particularly within the Person-Centred Approach, we seek to empower, to place the person at the centre of the process. It is hard sometimes to know if someone with moderate or severe learning disabilities really wants to be there in the counselling situation, since they have usually been referred by someone else, brought by someone else and will be collected by someone else.

We are called upon to honour our personal integrity and check out, by whatever means of communication we can, whether the client wants to be there and what they might want to focus on.

Communication aids can be anything from speech, sign language, music, art materials, toys, bits of dust floating in the room — but most importantly a willingness to really learn the other's language — it is there in whatever different or restricted form.

Carl's story

As with so many clients with severe learning disabilities, Carl was referred to me as a last resort. With a long history of extremely challenging behaviour, he had endured endless behaviour modification programmes, which had frustrated his carers by their continual failure, even where there had been initial promise. I am always greatly inspired by anyone who can, by their wit, ingenuity or even sheer stubbornness, outwit those who have laboured over base lines, schedules and reinforcement programmes. So often the behaviour being 'modified' has not been subjected to the most important test of all – to really try to understand what the behaviour is communicating.

Carl, a young man in his thirties, was profoundly deaf, and partially sighted, with only a very few signs to help him communicate with those around him. However, he was a brilliant communicator, making clear in no uncertain terms when he was angry, happy, frustrated or through his behavioural signposts, always assuming people were willing to try to understand them. Sadly, too often, his behaviour was noted under the heading of 'attention-seeking', and its real communicative content missed altogether. When we met, I invited him into the room I used then to work with clients who might need a variety of materials and objects to facilitate their communication. My purpose was to allow him the opportunity to choose freely, and to develop our relationship through his own choices of activity. A piano stood on one side of the room, and Carl made straight for it, after his carer had left. He selected from the music on the stand, opened it, and began to play. With evident joy his hands ran up and down the piano, and if the sound had been switched off, he would have passed, for all the world, for a thoroughly competent pianist. I simply observed, allowing Carl to find his own sense of where he was in this new place for him, with a strange person, and the freedom to choose. After some time, he closed the music, and the piano lid, pushed back the stool with a flourish, and glanced at me cursorily, as he explored the room, before settling at the small table, where he found the paper and pens. So far, only a few glances had been exchanged, and I was unsure of how clearly he could see, and wondered how I would communicate with what was then my rudimentary sign language. Carl took a piece of paper and wrote laboriously 'Carl', still ignoring me. I decided to respond, and wrote 'Jan' on another sheet of paper. A sideways glance was my reward.

As always, I endeavoured to communicate what I could offer here in this space, and to convey a sense of privacy and safety as well as freedom to choose what we worked with, and what we explored in terms of things that might be troubling him. However unsure I am that a client understands these concepts, I must try to make clear the purpose of the counselling. Our first session ended with Carl having only occasionally glanced at me through bottle-glass-thick lenses on his National Health spectacles. I recognised, through our limited interaction, that my signing ability, rudimentary as it was, was way ahead of my client's. I determined to develop my signing skills.

Carl established a pattern for our sessions: firstly, he would play the piano, and I was definitely surplus to requirements during this performance. Sometimes, he would sing in his own inimitable style, simple sounds all of similar pitch, but definitely with a sense of rhythm about them. When he was satisfied with his performance, he would move to the table, pick up pens and begin to write or draw: always the same routine, and always the same repeated drawings and words. For several weeks we met, and spent forty-five minutes in each other's presence, and I struggled to offer the core attitudinal qualities of the Person-Centred Approach: empathy, genuineness and unconditional positive regard. The latter was probably the easiest to offer, as my desire was to allow Carl the freedom and space to make contact with me as he chose. I was very conscious of how rare an experience this was for him, and I trusted that in time he would direct the process in a growthful way. It was not too difficult to experience my congruence, and to share that as and when it felt appropriate, for example in sharing my pleasure at his enjoyment of his own music making. However, it was very difficult to demonstrate any obvious empathy, given the routine content of the sessions.

In the third session, after the already established routine, I mentioned (in sign) that I had noticed that he looked sad that day. He did not seem to comprehend my sign, so I drew a primitive face, a simple circle with dots for eyes and nose, and an exaggeratedly down-turned mouth, and wrote the word 'sad' underneath, then gave the sign again. He copied the letters under the word, without any sense of connection between himself and the picture. I drew a similarly primitive happy face next to the other, and wrote 'happy' underneath, and signed the word. Again he copied the letters and looked at me. It felt as if we made a breakthrough in that session, when he was interested enough in what I was drawing, and signing, to copy. Yet it was the following session that I learned how much of a breakthrough it had been. Carl's carer who brought him to this session informed me that my client had gone home after the previous meeting, and signed that he was 'happy going to Jan's house', and that he had never previously known the signs for happy and sad, and he had been using them appropriately over the week since. At one and the same time I felt encouraged that we had made a connection that was meaningful and useful to Carl, and yet I felt that he had learned them easily in one session – if it was so easy, how had he reached the age he was without ever being given the signs for his emotions before?

There were two very significant issues within our work: his repeated disruption in his residential home, especially repeatedly setting off the fire alarms, and secondly, within our sessions he repeatedly mentioned 'mummy'. To facilitate our communication, I had asked carers to help Carl select photographs of the people in his life, and any photographs of homes, and the long-stay institution where he had spent several years. I asked too for pictures of the fire alarms, as I hoped these might allow him to talk about what was happening.

Many months had passed in our regular weekly sessions, when Carl began to respond to the pictures of the fire alarm, and communicate to me via photographs, drawings and sign, that he was setting off the alarms. My efforts at encouraging exploration of the lead-up or after-effects were fruitless. He was fixed on the actual events of setting off the alarms, and signing 'bad boy'. I checked with him how it would be if I were to ask his carers about the alarms, and he agreed. As ever, I felt uncomfortable simply accepting that I had his consent, since so many people with severe learning disabilities comply as a matter of course. In Carl's case, he would show a definite preference for certain things offered (for example, particular colouring pencils), and refuse those he didn't want, so I felt I could take his word for it. This was a long way from feeling comfortable that I had his 'informed consent'.

I asked the carers if there was a pattern to the alarms being set off, and none had been noticed. I asked if they would make a note of the incidents, along with what happened before, during and after, as well as who was around at the time. On the following session, the carer reported that a pattern had been noticed. Carl was setting off fire alarms when there was a staff change-over. His disruptive behaviour was, in fact, a clear communication of alarm, as if Carl were saying, 'Where are you going? Who will look after me? I am alarmed'. With this information in mind, it struck me that if the team were able to explain, with photographs, who was going home, and who would be coming instead, that Carl might have no need to feel worried enough to set off the alarm. This simple suggestion produced positive effects immediately. My instinct is that disruptive and challenging behaviour is communicating important feelings, and that if we truly want to understand what those feelings are, we must listen carefully to the behaviour. Carl reported to me in his sessions that he was happy with photographs at home, and took pleasure in telling me who would be on duty throughout our work from then on. It struck me that if Carl were to be alarmed about anything else, he would probably return to using the fire alarms as a means of conveying this. My hope was that his carers, as the teams changed over the years, would recognise that as a distress flare, rather than wilfully destructive attention-seeking.

My request for photographs of family had resulted in Carl including a new element to his routine within our sessions. He brought books with pictures of himself and family throughout the years. I knew that many years before, both his parents had died, and that he had not been to the funerals, as it had been feared this would be too upsetting for him, and he would not understand anyway. From the time we began going through his books, he told me 'mummy heaven', 'daddy heaven'. He always used the same expressions for each picture, and I sometimes found I was struggling to maintain full attention with the repetitive nature of his utterances. For many months the routine nature of the work, his choice of materials and activity as well as 'issues to be explored' remained a challenge to my ability to maintain attention, and continue to believe in the work we were engaged in.

At the same time, during this phase, however, Carl began to show an interest in the rest of the house. During the summer he had taken to including some time in the garden as part of his routine. My role, as always, was to track his utterances closely, and allow his self-direction to lead the process. He began asking if I had a bedroom upstairs. I responded to this question by affirming that, yes, I had. I had not recognised that the sign he was using for bedroom was the same as the sign for heaven. For months this had been part of our work, and I was simply not making the connection.

Carl began talking of a planned visit to his sister. Carers mentioned that these visits had often been difficult for his sister and family, as Carl would become very distressed and often had to be collected before the planned end of his stay. This did not fit for me with what he was bringing to his sessions – he was looking forward to the visit. Then, he slipped in, 'go sister, see Mummy, Mummy heaven'. I finally understood something incredibly important to Carl. I checked again if he and I could ask carers for information. His consent meant that I gained the information that it was Carl's sister who had told him that his mother and father had died, only she had not used the word died – she had told Carl they had gone to heaven. Carl's sign for bedroom was the same as the one he was shown for heaven, which had confused him. Carl had, for years, on visits to his sister, been searching for his mother, and becoming distressed when he couldn't find her upstairs in heaven/the bedroom.

A new phase began in our work. I began signing 'dead', and sharing my understanding that Carl had been searching for his mother. We looked at dead flowers together, so that he could begin to understand what being dead meant. I explained, many times, as he continually repeated the same things during those weeks, that being dead meant mummy and daddy could not come back – they were gone. He quickly took on the sign for dead, and began using it whenever he spoke of his parents, and following up that they were in heaven. In time I conveyed to him that heaven and bedrooms upstairs were different concepts. And over the months he was able to communicate missing both his parents. This was facilitated by a member of staff leaving his home, so that we were able to work through Carl's feelings about this loss, and clarify that the member of staff was not dead, but would not be coming back anymore. Carl gradually put the two together, and understood that he felt upset and sad when missing his parents and those staff who left from time to time, and that feeling upset and crying were acceptable.

Our work together was painstakingly slow, mostly because it took me so long to learn Carl's language, and fully comprehend how it was for him. He very much enjoyed his sessions, and always happily engaged in them. Throughout the two and a half years that we worked together, he developed his ability to express his emotions through the signs I taught him for those. We worked on other issues throughout our time together, all-important to him, and all probably ongoing.

From time to time I tentatively joined him at the piano, and tried to respond to his playing with mirroring musical sounds from the keyboard. I was, each time, made very much aware that Carl was the sole performer, and that my efforts simply cramped his style! I remained close by, but respected his desire to have this time alone to express himself through the vibrations of the instrument. However, I was occasionally invited to join him in wonderfully expressive dancing, when the mood came upon him. In those rare moments, there were connections that transcended our differences in language, ability, or experiences in the world. We were simply relating as two human beings willing to meet each other.

Over the last few months of our work, I realised that we had probably done the work that we could do, and that Carl was becoming very comfortable with his routine within our sessions. Essentially I was providing him with one-to-one time now, instead of therapy, though clearly he found our time together therapeutic. Although we had an open-ended contract with his funders, I was all too aware, as ever, that his funding could be withdrawn at any time. It seemed that now was the time to work towards ending. I recommended to carers that Carl be given access to a piano at regular intervals, and that he would also benefit from art opportunities. Meanwhile I suggested to Carl that he come fortnightly whilst we thought about finishing our work together. He agreed to this, but I was not convinced he understood what it would actually mean. A fortnight later, when his carer brought him, he reported that Carl had been disruptive and setting off the fire alarms again. When we went into our session, after the obligatory recital, I conveyed to Carl that he seemed upset: he certainly had given an extremely loud performance at the piano. He took a piece of paper and felt tip pen, and drew faces, as we had at the very beginning, one happy and one sad. Underneath each he put '1 week happy, 2 week sad'. I found myself deeply moved. This man, whose history had been reported as disruptive, disturbed and challenging, was able to tell me directly that my need to finish our work did not meet with his approval. I recognised that it had been too sudden – in one session the explanation, and then a two-week gap. We had had gaps before due to holidays, or his illness, but he clearly knew that this was different. I agreed to work weekly for some more time whilst we gave space to the feelings of loss of his space and relationship with me, and look at what would be happening in that space after we had finished. Gradually we were able to lengthen the time between, till we finally said goodbye.

When Carl left for the last time, it was not a momentous occasion. Just the usual routine hug from him, thanks from his carer, and off he went to his taxi. It has been some years since we worked together, and as I write this, it feels as if he has just left, the piano vibrating from the energetic interlude, followed by the firm closing of the music, upside down as usual.

I learned much from him, and his patience with me was infinite, as I took so long to make sense of his struggle. One of my fondest memories of him was once, when he had needed to use the bathroom, and seemed to have been gone for a long time. Just as I was preparing to go and check that he was OK, he emerged, and strode down the stairs with a royal air, with an incredible waft of fragrances surrounding him, and his hair slicked to one side with what must have been Vaseline. Later, on inspection, I found every toiletry article open in the bathroom, where he had obviously enjoyed exploring and preening himself. His delight with himself as he came down the stairs, head high and smiling, remains as a snapshot in my mind, and always makes me smile. I hope he always has access to music. Though he cannot hear, it is terribly important to him – he feels it deeply. I hope too, that he always has around him those who are willing to work out what it is he is communicating, even if he is not able to find the sign or expression for it, other than through unusual or disruptive behaviour. His soul and his touch were always gentle beneath those outbursts.

Interview with Marie Cradock:
On dinosaurs and other animals

Marie has chosen not to use her real name as an additional measure to ensure her clients' anonymity. A first career in teaching gave way to her training in Person-Centred counselling. She works for a youth counselling organisation, as a school counsellor, and has a private practice where she works with adults.

Jan: What I am actually particularly interested in capturing is how you enter the world of children you've worked with, who have special needs. How you enter their worlds and how you learn their language?

Marie: Yes, I suppose the thing that I learnt pretty quickly when I was working as a school counsellor was that the young people were expecting that this counsellor, who they didn't know anything about, was going to tell them off, be telling them what to do, telling them why they were bad, just another part of the school system really, how to be a good boy or girl . . . That they were going to be in trouble.

Initially with all of my clients in the school there was a lot to get round in terms of their expectations and they would shuffle into the room and look fairly hostile, and actually one little chap, I think he was in year seven at the time, just came in and sat with his fingers in his ears and was going 'errrrr errrrr errrrr, I'm not listening I'm not listening' and that was possibly the most interesting start to a counselling session I've ever had. Not something you tend to encounter too much with adults. And having been a teacher there was a teacher instinct saying, 'take your fingers out of your ears and start behaving sensibly'. I managed to resist that, and just let him sit there with his fingers in his ears making his non-verbal noises, and he kept looking at me to see 'are you going to — when are you going to tell me off — when are you going to send me out?' and I didn't. Eventually he took his fingers out and I started being able to talk to him about how the counselling time might be, and about what we might actually be doing.

He listened and looked very suspicious, and very wary but surprised as well, that I had certainly thwarted him in his expectations of being sent away and being told, 'you're just bad — go away'. I actually worked with him for probably about a year, though he was often out of school: he was often excluded, because his behaviour was not acceptable. He did have learning support teachers but he did not get on with his particular learning support teacher, and she seemed to tell him off more than anybody else. It was about a year of sessions, and over that time we started slowly to communicate. What I did in the beginning was to invite him to tell me something about what was going on, about who he was, about what he liked, what he didn't like. And sometimes using paper and pens and sometimes colours. Sometimes with my 'box of tricks': I've got a whole range of objects and little dolls that I've borrowed from my supervisor who's very generous, to actually find out what his world was like.

It took a long time. He was very cautious, very wary, but he kept coming and slowly, over many months, he began to get the sense that actually it was OK here to say what was happening in his world and to say he hated his sister and he didn't get on with his parents and that his life wasn't particularly good outside or inside of school and over the year we started to play. He actually started to make up games which felt so rewarding to me that he was beginning to trust, that this was a nice place where he was going to be heard. We made up some really wacky games like Plasticine darts. That was quite fun, and we had a real fear that the deputy head, whose room I was in, would come in and see us hurling Plasticine at his wall. 'What on earth's going on in here?!' He didn't. We played skittles and built little houses out of bricks and all sorts of things. In time he started to — I suppose to become himself in a way, to become somebody who would say what was going on in his world, say what he was feeling. Not all of the time, I'm not making life-transforming claims here but during sessions he would often be looking like he was in a very bad mood when he arrived, plonking himself down and then I'd just gently invite him to tell me what had been going on and how he was. He always expected there would be a telling off and that I was an agent of the institution, which I made great efforts not to be.

Jan: He was part of the behaviour unit?

Marie: Yes. Part of the learning support centre and the school very much still see the counsellor's role as behaviour modification which it was never going to be. Not in my mind anyway, and not in the minds of the learning support staff either. They knew that the behaviour modification stuff they were going to be doing would not be part of my work. I think the most joyful moment with him was when he actually started to tease *me* and to joke around and to be playful and that felt like such a triumph that he felt he could actually do that, and, yes, that was the thing that was most exciting for me working with him, was that he became playful and while we were playing managed to talk about all sorts of things about what was going on in his life. Particularly about his sister who had some sort of special needs, some sort of physical disability, but *she* was a good girl, all the teachers loved her, she was very bright and very keen and very studious. Everything that he wasn't, and he was always being told, 'you should be like your sister'. So there was quite a lot of anger released with what we did as well. I think that is where the Plasticine darts came in: we drew a darts board and put the numbers and rings on it and hurled Plasticine balls at it and that was quite fun. In fact, thinking back now, it's all flooding back. We did all sorts of throwing things around the deputy head's office! We had sponge balls and Plasticine and cushions as well. We played a version of shove ha'penny. We used to put goals on the table and have to get the rolls of Sellotape past each other. That was quite a fierce game. He was very pleased when he won, which he invariably did. I never got to be very good at roll the Sellotape. So that was him, that was Eric. I think with lots of them it was actually a case of entering into their world and that was something that had to be done very gently and very cautiously because it wasn't at all what they were expecting: they were expecting basically some telling off.

Jan: Could you just say a bit about the context of what their world in school in fact — learning support etc.?

Marie: They were all in year seven or year eight, one or two in year nine.

Jan: What sort of age is that?

Marie: Twelve, thirteen, fourteen, and they were all young people who had been identified as having moderate learning difficulties and behavioural difficulties and had then been referred to the learning support centre which was a new project which had been set up within the school, and did actually run for three years altogether. I was there for most of that time. The plan was to support the students experiencing difficulties and to provide one-to-one counselling for those who they considered to be in the most trouble, the most wounded and the ones who were really struggling. Those were the ones that made their way to the various little cupboards that I worked in while I was there. Most of the places we worked in were windowless and airless.

One of the classrooms was sandwiched between music and technology so you can imagine how peaceful that was. Most of the young people I was allowed to work with fairly long term if I made a case for it, and it seemed totally necessary to me. Nobody stood in my way, which is quite rare actually. So I suppose my goals in working with these people was to help them to find a way of articulating what was going on in their lives and to find ways of expressing and releasing their feelings, to look at how they did that and maybe a little bit about what they might change and what choices they might make. How to feel that they had a little bit of a sense of control over some things. To look at the demands of the school environment on them and how they might actually come to terms with that and how they might manage to change things slightly so that they would have a better time in school. That was certainly not the main focus, certainly not for me, but it did come up from time to time. There was, I suppose, with most of the young people, a lot of anger and a lot of anger work that we did with all of them but that was always something that came further down the line. Initially it was very gentle tentative beginnings, you know, tell me about your world was the spoken or sometimes the unspoken question.

Jan: I know you mentioned Eric — his sister was bright — but did any of them ever talk about what it was like to be in the learning support and about their learning difficulties?

Marie: Yes, most of them talked about their learning support centre — as a haven, as a place where they felt encouraged and supported and accepted and that they had some sort of value.

Jan: That's interesting that they didn't see it as something awful, that they saw it as something safe for them.

Marie: I think that was down to the staff, that there was the atmosphere they worked very hard to create. You could hear the difference as the child came through the door to the learning support centre, which was just a room: the teachers' voices were different, it was very boundaried but it was very encouraging, very positive and the minute sometimes they would step outside the door you could hear someone screaming at them down the corridor calling them a horrible this, that and the other, and what are you doing and you should be there etc. So I think all of the young people I worked with saw it in a positive light and it was a place they would literally run to when things got too much in the main body of the school. I think the school had a very ambivalent relationship with the learning support centre. They wanted it because they thought it would deal with the difficult, disruptive pupils. But there was also a sort of suspicion and a sense of you just go along and get mollycoddled and people are just nice to you but you don't deserve it because you have behaved badly. But we want the learning support centre because when we can't handle these difficult students then we need somewhere to throw them. So there was always that going on in the background which I attempted to keep out of my work.

Actually most of the young people did understand how things were different in the counselling room from out in the school. Maybe I did bang on about it quite a bit saying that in here this is how it is, this is what we do, these are the sorts of things that we are going to be doing but you do understand that out there, there are very definite school rules and that things are different and that is something that I have no control over and they did get the idea. A very simple idea is that they knew they could use any language they needed to when they were with me in the session, but once they were out of the door they went back to the school rules. I was quite amazed that they all got that because some were only eleven and some of them emotionally much younger than that, but they did get that. So that over the more-or-less three years that I was there, I entered all sorts of interesting worlds and knew very little to begin with but was keen to find out.

I think that was the one thing that struck me about the young people was that what they responded to was something real, something genuine, something where they were actually encountering a real human being, not somebody who is a teacher, who is nice sometimes, but somebody who is actually there for them, with them, who doesn't have a hidden agenda, is not trying to make them do anything or say anything they don't want to do or say. I think this is where the Person-Centred Approach is a uniquely potent approach working with young people because it is about going in, going alongside and being real. My experience is that young people have responded to that. I'm not making incredible claims that there are all these young people with their lives totally transformed, but I know from feedback from the young people themselves and from various people from the school and sometimes from social workers that they did experience it in a very positive way.

Jan: It's not like Hollywood, is it? — but on the other hand for many of them it may have been their first encounter with somebody real, somebody who was willing to enter their world.

Marie: Yes, I think so. I suppose that what was lacking in their own lives was anybody who was remotely interested in them at all. It just wasn't really there, and a lot of the home backgrounds were very disrupted: separations and divorces and unsettled families and a lot of upheaval in their backgrounds.

Jan: You mentioned one particular young person and I think you were talking about the feedback from social workers?

Marie: Yes. Susan, who I saw for about a year, who was a very bright girl with a very difficult home life, with an alcoholic parent and actually was permanently excluded some time after I had finished with her and moved on to college and was given some sort of social worker. I'm not entirely sure what kind of support it was but I think it was a social worker who contacted me, because she was trying to support Susan and was finding that she was being very hostile and difficult and she wasn't letting her anywhere near. She said she had asked Susan if there was anything at all positive in all the years at school, and she said the only thing was the counselling. I thought, 'ah, that was good'. And I'd been aware, whilst I was working with her, that she was finding it useful, but I hadn't realised that she was finding it that significant. I heard from the school later on that she had gone on to college and was very artistic and was doing well. I'm not saying that is all down to the counselling but the thing that struck me was her comment that that was the only thing positive about school.

Jan: She had really recognised the value of the relationship, and saw that as the thing that had given her something in education where everything else had not.

Marie: Yes, and she was a very lovely girl, very bright but very troubled, and responded to the relationship that was being offered, and it was a good feeling. I'm just thinking about some of the worlds I entered in with some of these people. One particular chap, I think he was year seven or eight when I started working with him, had been referred to the learning support centre and then to me because he seemed very switched off from everything. His home background on the surface appeared to be fairly stable. I think things were OK with both parents and siblings and they were comfortably off. There were obvious things going on that might suggest distressing difficulties, but he just always seemed to be on another planet, with completely flat affect and deadpan face, and did not seem to connect what he did with the trouble that he got into; he didn't seem to link anything.

Jan: Didn't seem to understand the consequences.

Marie: No, and I think his parents had had him tested for various things and someone mentioned possible autism but that is as far as it had gone. So he came along. He was about twelve/thirteen and sat fairly impassively and looked as if he was expecting somebody to talk at him or give him a lecture or something, and slowly, just by my persistence in asking him gently about himself and his life, he started to talk about his absolute passion which was reptiles and amphibians and it was something I knew nothing about, and I genuinely wanted to know — and it was like a different boy.

Jan: I remember that. I remember you saying, 'what do I do?' All he wants to talk about is reptiles, and I said, 'if that's what he wants talk about, maybe you could talk about them'.

Marie: I actually know quite a lot now. I could actually keep amphibians now. I know what they need and I know what sort of climate-controlled cage they need. His face started to light up and become animated, and for some weeks it was very much 'tell me what you know about these animals' and he did. And he bought books in, very complicated adult books about these animals.

Jan: So this learning disability thing he'd been in the unit for — he was all right in the area he was interested in. Which is actually consistent with autism, isn't it?

Marie: There were characteristics, but there certainly was a little boy in there who just wanted somebody to listen and to be interested. I suppose what happened over time was that I got to know about his animals and creatures, and then it seemed a way in to start to explore relationships and human needs and specifically his relationships and his feelings. Not a huge amount. I don't think there was ever going to be a huge amount, but a little bit of what we hope for or what we're frightened of, what makes us feel good, what makes us feel bad. I think if I hadn't gone into the reptile house with him we wouldn't have got anywhere. He would have sat and he wouldn't have been accessible. Probably wouldn't have been anything. He came to life through the animals and there was another dimension to the work with animals. He had one of the cyber pets. You had to feed them at the right time, and give them water and praise by pressing things on a tiny computer or they die.

A huge amount came out of that, because again there was an obvious connection between what a little creature needs and then building that into what do we need — what is missing and what is good and what is bad — and he did talk a little bit about relationships with family and with friends and with people from the reptile club. One of the times he had his cyber pet going and if you don't feed it at the right time and attend to it when it's crying it dies. You actually see it going up to heaven on the screen with little wings, so that was a way into looking at how you feel if you are not getting any of those things. You don't feel that there is anybody really interested in giving you any attention. I think this was one of the things that were going on at home, and so he switched off and just got on with relating to animals. He far preferred animals to people, there was no question.

Jan: That was his passion.

Marie: Yes. You know where you are with an animal. If you treat them a certain way, this is how they respond, and yes, I got to know quite a lot really about reptiles and things and it was genuine — I wasn't pretending to be interested, I really wanted to know. He seemed to be a very fascinating young person with this absolute passion and almost a photographic memory for facts and figures about the animals and what they ate, and he was saving up to buy a particularly elaborate form of lizard. I am not a great lizard fan; I wouldn't really want to cuddle them.

Jan: Wouldn't like to meet the lizard yet…

Marie: Noooo. I suppose it's quite interesting that he chose animals that other people wouldn't obviously go for. They're not furry or cuddly; they don't run and fetch sticks or do tricks or anything. But there was a real bond between him and the animals which was something that we could work with.

Jan: It's very interesting also that they are cold-blooded creatures and they seem impassive and they seem kind of vaguely not of this world, which is exactly how he presented when he first came.

Marie: Yes, a real appearance of remoteness, and they are very contained animals because they don't need fussing over. Yes, absolutely an echo of how he appeared. I suppose, maybe as a consequence of some of the work, he seemed happy enough to come to sessions. He coped in school; he survived more or less to the end of the compulsory schooling years though he was excluded from time to time.

Jan: What was he excluded for?

Marie: I'm trying to think back now — just fairly routine misbehaviour in the classroom, messing about, taking somebody's pencil case, not giving it back, answering back to teachers in quite a hostile way.

Jan: It's interesting that he did not do that with you, never ever did that with you as though somehow that meeting was different.

Marie: I used to have this fantasy that if the teachers could see — if only they could see how he really was. If he was related to in a different way, and you know full well that teachers can't do what I was doing, but they can offer a relationship, and the ones who did, he worked quite well with them. But yes, I think as well, once you have got a reputation in school, then anything you do gets jumped on from a great height and he did. But he did also began to be able to connect cause and effect and to see that if you don't feed your pet he will die; if you cheek the teacher you will get sent outside, you will get into trouble. And that non-awareness of consequences seemed to change very slightly: he became a little bit more aware and sometimes able to decide how he was going to react in a given situation and to think it through and reflect on it so something useful seemed to happen there. But it certainly was a strange and mysterious world of animals.

Jan: Quite a learning curve for you both in terms of his gradual glimpse of understanding about cause and effect, and your developing knowledge of reptiles, but also in your relating through different language entirely, one you had to learn.

Marie: Oh yes and something that instinctively I wasn't drawn to — I was drawn to him and that meant that I genuinely wanted to go into this world. I was just thinking about another of the young people, this was a young girl called Janine. I'm sure that name rings a bell.

Jan: I remember Janine.

Marie: She had some learning difficulties but could get by and she had some sort of extra learning support and came from a financially well off family. A huge family of seven children. They sounded like an East London Mafia family but a real emotional vacuum at home. A lot of material things were thrown at her. I think she was the youngest of the seven offspring, but she was pretty much left to get on with it. Entering Janine's world was entering the world of designer clothes and peer pressure, make-up, hair colours and in a way less unusual than reptiles and amphibians, but a lot came out of her talking about clothes. She seemed to have endless amounts of money: each time she came she would talk about 'I've got £100 and I'm going to have this designer and that, designer make' — half of which I wasn't aware of — I'm Mrs non-designer, Mrs woman-at -BHS — so I got to know what was in and what wasn't. I'd actually expanded this out to be work around values and what was important in terms of clothes and how you look and what messages that sends out and then to the next level, what matters and what actually makes somebody a good friend or a good parent or a good daughter. An awful lot was done around that and I think if I hadn't entered into that world of 'let's talk clothes and make-up' I probably wouldn't have done it. If I'd said, 'well, let's have a think today about relationships and significant people in you life' she would have said what? And we had an agreement: she was a compulsive chewing-gum chewer. She was constantly in trouble with it at school. We had an agreement she could put it in and chew happily through the session, making loud unappealing noises, which she did, as long as it went in the bin as the bell went. She happily stuck to that. It was fair and made sense. So we did that — I got to know a lot about mobile phones and what sort you are meant to have.

Jan: Umhm. Have you got one, by the way?

Marie: Yes. I have a deliberately unfashionable one, apparently the only mobile phone that is worth having is a Nokia and they have got to be ones you can play games on and do the texting stuff on and usually they have to be bright colours.

Jan: Ah. Otherwise they don't count. I see, yours didn't count.

Marie: Absolutely. At the time I was working with Janine, I didn't have one, which she found bizarre in the extreme — how could you possibly survive without a mobile phone? How could you possibly wear a BHS T-shirt that cost £8? How could you hold your head up? I think she was really intrigued by that. I suppose with all of the young people, but mainly with Janine because she was a girl, I talked about myself a bit at her age and myself now and about what was important to me — not trying to convert her but to show that there were other ways of looking at things. Because we talked about what she wanted, it was through her passion for clothes all sorts of things were possible, and make-up as well. That was an ongoing battle. She was always trying to wear her eye shadow and mascara at school and the teachers would make her go and wash it off, and she would put it back on again when she left the lesson — that was quite fun too — I got to know a lot about make-up styles and the right sort of things to wear and a huge amount about her world of boyfriends and social pressures and sex — which she was definitely not going to be involved with probably until she was about 20, she thought, unlike a lot of her peers. She had very definite views on that, which I have to say was a relief, and was very up on things like sex. She knew all the safety stuff. That was, for me, almost an experience of feeling about thirteen again, not losing my adult self but really feeling those pressures and how your life could actually depend on having the right T-shirt and part of her could see that it was all a superficial thing but she couldn't opt out of it.

Jan: But the other thing is that it shows how, if you hadn't been willing to engage in that language and world, that the relationship would have been a non-starter, and there is something about you being willing to feel thirteen that allowed you and her to explore so much.

Marie: Yes, and not being shocked by the odd swear word here and there and just allowing her to be. Certainly not coming over as a parent — I don't think any of the people I worked with ever saw me as a similar age to their parents. In fact I know they didn't because we would play guess how old the counsellor is? I always told them if they asked and they wanted to know, but you could see them thinking, 'oh that's about the same as my mum'. I liked it because it was one of my aims not to come across as another person doing the telling. I entered the world of horses as well with a young person, that was not in the school but with the youth service, and a lot came out of the world of horses, I mean similar as with the amphibians and reptiles.

Jan: Did you feel more comfortable with the world of horses having come through the world of dinosaurs and reptiles and so on?

Marie: Yes, I think so. Just getting to realise that this is where we are going in a young person's world and we are going to jump right in, and I suppose also knowing in my mind that there is so much going to come out of this and it is not just going to be about 'I went riding and I did this and I did the grooming'. There is so much about their relationships and their feelings and it does all emerge. There's just a couple more worlds that I entered that I thought were quite interesting — one of which was WWF wrestling. That was a youth service person, a young chap called Gary who thought counselling was OK, but the really good thing about coming was that he got a McDonalds at the end of the session, because his dad picked him up. So it was worth it to get out of school and having a McDonalds, and the bit in the middle was OK.

I only saw him about five times and he had actually been referred because his hair was falling out, and there wasn't an organic cause. It was stress.

There had been bullying going on at school. He was very withdrawn at first and didn't really say very much at all but I think in the first session, he got the message that this was a very non-threatening environment and he got a McDonalds after, so it was worth coming back. This is an interesting one — bribing with food. And he really took to the idea of drawing things. He really liked drawing, it was something he felt he did well — possibly the only thing he felt he did well, and he did all sorts of drawings: scenes, members of his own family, trees — just because he wanted to.

As we were nearing the end of the few sessions, he moved into his whole lifetime favourite thing of this wrestling, incredible theatrical stuff. They were wearing incredible outfits and had all got names and personas and so on. I knew absolutely nothing about it, except it exists, and in one session in particular we did a huge amount of work about just explanations of what it was he liked about it so much. It was the sense of power these people had and the drama and the confidence. Showing off and feeling good about themselves, and showing everybody else. Flamboyant stuff, and that was a part of him which was something he really wanted, but didn't feel that he could have. He desperately wanted to go to a 'normal' school to just be like 'normal' people and to feel strong and confident and powerful like these absolutely awful wrestlers, and quite a bit came out of that just talking round why it was they were so appealing and why he wanted to be like them.

I think in that fairly short term — it was only about five sessions — he started to feel a little bit more positive about himself and I think that was maybe largely due to the fact that he did a large amount of drawing, and felt good about it. And the drawings were lovely, some of which he wanted me to keep and some he wanted to take away. One of the funniest ones was a picture of me. He put me in a Tesco's uniform. I never quite worked that one out. I'd got my name badge on a Tesco label and pens in my pocket.

Jan: And you never understood that, but you accepted his drawing.

Marie: But I thought that was interesting. I said, 'that's nice. I've got a job, I've got a place in life. I feel useful', and he just smiled.

Jan: I wonder what he associated with Tesco's.

Marie: I have no idea!

Jan: Mind you, if he is very motivated by food?

Marie: Possibly. I got a slight sense that he did it and looked at me as if he thought I might be angry.

Jan: Right — just a test.

Marie: Yes, to see if I minded being put in this, not a flattering uniform — it had a sort of bow round the neck and a hat. I think it was him being maybe a little cheeky or to me — it was playful and I thought it was fabulous — I kept that one. Another one of the young people was Stephen, who had an absolute passion for disaster movies and disaster monsters and people being wiped out in large numbers.

Jan: I remember Stephen. Wasn't he the little one that you were worried about with his tendency with violence?

Marie: Yes, this was back at the school and he was such a lovely boy, very open, very quickly trusting. He had no reason to trust anybody because there was a lot of violence at home and social services were involved, and sort of broken families and horrendous things going on and he had been diagnosed ADHD[1] and was on a whacking dose of Ritalin[2] that made him feel ill, and gave him stomach ache all the time. Yet through all of that, he was happy to come, and very quickly picked up that this was a different place. That this was somewhere where somebody wanted to know about him and he was probably the only one when the centre was closing and they were getting ready to leave who really registered it, because he was saying, 'who will I talk to, who will I listen to if I don't have this?' and there wasn't an easy answer. There were some designated people in school who were trying, but I didn't want to end there and he certainly didn't want to. But — disaster movies. Titanic, he had the movie and knew it word for word, every single bit and he loved it when it started to sink.

Jan: That's interesting. What did he make of that, what did you and he make of it?

Marie: It seemed to be all about his anger; they've got that coming to them — ha. Mostly, I suppose, it's all adults who were being killed off. I don't think any of his drawings showed children being hurt, but it was about the inevitability of these bad things going to happen and it was going to happen to these grown ups and there was nothing they can do, and ha! — they've got it coming. You could just feel the excitement building up in him as he drew. He drew the Titanic going down, and he would get the blue pen and he would start on 'the water's this level now, and now it's coming up and those people can't get out and now its getting them, and now its getting them', and he was just wiping out large volumes of people.

Jan: All adults.

---

1. Attention Deficit Hyperactive Disorder
2. The drug commonly chose to control ADHD

Marie: Yes. So we did talk about that, and yes it was about his anger and his frustration and powerlessness and wanting to be in a position of power which, as the person telling the story and drawing it, he was. That was very much what it was about with him and the same with Godzilla — I've got a lovely picture of Godzilla — he comes into New York and splats everybody, I suppose *he* was Godzilla. There was the Titanic, Godzilla and there were the volcanoes. I think he had seen a programme about Pompeii. He liked that, that was particularly good, death coming randomly and people just falling in the streets and some of them running to get away and being got by lava — I've seen a very graphic picture of that one.

Jan: He allied himself with the volcano or with the people running? There's something about the theme of him having some power and retribution.

Marie: He didn't have any power at all. He would have a social worker who would come in and tell him what had to happen. And the social worker would say it was all about *him* being manipulative, and this is a small boy and of course he is trying to meet his needs. But, of course, it is never seen that way. Its always seen that the child is just being difficult and demanding, and when he behaves this way, just shut him in a room and make him calm down or take his things away from him, which routinely happened, and Stephen would explode at home and smash things. But there was never any sense of that in a session. There was no sort of . . . yes, anger *was* there, but it was being released through drawings really, and being talked about and understood and heard and contained. We did talk a lot about things that he might do to release some of the feelings that were built up, but mostly it was just understanding it. I think it was, for him, having the things accepted and not being told he was bad. He looked so unwell some days. He looked so pale some days. He had not had breakfast, just the tablets. His stomach was really hurting — he had some huge doses and I suppose the views from all the adults around him were that the problem was located in him. I've got all the pictures — they really are quite bloodthirsty, there are people actually being squashed by Godzilla and their heads coming off.

Jan: How did that feel for you to actually have to bear witness to that?

Marie: It felt OK. I suppose mainly because before I was working with Stephen I was quite used to things of this nature coming out on paper. I've quite a lot of violent drawings. I suppose it was fine at the time and it was good to understand it and I was pleased that the feelings were coming out in a healthy and safe way, but a huge sadness that that was how it felt for him — that was his experience. Not the kind of life you would want any child to have.

Jan: And that relationship you had with him was interrupted arbitrarily by the ending of your contract and that was awful too because you were not able to follow that through with him.

Marie: No — he knew that if he wanted to write a note or letter the school would pass it on, which he didn't do. That didn't surprise me, because writing was very difficult for him. In the school he was seen as this real hard nut tough little kid who would just go berserk, and wasn't really safe to be out. I suppose it did take a little while for him to trust me, and to see that what was being offered in that relationship was real, and at the end of term when everything was winding down and ending, he was one of the ones who came out and gave me a massive hug in front of peers which is really a big thing to do for a twelve/thirteen-year-old boy. That meant such a lot to me. It was just totally spontaneous and just for me felt like, well, we did something that mattered here and it was, I suppose, a drop in the ocean, and then nothing.

Jan: And maybe like Susan something that in time he would be able to reflect back on and recognise that counselling is useful to him.

Marie: Yes, I'd like to think so. I think he would. I think he will take that along with him. I wasn't able to work with some of the young people long term, because they became permanently excluded from school, and that was it. One or two, I think, when I first started there were so far down the line of almost being excluded that I almost felt like I couldn't reach them in time. If they'd been around long enough then something might have been possible. Actually, Martin — you might remember him?

Jan: I was going to ask about him — this is the young man who was actually moved to a different school?

Marie: Yes. He'd been in and out of foster homes, and there was violence at home and I only saw him a few times. They seemed quite positive, as in he seemed quite OK to be there. He didn't find it easy to talk and I don't think we got to a point where he wanted to talk about his life, mainly because his life was unmitigatedly awful. I don't think there was anything positive in it except possibly computer games and TV — we talked a little bit about computers and I got to know a bit about those things but it was sort of too late — if he'd survived in school, and I did my best to hang on to him, then something might have been possible, but it takes time and time wasn't there with Martin.

Jan: That strikes me about all of the young people you have talked about — how long it took to actually figure out what their language was and then actually learn it along the way. It's almost like, because they were young, and also because they were referred rather than asking to see a counsellor, that somehow you had to pass quite a few tests before they were going to trust enough to see you as something other than a teacher.

Marie: Yes — I think so; yes, and some of them also learnt my language as well — no way was I trying to teach them, but alongside in exploring, I would, I suppose, disclose to them more of myself than I would maybe working with adults, and they remembered little bits and pieces about that and they would say, 'oh yes, that's like the time when you did this when you were thirteen' or whatever and that was nice because it felt natural then. They were actually seeing me as well as me seeing them. That was a good feeling.

Jan: I know you mentioned one of the little ones who just wanted to be normal, but I'm wondering if they, themselves, ever referred to the labels (like learning difficulties or ADHD) they had acquired or whether that was just what the adults were referring to.

Marie: Yes that was quite interesting, working with Stephen, because when he first came he was saying, 'this is the illness I've got, this is the problem with me, this is my problem', and yes, he was saying, 'this is what is wrong with me', and I challenged that right from the start and encouraged him to try to talk about *his* view on things, and what his life was like and to encourage him to see that he was being told all sorts of things by all sorts of people, where really *he* was on the inside of it and *he* knew how *he* felt, and *he* knew what was going on, and this was like a bolt out of the blue for him. I don't think that anybody had ever suggested that at all before, because they are all adults and they know what they are talking about and they tell you that this is the problem with you. He had accepted it; I think at the start, he completely identified with his label. But he wasn't by the end.

Jan: Aah, that's interesting.

Marie: I mean he was still taking the tablets because they said that he had to, but I think that what he did get was a sense of the whole picture. That he is not this label — that's what I was trying to help him to get the sense of that, and to try to help him develop some smidgen of a sense of his own value — which in a sense I was trying to do with all of them and trying to create this environment for growth. For them to actually start experiencing themselves in a different way and I think there were glimpses of that with most of the young people but I'm certainly not making Hollywood claims. Yes, he certainly did experience himself as 'yes this is me. I am a problem child'. So I said, 'really, tell me more about that', and he did. We did some really useful work and I just really liked all of them. They seemed such lovely interesting young people with so much going for them and so badly treated. I didn't find it difficult being with or aligning with them. Not all of the teachers were negative and hostile to them at all, I mean some of them were extremely good and they related well to them. If a relationship was offered the children would grab it. It doesn't mean that they wouldn't test the boundaries sometimes.

Jan: That says something really important, doesn't it? What they really needed, and what they got in the counselling, was a relationship.

Marie: Yes and it was just theirs, nobody else's. Just for them to do whatever it was they wanted to do. Whether it was just talking or making Plasticine Teletubbies. I'm not quite sure why that happened — somebody said, 'here, you make something', and I couldn't think of anything I'd have a chance of making, so I did a Teletubby 'cos they are easy shapes (Jan: and you knew what they were). Yes. They thought that was really funny — there was a lot of teasing about that, which I absolutely loved. I think one of the young people made the whole Teletubby bit, the dome and the valley, but that was just for 'Miss', just to keep me happy! Over the years a lot of them made pictures that they wanted me to have and they couldn't quite believe that I would take it home and put it up on my fridge and I did, and I still have them all. And cards and things which were really lovely and when we had finished, when the whole thing finished, I gave each of them a little card with a sort of open testimonial saying how I had really enjoyed the time that we had, and valued them, and one or two things about each individual to say how I'd experienced them. I suppose it felt like giving them something to hang on to if they were feeling appalling. At any time just hold that thought — maybe trying to extend my influence beyond what is humanly possible. So they all had a little card and they all had a finger of fudge which went down well — 'can I eat it now?' — So I said, 'this is counselling, it is not school, so yes you can eat your finger of fudge'.

Jan: And on that happy note, thank you.

'I'm angry'
Christopher's story

Christopher was in his fifties when I began working with him, and our work together spanned sixteen months. He was a mild-mannered man whose greatest pleasure was his pipe. People don't usually smoke during sessions with me — I keep a smoke-free house for family health reasons. Christopher's pipe-smoking opportunities were rare and not within his control. I remember explaining the possible purposes of counselling to him and he seemed to be taking it all in. However, in response to my enquiry 'Is there anything you'd like to ask before we begin?' he simply said, 'pipe'. I invited him to smoke his pipe in the garden and learned quickly that pipe smoking was a private affair for Christopher. He established a pattern on arrival of barely acknowledging me at the door, walking straight through the house for a careful pipe filling and lighting ceremony and then wandering around the garden. At first it seemed that he was a man with an interest in flowers, but not so — he simply walked around freely in the space, murmuring quietly and smoking his pipe.

The smoking completed, we would move into the room I used for people whose special needs required a variety of options to facilitate communication. Christopher, like Carl (see p. 150 ff.) was attracted to the piano, and began each session with a few hymns accompanied by a handful of notes which, though disharmonious, took on an unusual musical quality, due to the sensitivity of his movements. Unlike Carl, Christopher seemed happy when I joined him in singing and we established some contact with each other through his chosen medium. A guitar lived in that room too and sometimes Christopher would ask for it and strum it gently or hum when I played for him. He had some writing ability which he enjoyed using in our sessions. Both what he wrote and how he formed the letters were of a stage of development I knew from children around the age of seven. Certainly his ability was sufficient to communicate his feelings from time to time, and was especially important when he wanted to tell particular events.

Whilst Christopher's speech was reasonably clear, he frequently lapsed into repetitive phrases and mumbling so that our work was interrupted many times over in each session. He had been referred by his key worker at the day centre he attended. He seemed sad and there was a feeling that he was locked into some kind of bereavement.

It became apparent in some of his mutterings that the loss of his father had had a major impact on him. He talked frequently of his desire to visit his parents' home address to see him though I had been informed that he had been dead for many years. The very few background details that I had were that Christopher had spent a lot of years in Longwood Hospital before 'dispersal' to a community house only two years before. He had some contact with a couple of family members but it was unclear to me whether his mother was still alive — Christopher talked a lot about 'mummy' too, and it seemed he was searching for her as well.

Our work really began with me attempting to meet him not only in his lucid moments but also in his less coherent mumblings. It was difficult work session-by-session, because of the interruptions of his muttering ramblings, and I needed to concentrate very hard to shift gear alongside him.

Over the months I learned that he was a nervous and sometimes fearful man. We worked with his loss issues as they arose for him and I attempted to help him understand the concept of death, using line drawings and pictorial resources. He gradually understood that his father had died and the process of funeral (which he had not attended) and that he would not find him at his parents' home any more. Gradually Christopher understood this and seemed less sad, as if somehow knowing he'd gone meant he didn't have to search any more, nor be sad at not finding him. His sadness lifted as he talked of missing 'daddy'.

As I write I realise how coherent the process seems to have been, but it was not coherent, nor linear in progress. Christopher's sadness and searching for his father came out in snippets like passing driftwood on a winding river. I attended to each piece of driftwood as it floated by, tracking him as closely as I could.

From time to time, a care worker would ask me to do some focussed work with Christopher on particular behaviours the staff or carers found concerning. One of these issues was a new behaviour for him. Christopher had begun raiding litter bins and eating bits of food in the rubbish or off the floor. When I gently enquired of him if we could talk about litter bins, he responded with an expression of disgust. 'Dirty boy', he said. He had obviously got the idea that he was dirty even though he was continuing to do it. He asked me for a biscuit. I asked, 'Are you hungry, Christopher?' 'Yes', he responded. I encouraged him to tell the staff in his day centre and his home when he felt hungry and asked if I might mention this to the worker who collected him. With his agreement I mentioned this information and the worker then said she'd thought his packed lunches were very small for such a big man. It transpired that Christopher, like others from his residential home, was sent to his day centre each day with only a small jam sandwich and an apple. There was concern too that he and the other residents were not getting adequate meals, yet little could be done, it seemed, because the residential staff were not approachable.

The boundaries of therapy felt restricting. However, it was not my role as therapist to take this on, but to work with my client to empower him to get his needs met.

Christopher's 'inappropriate' behaviour was actually communicating something very important for him. We did some drawings of bins and rubbish and talked about what he'd really like instead, drawing plates of egg, bacon, mushrooms and sausages. Christopher knew what he wanted, but needed encouragement to say what it was. It is very easy to disempower in the name of caring. If an individual is as amenable and compliant as Christopher and as slow in considering what he wants, then it is easier to simply offer whatever is practical and easy for a group. I understood that, but I am sad it is so, and especially sad that Christopher had to resort to finding bits of food in rubbish because he was hungry, and taking on the idea that he was a 'dirty boy'.

Christopher's experiences disturbed me. Among the issues we explored were frequent references to the 'domestic cupboard'. Whenever he mentioned this he would become agitated, sometimes showing his teeth — which made me nervous! I knew he had sometimes bitten people in the past and I was not keen to experience that again (see Danny's story, p. 1 ff.). Over many months he would mention, and sometimes draw, the 'domestic cupboard', and get anxious and drift off into mutterings or other subjects. I was unclear for a long time if the 'domestic cupboard' was in his current home or day centre or his own family home, until he eventually made it clear that it was in Longwood Hospital.

He once assumed I had a 'domestic cupboard' and if he were 'naughty' I'd take him there and beat him and kick him. I reassured him that I would never do that and no 'domestic cupboard' existed in my home. I felt painfully touched at his direct expression, a real relating to me in the here and now, even though it demonstrated his fear of me.

Christopher often drew the 'domestic cupboard'. It seemed to be less a cupboard and more a small room. He frequently began to mention a nurse, here called nurse Adams. As the months went by the full picture emerged. If Christopher or any of the others in his ward were 'naughty' they would be taken to the 'domestic cupboard' and punched, kicked (he drew himself on the floor being kicked) or hit with the vacuum cleaner hose. Christopher assumed that all places had a domestic cupboard and feared being 'naughty'. The snippets of the story came over the course of about fourteen months.

During this time, due to transport problems, I had begun to see Christopher at his day centre. This represented a loss for him in that his routine of including some musical moments within his session was not possible. I always took drawing materials and a collection of pipe-cleaner people which some clients liked to use to tell their experiences. But it was a loss for Christopher — he missed the few private minutes with his pipe in the garden, and he missed the piano and guitar. Occasionally we would still sing quietly together, but he accepted the situation without complaint, just wistful comments about my room.

Due to day centre holidays, trips and my own holiday, there came a six-week break, which I had not been able to prepare him for — day centre trips would just happen, and I'd arrive and find that my clients were off somewhere on a trip.

The first time we met after that break, for the first time in our work together, Christopher ignored me completely when I arrived at the day centre. He then refused to come into the room for his session. Staff at the day centre were as bemused as I was about this, but I told him I'd be here for him the next week as usual.

The next week he refused again. He was quietly resistant — no stamps or screams, just quiet, eyes averted. On the third week, Christopher came into the room with me and still seemed rather distant. I had a feeling that he was angry with me for the long gap with no explanation. I shared this with him and received his response through his eye contact. Mixed with recognition of what I was saying was his anxious, fearful look. I affirmed that I understood now he was angry with me and hadn't wanted to talk with me the last couple of weeks. That session he kept short, deciding to leave after only twenty minutes or so. He quietly muttered 'angry with Jan' as he left the room. 'See you next week', I responded. As I left the day centre later that day, as always walking through the group of day centre users, Christopher looked up at me from where he was sitting. 'Bye Chris', I said, and he gently took my hand, looked me in the eye and said nothing. I can feel that connection now, however brief, it being the only physical contact we ever had. We connected deeply in that moment — our relationship and our work together had changed.

The change was not of Hollywood proportions, of course — we still worked on the issues as they drifted in and out of his mind — but Christopher knew now that being angry was OK with me and that I was not going to beat him or tell him that he was bad.

Shortly after this came a session where we were focussed on the 'domestic cupboard' again. Christopher had drawn his most complete picture with extra 3D touches to cupboards and vacuum cleaner as well as the man holding the broom and 'the boy' lying on the floor being kicked and hit with the broom. Christopher stayed with the issue for longer than usual and managed to explain it in fuller detail with less anxiety than he normally exhibited when talking of the 'domestic cupboard'. So focussed was he that I was able to ask, 'What does the boy want to do?' His response was immediate, focussed and almost gleeful. He turned the paper over and drew the boy with the broom hitting the nurse Adam's figure. 'Boy is angry', he said, over and over.

This session took us to a different realm — it was a long, long time coming, but Christopher could now be angry about what happened in the 'domestic cupboard'.

On my journey home, I sobbed with despair and grief that such things had happened to him. What additional damage had he suffered as a result of those beatings? What kind of life or ability to function with more independence might he have had, had he not suffered daily from the terror of the 'domestic cupboard'? Was it too little, and too late, that he had finally been able to tell his story, and transform his fear and anxiety to anger?

Not long after this Christopher decided he would do pottery instead of counselling! Pottery work with clay sounded great — and him making his own decision about ending with me and beginning something new felt important.

A voice for the voiceless:
the joy of communication

People with severe learning disabilities, and many with mild learning disabilities, have very little power to influence directly those who make decisions on their behalf. Their treatment or care tends to reflect trends within societies. The era when 'the village idiot' played a part in the local community, and received varying degrees of care, gave way to the institutionalisation of the insane and retarded along with those whose misfortune it was to be born illegitimate. Once institutionalised, if they didn't have learning disabilities and/ or mental illness before they entered, the mere fact of being there would have created both. Being deemed at an early age ineducable brought with it the self-fulfilling prophecy of lack of attainment. Early institutionalisation brought its own perils, with even the best of care restricting people in terms of any development they might have achieved given relevant programmes for learning. Many of the clients mentioned in this book had lived for decades in long-stay mental hospitals, with no access to education. Their only homes were the wards they were familiar with.

It was not until the 1970s that children with learning disabilities were actually entitled to an education at all. So all of my older adult clients had missed out on that possibility. To manage their behaviour many were drugged, and most of those I worked with had experienced physical abuse which had kept them managed by fear.

When the new trend of care in the community (DoH/DSS, 1989) required the 'dispersal' of those living in long-stay hospitals, massive adjustments were necessary. Those with the power to decide and make the changes made assumptions about how much better life would be for people to live in houses and have a life within the community, rather than living in a hospital. But for many who have shared their stories with me, the move was sudden, and represented loss of security, familiar faces and a degree of acceptance which is still rare out in the community. 'The community' summons up images of a cohesive group with shared ideals and a degree of caring for each other, where people with learning disabilities would be welcomed. But our society is not actually like that, and all the people with learning disabilities with whom I have worked remain isolated from the rest of society because they are unable to speak the language or because they behave 'oddly'. 'The community' contains few individuals who make it their business to learn British Sign Language or to spend time with people with learning disabilities. An Anglican priest who offers regular services for people with learning disabilities beautifully considered how to empower the congregation to play their part in the proceedings. An art in itself, this priest took the time and thought to adapt the service to allow enjoyment and fellowship in a way that seemed nourishing for all. Following the service there is a tea and some entertainment. There is never a shortage of people to make cakes, serve tea or entertain, but fear prevents there ever being enough volunteers to actually spend time talking with individual people.

For many, it is difficult and strange to meet people with learning disabilities, especially as most people have gone through their whole lives without knowing someone whose learning disabilities place them outside the familiar communication zone.

Professionals supporting and making decisions for people with learning disabilities rarely have time to develop relationships and communication between them so that decisions are often made based on financial issues or what is in vogue at the time, rather than on what that particular person might want. When closing mental institutions, what might have happened if some individuals had a real choice and refused to go? For some, their whole community was a long-stay institution and that felt safe, whereas having a room alone in a small house where they could not walk out of the front door without a staff member with them might actually feel frightening.

Some of the people mentioned missed their wards and nurses, and some, like Hope, lost her sister when moved from the hospital. Others made the transition well and liked their new houses. Those who either didn't like their house or didn't like the people they lived with — usually because they were frightened of them — were never moved to different places. There were no real choices for them.

Choice, though, is one of the things missing in the lives of those without a voice. These range from simple choices, like when to get up or go to bed, to what to eat or wear, or what to do each day. Logistics for staff support and funding problems are major obstacles. But many of the people I worked with who had severe learning disabilities had little capacity to make choices, so used were they to either not having a choice or not exercising an ability to choose, so losing that ability. There are pockets of inspirational good practice, and these are to be celebrated. Unfortunately how much access people with learning disabilities actually get to those services depends on individual health authorities and social services policies, and changes they make from time to time. Vic Forrest's work (see p. 33 ff.) is among the pioneering few, the aim of which is to promote real choice at a citizen level for people with learning disabilities.

There being little political voice for the majority of people with learning disabilities, it is difficult to know what they might want, given the choice. Advocacy projects like Kith & Kids and Vic Forrest's are rare and are beginning to encourage some people with learning disabilities to find their voice, and therein is hope.

Many have limited or no language to communicate. It is easy to assume they therefore have no serious concerns, feelings or needs and that caring for them in practical ways is sufficient for them. But even the most profoundly and physically disabled people have ways of communicating if we take the time to listen. We must listen with every part of our being to hear what is there to hear, and test back to see if we really have understood

In offering massage therapy to people with learning disabilities and with profound learning and physical disabilities, I was taught by those individuals that even the muscles individually can communicate that they like or dislike being touched in a particular way. That learning has intensified my work in massaging clients whose bodies and minds are free, not restricted by disability.

It is the same with counselling. Through learning to wait patiently, and listen to even an eyelid flicker or expression and find ways of checking that understanding with clients with severe learning disabilities and no speech, I find I am more able to listen fully to those who do use speech.

Those moments of connection, when two people are in psychological contact (Rogers, 1951), when one communicates and feels fully understood by the other, allow the full range of emotions shared by each and in the space between. There is great joy to be found there. Whether the other is bright, articulate and exploring issues of great complexity or severely learning disabled and sharing the quietest feeling of sadness, the feeling of connection can be tangible. Great healing occurs there.

The Person-Centred Approach offers something unusual for people with learning disabilities. Its practitioners do not seek to measure, label or judge behaviours, devise treatment programmes or decide success or failure based on 'good' behaviour. There is no desire to assume motivations or feelings that might be present, but to track closely the client's own expressions of experiencing and communicate empathic understanding. It offers a degree of respect rare in the lives of people with learning disabilities. Those who have contributed to this book have demonstrated that there are many ways in which the Person-Centred Approach can be applied to supporting the lives of people with learning disabilities, not simply within the counselling context. They have all expressed a passion for their work and contacts with people who have learning disabilities, and I would suggest that this is partly because there is such responsiveness and development possible when people are met where they are, and accompanied on their own particular journey, wherever that might lead.

As Michael Farrell has highlighted (see p. 70 ff.), the government is now insisting that services for people with learning disabilities are devised on person-centred principles. This relates to placing the person at the centre of the plans, though is a long way from including qualities of empathy, congruence and unconditional positive regard. But the beginnings are hopeful.

Without pioneering support workers, none of the people mentioned in this book would have had access to therapy at all, and their voices would remain unheard.

Their ability to communicate, through the only means possible — difficult, destructive behaviours sometimes — shows the creativity of the human psyche, however limited. If those communications are received and understood, development might more often occur.

I began this book by mentioning that I didn't understand, twenty years ago, why I had an affinity with those who cannot speak. Some years later I recognised that parts of me could not speak either. And often those parts of me who could speak were misunderstood or ignored. It felt as if I had arrived on an alien planet with a flower in one hand and the wrong phrase book in the other. The flower was wilting. Then came the time when I was tired of trying to communicate, tired of trying to learn the language of those around me. I wanted someone to understand me. There's my affinity. Why should people, already impeded in life, have to do all the work in gaining a voice, in learning the prevailing language — speech? Some are doomed to fail, however hard they try, as they don't have intact speech mechanisms.

It is time we learned the different languages of the voiceless. No matter how disabled physically or cognitively, there is a core of wholeness that connects us one to another if we are willing to open ourselves to hearing the voiceless speak in whatever way they can.

The research study

The experiences of Person-Centred counselling practitioners with clients who have severe learning disabilities

There is very little provision of therapy/counselling for people with learning disabilities, and what there is tends to focus on behaviour management/control (e.g. McBrien, 1994; Watson and Gresham, 1998), or on a psychoanalytic approach (e.g. Waitman and Conboy-Hill, 1992; Sinason, 1992). Therapies which aim to uncover personal meanings are still rare (Lovett, 1996). The person-centred approach to counselling is in stark contrast, in particular because the counsellor does not take the position of expert but rather considers the potential for growth and change to be at the heart of the work. In providing all clients with an environment of safety, a relationship can develop between client and counsellor, and healing growth can begin. Person-centred theorists argue that the relationship develops because of the counsellor's attitudinal qualities of unconditional positive regard (or acceptance) genuineness, and empathy (Rogers, 1951; Mearns and Thorne, 2000).

> *We believe that human beings flourish best when they can experience acceptance and understanding rather than adverse judgement and a lack of informed responsiveness from others.* (Mearns and Thorne, 2000, p. 15)

In contrast to the approaches mentioned above, the person-centred counsellor does not seek to set goals, analyse or interpret the client, but endeavours to enter the client's world, to understand it from their point of view, and to share their own experience with transparency, respect and acceptance. These are deceptively simple, yet profoundly difficult, aspirations.

My interest in exploring the experiences of person-centred practitioners in providing therapy for clients with learning disabilities sprang from my own work in this field. I was particularly interested in learning of practitioners who work with clients with severe learning disabilities. Since the 1920s the definition of 'severe learning disability' has referred to those with an IQ of less than 50, whereas those with mild to moderate learning disabilities are defined by having

IQ scores in the range of 50–70 (Sinason, 1992). It seems unhelpful to me that people are classified in this way. In my experience, IQ scores give very little indication of a person's functional ability. It is also very difficult to describe people who have learning and/or functional disabilities, as the description within the services which make provision for these clients continually changes. For a discussion of the euphemisms and labels applied to this group of clients, see Sinason (1992, pp. 39–54).

Personal notes (May 2000)
One of the difficulties I anticipate in this research is the different ways of labelling people as having or not having learning difficulties. There is, in some areas, an emphasis on IQ scoring as the determining factor, with those who score less than 50 on a global IQ test being deemed to have severe learning difficulties. At the other end of the scale are those who have 'specific learning difficulties', often with an average or higher than average IQ score (sometimes globally called dyslexia), which affect their abilities in certain academic areas, but not in other areas of life. My own anger about the reliance on IQ testing will need to be held, as it is this kind of test that defines whether people have their needs recognised, often rather than focusing on their functional abilities. **For the purposes of this research I shall define severe learning difficulties as being those for whom most or all areas of their lives are affected by their difficulties in functioning independently. For many of these clients IQ scores will have been either unobtainable or below 50, and many of these clients have either restricted or no verbal abilities**.

I have often felt very isolated with my work with clients with learning difficulties. When I began counselling some thirteen years ago, I didn't know anyone who worked with this client group, and those few people I discussed my work with had some quite extreme reactions. I was one of several colleagues who had a few hours each week on our timetables given over to counselling, within a Further Education institute. Our training and approaches to counselling varied, though we shared group supervision. Within the college, I also contributed to teaching groups of students with severe learning disabilities. After some discussion, there was a willingness among the team and supervisor to allow me to offer a counselling service for our students with severe learning and communication difficulties. I remember especially the colleague who told me she felt it would be impossible to counsel clients who could not speak (several of my clients at the time had no speech) and who were 'not intelligent', because counselling relies upon speech and intelligence. This reaction, while being extreme, was not unusual.

It felt important to engage in some research which would reflect my passion for working with clients who have severe learning difficulties. In part I realise now that this was to explore my own experience of working with this client group, and to share with colleagues, hopefully drawing together some useful material and insights. It was also to honour those clients with whom I have struggled, connected with, come alongside just briefly, or for whom I have been the witness to terrible pain and suffering. Although I have not been the Hollywood therapist who makes things right for them, the fact that my clients have trusted me to share a part of their world or experience is testament for me to the endurance of the human spirit, no matter how entrapped it may be.

I was particularly interested in differences in working with this client group and with those who are not learning-disabled. Coming alongside those whose lives are organised and maintained by others is different from working with those who have the opportunities to make their own changes in life. What is the cost to the therapist of having a philosophy of empowerment with people whose lives are constantly disempowered? The nature of the Person-Centred Approach (Rogers, 1951; Mearns and Thorne, 1988, 1999, 2000) means that practitioners endeavour to keep themselves open to experience – their own and their clients'. My experience of working with people who have severe learning difficulties is of constant dilemmas, continual pressure from carers, support workers and funders to breach confidentiality, pressure to 'work on' particular issues with clients and ongoing abuses of clients where little or no action is ever taken. The therapist needs the capacity to communicate with the whole of their being, and adopt creative and imaginative ways of working with clients who may have no verbal language. It demands:

> . . . *a different conception of themselves on the part of the carers [therapist].*
> (Pörtner, 2000, p. 62)

Generally, adult clients in counselling have the power to effect changes in their lives. Adult clients living in care environments with severe learning disabilities generally have much less personal autonomy. The very slow development of many people with learning difficulties can lead to considerable frustration, and the lack of support for the changes clients identify wanting to make can lead to feelings of anger in the therapist (against care workers or families). These feelings can be all the more complicated because the client has severe learning difficulties. I was interested to investigate other practitioners' experiences with this client group, and to endeavour to clarify any differences there may be between this client group and those who do not have learning difficulties.

I began by developing a questionnaire (see Appendix 1) as a way of identifying some of the important issues for interview. My experience in undergraduate research was mostly in the quantitative arena, with few qualitative investigations. I had learned to attempt at all times to be objective, and though the recognition of the impact of our own emotional reactions and experimenter effects were explored, it was from objectivity first.

I felt divided about loving the intellectual challenge and rigour of working with ideas and delving through variables to gain understandings, while also feeling passionate about the importance of experiencing and that bringing a different rigour and challenge to data. There also felt to me a parallel process (Wosket, 1999) going on, in that I had chosen to look at the experiences of an isolated group of practitioners (those few who work with clients with learning difficulties), who work with a marginalised group of clients. I felt as one of those clients might – I did not know where to begin, and my language and thought processes were different from those being expressed and understood in methodology workshops I attended. Thorny issues of how to analyse the data remained. How could I be certain that I would select the most relevant data to highlight? This all seemed perilous: I had embarked on a journey, having thrown aside my map and compass.

In preparation for the investigation I was encouraged to examine my own assumptions about what the responses might be. As Moustakas (1994) suggests, one must reflect on one's own meaning first, then look outward.

> . . . *where the researcher brackets his or her own preconceived ideas about* the phenomena *to understand it through the voices of the informants.* (Field and Morse, 1985, cited in Cresswell, 1998, p. 54)

The questionnaire provided the framework for considering my own perspective before looking at others'. I endeavoured to gather my thoughts and experiences together, so that I would feel freer to listen to the voices of respondents to the questionnaire, and to interviewees. My own initial responses to the questionnaires can be found in Appendix 3.

Personal notes (30.03.00)
I am again rather stunned by the intensity of my feelings, and how terribly important I feel the whole issue of offering counselling/therapy to people with severe learning difficulties is. Somehow, having made such connections with some of my clients, I can feel an energy almost outside of myself in even choosing this topic to investigate. And in some of my assumptions, not only is my own voice present, but also, I feel the concerns and insights my clients have offered me.

The foci for the investigation

- What were the experiences of person-centred practitioners working with clients who have severe learning disabilities?
- Were there differences in working with clients who have severe learning disabilities and with those who are not learning-disabled?
- Was there a cost to the therapist of having a philosophy of empowerment with people for whose lives are constantly disempowered?

Because I feel passionately for this group of people who are so easily ignored, disempowered and/or abused, I aim to clarify any particular issues relating to the work of person-centred therapists with clients who have severe learning disabilities. Through adding to knowledge about this client group, I hope to stimulate an improvement in services.

As practitioners will be offering their experiences, I anticipate an awareness of the importance of confidentiality on their part and that they are capable of giving informed consent for this purpose. I invited anonymity with the questionnaires to cover confidentiality and power issues and carefully ensured that no potentially identifiable details are included.

Methodology for questionnaire phase

I advertised in *Person-to-Person*, the newsletter for the British Association for the Person Centred Approach (BAPCA, for address see p. 206) for anyone who would be willing to respond to my questionnaire and specifically mentioning severe learning disabilities. BAPCA has a membership of almost seven hundred (as at July 2000). I hoped that a reasonable proportion of members might be working with clients with severe learning disabilities and be interested in supporting the research. In the event, there were twelve respondents, each of whom were sent the questionnaire and covering letter (see Appendices 1 and 1a), along with stamped addressed envelopes. Eight completed questionnaires were returned.

Personal notes (16.04.00)
A short flurry of responses to my ad in the BAPCA newsletter. Four respondents, all already expressing feelings of solitude with their work, and delighted to see the ad. All expressing similar feelings of isolation, difficulties in finding others to discuss their work with, and a desire to share in the findings of the research. I have collected eight questionnaires, and shall interview shortly.

Considerations of methodology led to exploration of a plethora of possibilities that qualitative researchers have suggested (e.g. Howard, 1983; Cresswell, 1998). I felt drawn by the phenomenological approach (Dukes, 1984; Moustakas, 1994), because it is very much in keeping with the Person-Centred Approach, being focused as both approaches are in the meaning of experience for the individual. In offering procedures for 'verification' of a study, Dukes focuses on the 'lens of both the researcher and outside reviewers' (cited in Cresswell, 1998, p. 207), describing the outside reader verification as 'the eureka factor' (p. 201, cited in Cresswell, 1998, p. 207). In examining the data, I have endeavoured to keep in mind five key questions on validity (Polkinghorne

1989, in Cresswell, 1998). In summary these are:

- Is the data reflective only of the researcher's opinion?
- Are the transcriptions accurate?
- Could other conclusions be offered?
- Can generalisations from the data be applied and tracked back to the original transcripts?
- Can generalisations be drawn?

I certainly do 'relish the interplay between [myself] and the data' (Strauss and Corbin, 1998, p. 5), and spent some time trying to decide if grounded theory was a more applicable approach than a 'phenomenological' one.

Personal notes (May 2000)
Reading this book (Strauss and Corbin, 1998) has been quite a struggle — I feel stupid and can't quite make sense of what is being said. I *think* the idea is to explore *all* aspects of the data and continue re-examining and re-exploring it in the light of the process, rather than waiting till the end of the study to deduce or analyse. Theory grounded *in* the data – is deduced *from the* data.

I felt then that the most important thing was to return to the reasoning behind the study, that I was interested to learn more about other person-centred practitioners' experiences in working with people who have severe learning difficulties. It has also come to me only through involving myself in this study, that I wanted to find a forum for the voices of those clients I have worked with, to bring their experiences to the world.

In designing the questionnaire, and carrying out the interviews, I was aware of the ethical considerations relevant to this study; for example, identities of respondents were not to be shared unless written consent was given. I especially wanted to have 'the sensitivity to identify any ethical issue and the responsibility to feel committed to acting appropriately in regard to such issues' (Eisner and Peshkin, 1994, p. 244, cited in Kvale, 1996, p. 117). Anonymity has been offered and maintained to all respondents to the questionnaire, and to the two interviewees. A summary of this study was sent to all of who participated, and the full text made available upon request. Client anonymity has been ensured by changing names, or omitting names altogether where possible. All respondents to the questionnaires and interviewees maintained the confidentiality of their own clients — a reminder having appeared at the beginning of the questionnaires. Any possible identifying material has been removed, or altered to maintain confidentiality. I hope that this research will give information and encouragement to person-centred practitioners to offer services to more clients with severe learning difficulties.

Responses to the questionnaires

In an effort to maintain the reality of each respondent's experience, treating all statements as having equal worth, I present here a 'horizontalisation' of the data (Cresswell, 1998, p. 147). The responses are collated verbatim to give the fullest possible account of their contents and richness. As the focus of the study is the experiences of person-centred counselling practitioners with people with severe learning disabilities, it feels important to allow the reader full access to the responses, so that a flavour of the range of experiences comes through. It also seems important to show the process of collation, as many voices of my clients came through from my time working at the day centre, counselling clients with severe learning disabilities. These reflections would not be quieted, and need to be seen in the context in which they arose. The fuller accounts of those relationships have appeared throughout the book.

Instructions to the reader

- Those questions and responses specifically relating to the foci of the study (see p. 190) are presented here (questions 5, 9, 10, 15, 16, 17). The complete collation, including the supporting questions and responses (questions 1, 2, 3, 4, 6, 7, 8, 11, 12, 13, 14), can be found in Appendix 2.
- The letters relate to each questionnaire, i.e. all responses marked (a) relate to one respondent, and are in corresponding order.
- My own reflections, as they were stirred during the process of collating the material, appear in square brackets.
- Short reflections follow the gathered responses to each question, and there will be a fuller discussion of the questionnaire following.

> **Personal notes** (Dec 2000)
> I had become lost in my own perspective — a problem I had not anticipated when considering how to analyse the data. Though a danger with the quantitative approach to research, I certainly never became as lost as I have here. Much rethinking required . . .

5. **How would you say clients are, or can been classified as having mild, moderate and severe learning disabilities, and does this classification have any usefulness in describing the work you do with clients who have learning disabilities?**

   (a) I apply no label to them at all — first and foremost they are individuals in their own right. I feel I do nothing different to what I would do with 'normal' clients

(b) Having to emphasise the communication

(c) I think the classifications are very outdated, as people who are said to have severe learning disabilities often have skills and abilities in certain areas, which do not conform to the stereotype. I think it would be more useful to me, as a counsellor, to know more about a person's abilities to communicate rather than what is perceived to be their intellectual ability

(d) I do not find it relevant and therefore would not try to do so

(e) We classify by clinical impression and IQ testing. I would classify (broadly): Mild: those living independently and who are able in everyday living; Moderate: those living perhaps in residential care and/or living with some support independently; Severe: those needing 24 hour support, physically severely handicapped or with severe challenging behaviours

(f) The only usefulness of labelling degree of disability is that it can facilitate the process of attempting to provide appropriate support. I have no experience of students with severe learning disabilities – so assume that these are excluded from mainstream schools. My clients have had mild–moderate learning disabilities

(g) To be honest I am not quite sure where in this spectrum my client would be placed. I would guess at moderate, possibly. My client is an adult under 30, can tell the time only by the hour and with some uncertainty and reads only a tiny amount. However she can speak clearly and is quite independent in many areas of her life

(h) Little help to me

Of these, four respondents (50% – a, d, g, h) either actively resist use of the term 'severe learning disabilities' or any labelling at all or find the terms of no help at all. Of the other four responses, two (c, e) indicate specific knowledge of the terms, while two (b, f) suggest ways in which they may be useful in preparing themselves for the sessions.

9. What are the particular difficulties and dilemmas you have found working with this client group? (you may wish to select three key points)

(a) (i) they tended to reach a plateau of learning. It appeared to me that they became aware of certain factors in their lives and their learning to come to a temporary halt (ii) Because of a combination of learning difficulties and mature age, their beliefs rarely changed! One, in particular, thought that women did the cooking and were there for sex (ouch!) (iii) I learnt new levels of patience! They did tend to wander in their thoughts and words . . . the sessions often went onto the latest rugby scores, football, Christmas presents . . . [I'm remembering May (see p. 8) interrupting an intensive session when she heard the ice cream van.]

(b) (i) Confidentiality — has always been a big issue for me in that organisations/ local authorities want information and proof of the benefits of counselling which is not always easy to quantify.
(ii) Other people's doubts of the usefulness of counselling for people with learning disabilities especially those who have no verbal/or little verbal communication.
(iii) Having an environment that communicates the value of the individual (when not working in an environment of my choosing) [The movable room — never sure at the day centre where we would work, once we were reduced to the store cupboard. Me feeling at the time incensed for the clients, they didn't seem to notice the room, and used the sessions as usual.]

(c) Confidentiality has been an on-going issue. I have found that the house staff ask for a 'progress' report at the end of sessions or want to tell me things about the client before a session. Also where the sessions take place is not ideal, resources for clients with learning disabilities are usually limited and sessions take place in the client's own room. I have found this to be difficult at times and not how I would like sessions to be. There have also been language and communication difficulties, both of my clients have speech impairments and it has taken me a while to 'tune' in to the way in which they speak.

(d) Lack of social awareness which we tend to take for granted

(e) Organisational difficulties and under resourcing are big difficulties. Travel and transport are quite often a problem. Clinically I have found quite often the client needs an advocate, but we have not got an advocacy service in the area. The need at times to talk to staff members involved giving me dilemmas. I overcome this by agreeing with the client the need to do this and involve them [My client Carl (pp. 150), who would set off fire alarms, eventually I learned that he would do this when new staff came on duty. He was, quite literally expressing his alarm. Carl had no speech, and very few signs — we did agree that I would talk to staff in his house, and I asked them to show photographs of who would be coming on duty when they went off. Carl stopped setting off fire alarms.]

(f) Counselling philosophy and practice runs counter to the school's philosophy/ environment — it is personally difficult to offer a positive experience and then to hear the client being bellowed at as they leave the counselling room — working as a minority in a large school is isolating and being viewed with suspicion doesn't help — i.e. regarded as a 'soft touch' . . . 'woolly liberal'

(g) The initial challenge was whether I could allow myself to believe that the core conditions were sufficient for her, even given her disability. After this came a consideration around boundaries, concerning where and when it was appropriate for my response to her to be practical, given the limits of her ability to e.g. find out about agencies for herself. Always, though, I need to do this in a way which does not take away from her very real abilities

(h) (i) Disempowerment of presenting person — usually significant other whose voice is heard.
(ii) Trust — accustomed to being labelled and sorted and judged.
(iii) Tiredness — 50 minutes for two with health problems in addition — is long.

The responses to Question 9 give a flavour of the session-to-session experiences of these counsellors. It shows the range of ability being worked with under the umbrella of 'learning disability'. Here the particular issues which emerge when working with clients who have severe learning disabilities are highlighted: rigidity of thoughts and beliefs in the clients; slow pace of the work; pressures to breach confidentiality; expectations for outcomes placed on the counsellor; communication difficulties; philosophy of counselling practice at odds with institutional philosophies; continual institutional disempowerment of client; tiredness of counsellor. Despite some respondents' preferences not to use the term 'learning disabilities' or 'severe learning disabilities', all gave accounts of the issues they are facing when working with clients who are hampered by learning difficulties.

10. What are the particular rewards of working with this client group?

(a) There were no expectations from any of the clients — they were selected by their 'key' workers at the day centre they attend. They were very open and trusting toward me which enabled me to appreciate the work I was doing. I suppose the word TRUST is uppermost in my mind . . .

(b) (i) Identifying points in the work where the 'normality', the non learning disabilities part of the individual, shines bright [Kay, who had no speech and communicated via minute movements or eyelid flickers — during a massage, when I was verbalising what I understood her to be expressing, she made eye contact, and one heavy tear dropped from her eye. It was a moment of intense closeness.]
(ii) Seeing small changes that I know are a result of my willingness to stick with the process — i.e. recognising they are important [Christopher (pp. 172), a week after I had acknowledged his leaving a session angry with me for leaving him over the summer, he looked directly at me, and reached out and held my hand. In over a year of our counselling sessions, he had never made physical contact with me.]
(iii) Seeing results/change that I have instigated i.e. my client moving to a new home and being so happy about it

(c) I don't think I'm experienced enough to make any judgement regarding rewards, so far I feel equally satisfied about working with learning disabilities and non learning disabilities clients
(d) Her emotional awareness, sensitivity and caring nature. Her capacity for fun and a willingness to address the issues at stake

(e) Watching them improve their lives and advocate for themselves. Building a trusting relationship

(f) Helping some of the most disempowered young people to find their 'voice' and to begin to experience themselves in a positive way – as a unique, valuable individual rather than as a learning disability (in mainstream schools this client group tends to perceive itself as 'thick', 'stupid' and 'failing')

(g) My client's simplicity [I'm reminded of Sinead O'Connor's song, 'Scorn Not His Simplicity, but rather try to love him all the more' (O'Connor, 'Scorn Not His Simplicity', 1994)] *and directness are very engaging. I know that she has very few outlets and that she faces many disadvantages in her life. Even more than with my other clients I am aware that just being there with her is worthwhile*

(h) The challenge of finding a way to really meet. The joy of the encounter [I'm recalling the shortest session I ever had with Paul (see p. 8)]. *The growth of their self-esteem and capacity to invite ideas and especially humour. A coming alive.*

It is interesting that those who did not wish to use the term 'learning disability' at all were able to respond to this question so clearly in terms of richness of experience, in particular relating to the rewards of working with clients who do have learning difficulties.

15. What, if any, are the differences in your work with clients who have learning disabilities and with those who have not?

(a) I feel there is none at all. Each client is an individual. Having worked with people with disabilities, it would be easy to categorise them into those with cerebral palsy, strokes, amputees, etc., etc., etc. I feel it doesn't work like that particularly with the feedback I have had from sufferers of disabilities. They want to be treated as a person, not as a disability, and as a result, I do my utmost to respect their wish. I have found that, although I am counselling a person with disabilities, the issues they bring with them are not tied into the disability itself.

(b) The main concern I have is the level of attachment my clients have in relationship to me. I fear what happens when what I am able to offer is no longer available to them. The process I feel takes a lot longer for a variety of reasons:- (i) Trust in my willingness to not give up on them (ii) Working with individuals who have been so disempowered all their lives (iii) Working with individuals who do not communicate on a verbal level and trusting myself that what is communicated in other ways has meaning and sometimes not really knowing if its my interpretation because they can't verbalise it. (iv) I see movement/change much quicker in my non learning disabled clients (v) the work is a lot more draining, I feel I have to work so much harder.

(c) I think that my basic attitude is the same; I still rely on the core conditions and myself. The biggest difference is in my willingness to be more flexible and patient enough not to assume that the relationship will develop in the same manner and the same speed as with a client without a learning disability.

(d) I found I had to be more real and therefore congruent. I couldn't get away with 'professionalism' which we may occasionally seek refuge behind! She challenged me to maintain the core conditions uncompromisingly!

(e) Clients rather than choosing themselves to have counselling are encouraged by staff/carers around them − Clients need more reassurance on confidentiality − it takes longer to establish a relationship.

(f) The only significant difference for me has been the challenge of facilitating communication − the necessity of developing non-verbal ways of articulating something (different feelings in particular). I've had to use more imagination and creativity to engage with clients [like the client who would only talk about trains − engaging through these became the therapy] *and have developed greater patience − i.e. I may have an idea of where it might be useful for a client to explore, but individuals will* do *it in their own time and must not be rushed!*

(g) The process of our work is similar but I feel the demands on me are subtly different. To enter into her world requires me to be able to let go of my own in some ways which are not necessary with other clients. I also have to be more aware of a need to communicate with her in ways that she can understand. This particular relationship has also demanded considerable openness from me − she asks some very unusual questions of me and I have not wanted to hide myself from her. In some respects she is quite childlike but of course she is not a child. The nature of the relationship in this case feels qualitatively different from other clients, perhaps in some ways more relaxed and unconstrained (which I find an interesting observation I will have to consider further). However, as relationships vary with each client I cannot say to what extent this does or does not result from her disabilities.

(h) Capacity to work while checking their understanding is needed. Their disempowerment encourages them to be compliant therefore need constantly to check where they are. Limited vocabulary/memory mean that sentence construction and sharing of ideas needs to be simple. Keep an eye on making assumptions about their understanding or meanings attached [Me: 'Would you like to meet an advocate?' − Client: 'No that won't be necessary' − Me: 'Do you know what an advocate is?' − Client: 'No!' − Me: (explains) − Client: 'Oh yes I'd like one of those'] *have to work very hard to check out my understanding of their world.*

16. What, if any, are the differences in your feelings in working with this client group, and others?

(a) I get much more enjoyment from working with these client groups. From feedback, it is obvious that there has been little work with individuals who have been considered 'not to have the inclination to want therapy'. There again it might be because of the lack of funding in this area. But there seems to be a much deeper level of appreciation.

(b) Feelings of responsibility seem much more apparent. For many clients they have not had a long-term attachment of the nature I am offering. They have not had a trusted individual who really listens and take time to hear their feelings and concerns. I often feel very inadequate in my work with individuals which I think has to do with what they themselves are after feeling.

(c) I don't think I can comment on this, I don't feel any different but that could be due to my relative inexperience.

(d) No difference beyond those mentioned in previous questions.

(e) There are no major differences. However I do find I feel more responsible for how the client is progressing etc.

(f) I tend to experience more anger — around the way these clients are treated by others — schools; parents; social workers . . . empowerment becomes a burning issue, and source of frustration — the odds are stacked against this. I experience a sort of fierce protectiveness (which I don't feel with the same intensity in my work with adults/people without disabilities).

(g) I am aware that my intellectual ability has always formed an important part of my self-concept and was the key to many of the opportunities I have had in my life. To work with and enter into the world of someone whose life is so different in these respects is, I am aware, potentially threatening. Even now I wonder to what extent I have really been able to engage with this in myself — working with this client has, however, been a great pleasure and I have from the beginning felt considerable affection and respect for her.

(h) Their challenge in different ways brings out different emphasis in me. They force me to track my responses carefully. Usually have very close emotional contact once trust has been established. Have to be v. aware of own feelings and not fall into wanting to 'help them'.

17. Do you have any other comments that you would like to add?

(a) I get frustrated that many consider anyone with a disability (mental or learning) as a case for different or specific consideration. The only reason for this would be

that they have not been considered before now for straightforward therapy! Having talked with a number of people with physical disabilities, their one wish is to be treated equally as those of us without any form of disability. They don't want 'special' treatment − simply to be accepted as a person with the same feelings and thought processes as everyone else . . . [I'm feeling irritated by this response − missing the issue around people who have severe learning disabilities, who cannot say what they want, either because they have no words, restricted communication skills, or so utterly disempowered that they couldn't begin to think in terms of equality].

(b) I feel very privileged in working with all my clients, learning disabilities or not. But I feel the patience and willingness to fully appreciate the needs of this group [. . . the patience of some with severe speech impediments, who repeated over and over for me, because I could not make out the word] *do not just happen and experience of the needs, the issues involved in terms of inter-agency understanding of counselling process and belief in benefits to people with learning disabilities need to be addressed.*

(c) [Blank]

(d) I felt highly privileged. I enjoyed a steep learning curve!

(e) [Blank]

(f) Look forward to reading your dissertation! There is definitely a failure in most counselling training to address this area of therapeutic work − non-discriminatory practice requires more than lip service!

(g) I have virtually no contact with people with learning disabilities prior to this. Working with my client has opened my eyes to the many ethical and philosophical issues in this area as well as making me much less likely to be afraid or awkward in interacting with someone with learning disabilities, although of course I have an incredible amount still to learn.

(h) There is something very special about working with this client group. I feel very privileged when allowed to get close. I often feel humble when I . . . I touch their difficult world. Usually enormous warmth and humour. They can begin to grow as adults rather than remain as dependent children. Very exciting − needs enormous patience!

Personal notes (8.8.00)
I'm surprised by the intensity of my emotional response as I have been reading and collating the responses to the questionnaires. Initially I approached the task as a copy typist, and very quickly began flashing to

ghosts of clients past! I pressed on for a while, and then had to insert short notes along the way to remind me of clients whose voices were coming through. Almost as if I HAD to write them in to do honour to them. I am shocked by the immediacy of sadness, joy, frustration, anger and powerful spiritual connections I made with clients, which still feel so tangible. It feels now more important to listen to those ghosts, and give voice to them, than to go interview more counsellors. The questionnaires seem to have tapped into a fairly broad experience of practitioners working with clients who have learning disabilities. But it has also brought back powerfully my own experience in this field. Perhaps interviews are not necessary now? I must spend some time reflecting upon this.

Upon completing the collation I feel a surge of emotion — how often I have worked with those society has wanted to forget. Many of my clients in long-stay institutions, their only home a hospital bed in a ward — May, who talked of the nurse who packed her bag one day and walked her out of her ward to the house she now lives in. No goodbyes, no discussions — a simple move. And Hope, describing a similar event, but she having spent years subsequently yearning for the sister she used to visit in another ward. She has no idea where her sister was moved to — no idea if she is alive or dead — no photograph — nothing. Both women repeated these events frequently in their sessions, as if they would never recover or move on, but simply needed me to bear witness each time to the trauma and bewilderment that comes from having no status in society. Though both women had restricted language, their emotional articulation was clear.

Discussion of the questionnaire data

It would have been useful to have asked what proportion of each respondents' clients came with severe learning disabilities, and I feel this was an oversight in devising the questionnaire. Had such a question been included, it might have been possible to discover whether those who were working with clients who have learning disabilities or severe learning disabilities focused their work entirely in this area, or whether these clients were part of a wider practice. On reflection now, I wonder if there might be particularly intense feelings if the respondents only work with clients who have severe learning disabilities. (It is possible when one's practice is focused on a particular issue to become deeply and passionately immersed in it. At times this may include some unconscious, or even conscious, identification.) The differences mentioned by those working with clients who have severe learning disabilities, as well as clients who have not, might have been compared with counsellors who only work with clients with severe learning disabilities or those who do not, especially on the issue of 'cost' to the counsellor. There are possibilities for further research here, it seems.

Self-referral was rare among all those who the respondents saw as having any type of learning difficulty, and this does differ from people who are able to access resources themselves, either via GPs or to private practices or specialised organisations. From the descriptions of efforts and abilities to establish contracts, the indication of work with clients who have severe learning disabilities was low. Most clients were able to speak, and had some degree of independence in their lives. This linked with the resistance of some respondents to describing people in terms of mild, moderate or severe learning difficulties. Question 3 asked 'How many clients with severe learning difficulties have you worked with as a counsellor?' There was a somewhat confused reaction to this because though some asserted that they had worked with people with severe learning disabilities (SLD) the subsequent responses implied that these clients were in fact in the moderate learning disabilities (MLD) range. Those who seemed to understand what severe learning disabilities might mean in real terms could see (with reservations) the usefulness of knowing in general terms what to expect and prepare for. None of the respondents had any formal training specifically in the area of learning disabilities, which was as I expected (see Appendix 3), but those who brought to their work some background experience of working with learning disabilities in other settings seemed most likely to be offering counselling to clients with severe learning disabilities. The attitudinal qualities of the Person-Centred Approach were mentioned as generally the way into communicating with any client, and certainly there seemed to be an emphasis on the relationship as the most important aspect of the work. This was mentioned by those who were obviously not working with clients with severe learning disabilities, as well as by those who clearly were. For example:

Response 8 (h): *By seeking to meet them where they are, utilising the core conditions in a way very similar to what I would with any client. Trust and empowerment. Really being here for themselves rather than their behaviours. Allowing them to lead.*

One of my interests in exploring this subject was to see if there were differences, as far as respondents felt, between working with clients who have severe learning disabilities and those who do not. From these responses, there was some confusion (e.g. Response 5(g)) about what the terms meant, and there were some who seemed angry or resistant to the whole idea of descriptions at all (Responses 5(d), 7(a), 15(a), 17(a)), while others felt there was something quite special about working with their clients who have severe learning disabilities (Response 17(h)). There was a split between those who knew the term 'severe learning disabilities' (respondents b, c and h), and were working with clients with those, and other respondents who were not. Respondents b, c and h all had a background in other settings working with people who have severe learning disabilities, and this showed in their contributions in different and fuller responses to their clients and the issues they face.

These respondents highlighted more dilemmas, concerns, and what could be described as feelings of frustration and anger, than those who were not working with this group. These differences, however, may simply be reflected in this small group of responses, and more extensive work would be needed to ascertain whether these are general findings, and if so, if it would be possible to do more than simply highlight the differences.

Respondents expressed their feelings about personally beneficial experiences from working with persons who had very different backgrounds than their own, especially intellectual backgrounds, for example:

Response 16(g): *I am aware that my intellectual ability has always formed an important part of my self-concept, and was the key to many of the opportunities I have had in my life. To work with and enter into the world of someone whose life is so different in these respects is, I am aware, potentially threatening. Even now I wonder to what extent I have really been able to engage with this in myself*

The richness and diversity of responses demonstrated that there is a lack of clarity about what is meant by the terms used to describe learning disabilities. My advertisement, which attracted all respondents, clearly stated that I would be looking at severe learning disability. Each of the respondents understood themselves to be working with people who have learning disabilities, but most were working with those who have varying degrees of independence, and were verbally competent. It is possible that the opportunity to discuss their work was so important that the severity of the learning disability was irrelevant. The continuum of ability from those of genius potential to those with severe learning disabilities is wide and complex. Abilities to function socially, and with reasonable levels of independence as adults, vary, not necessarily in parallel with measurable intelligence. It is possible to discern from the responses that there were some clients whose learning and functional abilities would put them within the range of 'severe learning disability', while there were many who would fall into the range of 'mild' to 'moderate' learning difficulties

Only respondent (b) had considerable experience in working with people with severe learning disabilities.

Personal notes (August 2000)
Have calmed down, and processed my feelings raised from collating the responses to the questionnaire. I realise that there's quite a divide between respondents who obviously have not worked with clients who have severe learning disabilities and those who have. So shall try to get a couple of interviews, to explore the subject in more depth.

The interviews:
dilemmas and passion

Methodology

A good interviewer is a listener rather than a speaker during the interview.
(Cresswell, 1998, p. 125)

In keeping with person-centred theory, I aimed to offer the interviewees those same attitudinal qualities (e.g. Mearns and Thorne, 1999) that I offer clients and supervisees — I wanted to be fully present and aware of what was happening within myself, and willing to share what was relevant. My attention was focused too on the experience of the person to whom I was listening. I wanted to understand, and to demonstrate that I understood, in order that the person may go deeper into their felt experience of their practice with clients who have severe learning disabilities. In interviewing, as in therapy and supervision, an asymmetrical relationship exists, with the interviewer's attention focused on the discovery of the interviewee's experiences, rather than on equal sharing of experiences. The interviews were semi-structured, in that a number of questions were prepared, and each interviewee was asked the same questions, but not necessarily with exactly the same words or same order, as would be the case in a standardised, structured interview required by quantitative researchers.

After completing the questionnaire phase of the study, and collating the responses, I invited two counsellors to interview. Both work with clients who have learning disabilities. One, respondent b in the questionnaire phase (here called Jill) has a background in social work with this client group, and offers counselling to adults with severe learning disabilities in a day centre. The other interviewee (here called Wilma) was recruited after the questionnaire phase was completed, because of her experience in offering counselling to residents in a residential centre for people who have learning disabilities and challenging behaviours, and because no other respondent in the questionnaire phase had worked with a significant number of clients with severe learning disabilities. Both chose to come to my private practice for the interviews, and both agreed to their interviews being tape-recorded. The interview questions were derived from some of my observations from responses to the questionnaires, and allowed for more in-depth explorations of the experiences of these two practitioners. The purpose of the study, and the expected length of time of the interviews, were explained, before launching into the prepared questions.

I knew both the interviewees as colleagues and this brought advantages and disadvantages. We share a language and an understanding of the client group under discussion, which hopefully has led to less misunderstanding or misinterpretation. To counterbalance this, I used clarifying questions during the interviews to ensure that I had not simply assumed, I had understood something, because it was part of my experience too. Platt (1981, in Holloway and Wheeler, 1996) points to the usefulness of interviewing colleagues or peers in that they are more likely to 'open up' to a person they know and trust; however, it is then important to recognise the danger of over-involvement and identification. With all this in mind . . .

Personal notes (Sept 2000)
Heavens! I had never realised, whilst engaged in it, how much easier quantitative research was! I had a map then, I could organise, control variables, and then interpret data in a way that was likely to match (well, that was the aim) any other reviewer of my data. I feel all at sea with the qualitative approach. It is both exciting and terrifying, and requires me to put so much of myself into it, when every effort had to be made to exclude myself from my quantitative work. I feel very nervous of interpreting the questionnaires and the interviews.

Qualitative research is endlessly creative and interpretative. The researcher does not just leave the field with mountains of empirical materials and then easily write up his or her findings. (Denzin and Lincoln, 1998)

These theorists refer to the 'art' of interpretation, which must be practised to gather the essence of what I have learned about the experiences of person-centred practitioners in the area of severe learning disabilities. The interviews were transcribed from their tapes verbatim, and then read a number of times to draw out the themes. Each transcription was marked with highlighter pens and it took much discipline to select only the most important parts to quote. Quotes were selected for their clarity in expressing the practitioners' experiences, although I am sure that my attempts to unravel myself from the feelings this investigation have stirred in me have not been completely successful. Quotes are collected from throughout the interviews, and follow on from some reflections on the material.

Interview responses

What is apparent from the two interviewees is their passion for this work, and what could be described as a rawness and 'unclutteredness' of their feelings in response to their clients who have severe learning disabilities. They both offered an openness to the experience. Each interview gave me the impression that a great deal of emotion had been held in by both counsellors, and that here was an opportunity to let go. Both were energetic, on the edge of their chairs during the interview, as if aware that the time I had said we would speak for would not be enough. Once again I had a sense of the bottleneck I had felt in myself sometimes when working with my clients at the drop-in counselling service — that I had so much emotional energy and somehow I was charged with holding and processing material that my clients could not. Only as I write this is that feeling from the two interviews now becoming clear — those two counsellors were also holding and processing, in some way on behalf of the clients they work with.

Wilma:
Often with someone with very limited understanding maybe you become the bridge.

. . . There is a gap between where someone is maybe trying to get and their ability to understand the processes along the way to getting there.

. . . He was given no choice about whether his parents were informed, he was given no choice about going to the police, he was given no choice about a whole range of things.

. . . There's no recognition of the effects of abuse perpetrated by the system itself on individuals or of the responsibility of that system, you know, as the perpetrators and maybe make some form of recompense . . . it's just not recognised.

. . . The sheer weight of oppression that has gone on, and also the sheer weight of oppression that still exists.

Wilma is describing the issues facing her clients and her own efforts to meet the clients and the issues where they are. There seems to be no way of empowering effective change yet in the client's environment, so that she must simply hold their truth, as well as her own anger about what happens to them.

Jill:
. . . the amount of loss and the number of changes in their lives that none of us could possibly imagine. And it never . . . it still doesn't cease to amaze me they manage to survive and come through.

. . . is it worth my while this person coming to me every week? and what's happening, she's sitting rocking in this room and then . . . maybe after four or five sessions something happens and I . . . a bit of eye contact or a movement of a toy, or a hand out to hold your hand, and it's those tiny, tiny bits of movement that make it worthwhile.

> *. . . every one of them has taught me something very important . . . communication verbally has become one of the least important things.*

Jill highlights the awe she sometimes experiences in her work, and this feeling of awe is present for Wilma, and some of the questionnaire respondents too. There is something of the realm of mystery in the way that their clients, who have such difficulties in existing, functioning and communicating, can still develop when given the opportunity in the counselling relationship.

Both Jill and Wilma had strong feelings regarding the differences they perceive in working with their clients who have severe learning disabilities, and clients who have not. They felt the pressure of working in their different environments, Jill in a day centre offering a drop-in service for clients with severe learning disabilities, and Wilma offering a counselling service to the residents in a residential institution. They felt that these environmental factors impinged both on their clients and on the work they could do with their clients.

> Wilma:
> *. . . to say that there's no difference between someone with learning difficulties and someone who hasn't is . . . like saying there's no difference between a black person and a white person. It's a . . . a . . . denial of who they are . . .*

> Jill:
> *. . . you can empower that person* [who has moderate learning difficulties] *to go on and do something whereas the person with severe learning disabilities is in a controlled environment . . . doesn't have the ability to go and say, right I'm taking no more of this . . .* [Explanatory note added in brackets]
>
> *. . . how can I help this client move on, it feels like they want you to do something, and you've your hands tied.*

> Wilma:
> *. . . you're sort of joined in their helplessness . . . put back yourself because you can't . . . the system is vast and it feels like . . . trying to take a mountain of rock apart pebble by pebble, it's overwhelming.*
> *. . . I find a difference even working with somebody with what you might term 'severe learning difficulties' and someone with more 'moderate' or 'mild' learning difficulties.*

> *. . . I have to work a lot harder in terms of understanding . . . you can't rely on the same sort of assumptions about knowledge, about what is understood and what isn't . . . I worked with someone who thought he could be sent to prison for swearing . . .*
>
> *. . . people who don't know the difficulties . . . have a great psychological armoury of things they can sling at them.*

Wilma highlights the complexity in the continuum of learning disability when referring to her client who thinks he can go to prison for swearing. Here is a client who can speak, but his understanding of the world, and lack of ability to function socially or live independently, mean that Wilma finds that she has to work much harder at understanding him, even though he may not be described as having a severe learning disability.

Concerns over institutionalised abuse, and lack of recognition and services for people with severe learning difficulties, were other particular differences mentioned. It would be almost impossible for some of Jill's clients to seek other help, or name abuse themselves outside of a relationship of trust, where time has been given to developing the relationship and communication and where such issues can be raised.

> Jill:
> *. . . issues of power − a lot of people with learning disabilities are used to being told what to do and never had a choice. I mean, it's starting from very basic things . . . like that a person's allowed to choose between tea and coffee . . . somebody with learning disabilities might never have been given a choice at all.*
>
> *. . . so you might be empowering somebody to go to a disco to make relationships but the person you're working with might not be able to travel there alone . . .*
>
> *. . . And initially I found that quite difficult because what I would have liked to have done would have been to empower the client to do that herself but knowing . . . knowing that she wasn't going to be able to do it . . . and having to almost be an advocate, or at least maybe not the advocate but I suppose raise those issues that she's, she's brought the issues to me, I've checked them out with her, and before I've related it back I've checked them out with her again − is it OK for me to raise the fact that you may want to think about moving?*

> *Wilma:*
> *The effects of abuse perpetrated by the system itself on individuals or of the responsibility of that system . . . make some form of recompense . . . it's just not recognised.*

There are significant expectations from referral agencies for reports and recommendations, and focus for the work poses particular dilemmas, as often the constraints of offering the service are that these expectations will be met (see Appendix 3, my assumptions). This of course is in conflict with confidentiality, as well as with the process of the work. Respondents indicate the ways in which they attempt to honour their commitment to their clients while giving only what might be responsibly in the service of the client.

> *Jill:*
> *. . . a whole audience of people: carers, psychologists, solicitors . . .*
>
> *. . . it's almost like you've got to have an end product . . . and I don't have an end product to work to with the other people I work with. The end product is what the client wants, but there's an expectation from others that there's . . . puts more demands on you and does tinge the way you work, if you're not very careful in handling it.*
>
> *. . . The work with people with learning disabilities is so much more public, so you're not only dealing with the needs of the client, but you're dealing with . . . the disbelief, the cynical views of other people, and people wanting things to change.*
>
> *. . . Something I've found really difficult is almost like struggling with what's expected of me against what I'm seeing in the relationship with that individual.*

> *Wilma:*
> *. . . [This client was] referred through the courts, so part of her bail conditions is to see me. So the element of choice for people with severe learning disabilities is severely limited.*
>
> *. . . the sheer weight of oppression that still exists.*

There seems to be a need for the practitioner to accept the power that is inherent in the situation, and to have the personal integrity to use that power responsibly. The sense from both interviewees was that they had to be extremely careful in supplying information asked for, in part because of those issues, and in part because of the fear of the service being withdrawn from those clients. A particular dilemma for these person-centred practitioners was the expectation of acceptable 'outcomes', particularly as improvements in behaviour, which conflicted with their own sense of needing to be with, and go with their clients. This created tension for both, in what they felt was the importance of process over product, while they were continually pressured for product in terms of outcomes.

Consent and compliance within this group of clients were important dilemmas for the interviewees, especially Jill.

Jill:
The recognition that as a group, these people are so used to being told what to do, where to go, almost what to feel – or not, that there is an awareness of the power given over to the counsellor, even when she is endeavouring to give the power to the client.

. . . like clients without learning disabilities will tell you off sometimes . . . they'll challenge you, a lot of our clients have been so squashed that they want to please you all the time . . . the majority will want to please you, and if you go on that sort of face [value] . . . accept it, that that is something about that individual, it's not, it's about the oppression that's been suffered by people with learning disabilities in a way that nobody else has, I don't think – not in the same way.

Again, the passion and compassion expressed by the interviewees was tangible. It was as if both had to 'play the game' in some ways, not making too many waves or demands for their clients, because they were aware of how easily their clients could be denied their services. This involved not making too much noise about the Person-Centred Approach and its emphasis on process, or self-direction of the client, because they could all too easily be replaced by nothing at all, or by 'treatment' that would leave the clients they both felt committed to in the same disempowered place they always had been. It was noticeable how a 'parallel process' (Wosket, 1999) often occurred, where the counsellors felt disempowered and helpless, just as their clients actually were.

Jill:
I can't make it stop [abuse] *because I'm not in the . . . I mean . . . I'm left with the same sort of feelings that the client must have. It's like I keep saying it and nobody does anything . . . so it's almost like you're in parallel with the client.*

> *Wilma:*
> ... [discussing her client's lack of choice] *unfortunately the onus was on me to have to act, which I was not happy about . . . but I had no choice.*

Discussion of interviews

It was humbling to hear the experiences of so many people with severe learning disabilities come through the voices of those I heard in questionnaire or interview. I had not expected the intensity of those voices, nor those that pressed themselves on my consciousness throughout the process of collating the questionnaires.

It has been very difficult to select from the interviews and also from the questionnaire responses, as inevitably there is such richness of experience. I have felt tempted to simply let the collated responses and transcripts speak for themselves, and bow out gracefully! What is clear is that the clients discussed by respondents and interviewees engaged with the process of counselling, and relationships developed between them and their counsellors. For person-centred practitioners and their clients, that is where the work happens. Whatever the costs, in terms of frustration, sadness and anger about the lives of their clients, when they had come into their clients' worlds and shared their experiences, respondents and interviewees felt that they had gained much from this work, and were clearly keen to develop services for clients with learning disabilities.

In considering the validity of this research, I return to Polkingthorne's (in Creswell, 1998) key points. I feel confident that the transcripts are accurate, and that my reflections on these can be tracked back to the originals. I have attempted to draw only those conclusions that another reviewer would recognise and agree with, and to reflect the opinions of the respondents. The latter has been made easier, because respondents presented many of the same dilemmas, opinions and feelings as I had explored in my own pre-investigation considerations (see Appendix 3). I have some concern, because of the small numbers of volunteers who presented themselves, that the responses may reflect a minority view anyway– and a view that I share. Further research would need to gather more data from a wider number of respondents (if possible). Because of the small number of respondents and interviews, it is not appropriate to make definitive generalisations. My hope is that what has been expressed may be of interest to other practitioners, and may especially act as an invitation to other practitioners to offer their services to those with severe learning disabilities. It might also be fruitful to compare views with counsellors practising from other therapeutic perspectives with people who have severe learning disabilities.

As I am nearing the end of my work on this exploration of person-centred practitioners' experiences of working with people with severe learning disabilities, the first book discussing the applications of the Person-Centred Approach for people with special needs has just been published. Marlis Pörtner (2000) focuses on everyday work in many different care settings, and points out or illustrates the benefits to clients and carers alike of developing the core attitudinal qualities as a way of being with people in communities. In the book she describes the work of psychologist Barbara Krietmeyer with Laura, a woman with severe learning disabilities and no verbal ability, 'a hopeless case'. Through the moving description of her patience with the process, Laura makes significant changes in her behaviour and ability to be with others: 'It shows how helpful and necessary it is, even with severely disabled and non-verbal persons, to never forget that they still have the potential to grow' (Pörtner, 2000, p. 112). This presents an optimistic view that I share, and feel affirmed to see in print. While Pörtner includes this important case study, there is, so far, a complete lack of other material discussing person-centred counselling with people who have severe learning disabilities. The purpose of this study is to begin looking at this area of person-centred practice.

In my struggle with the qualitative approach to research, I have felt very much in a 'remedial' position, often becoming confused, lost and overwhelmed with the task. At some level, I feel something of an affinity with those whose learning disabilities are so severe; that the world we ostensibly share together is hostile, overwhelming and confusing. The counselling practitioners who have offered their time to this study have described a rich variety of experiences with their clients who have severe learning disabilities. It seems that the more severe the learning disability, the more dilemmas arise for the counsellor, and they rely upon their personal and professional integrity to find the path forward in their work. This is particularly pertinent to issues of confidentiality, and accountability to those who have expectations of outcomes for clients they refer and fund. The oppressive environmental factors create intense feelings in counsellors, who feel as helpless as their clients to make changes.

Those counsellors who were working with clients with severe learning disabilities saw quite clear differences in their work with them, as compared with working with clients who do not have severe learning disabilities. These were due to issues such as: differences in understanding the world; difficulties with communication restricting their access to others who can 'speak' their language; reliance on institutional care rather than independent living; continual and sometimes institutional abuse of those with severe learning disabilities; extremely restricted personal autonomy for those with severe learning disabilities; and lastly development or 'progress' of people with severe learning disabilities can be extremely slow.

The interviewees described their own isolation, and a lack of understanding of their work with clients with severe learning disabilities, which they felt mirrored their clients' isolation. On the more positive side of the experiences shared here, much passion was expressed for the clients and the work, such as feelings of awe and wonder at the striving of their clients for understanding and communication, despite all the restrictions they live with. There was much discussion of creativity and flexibility, as well as willingness to meet their clients in whatever way this could be managed, through words, signs, drawing, Play-Doh, whatever would facilitate their clients' communication. Throughout an underpinning Person-Centred Approach to the work came through responses to the questionnaires as well as the interviews. Despite the feelings of frustration and anger expressed about the daily oppression of their clients and the continual demands made upon them from referring agencies, those working with people with severe learning disabilities felt it was rewarding to them as well as their clients.

Jill:
. . . [speaking for her clients] *don't be fooled by the mask we wear . . . what you might see initially it's like the words are not here* [points to mouth] *they're here* [points to chest], *they're all around you, just be prepared to keep your eyes, your ears, your senses, keep your whole self available to me and if you're prepared to do that, you'll help me. Lose your attention, and you might miss something.*

British Association for the Person-Centred Approach
BM BAPCA
LONDON
WC1N 3XX
www.bapca.org.uk

Appendices

Please give your responses to the following questions:

1. How many clients with severe learning disabilities have you worked with as a counsellor?

2. How long have you been working altogether as a counsellor, with this client group?

3. How was/were the referral/s made?

4. How did you establish the counselling contract/s?

5. How would you say clients are, or can been classified as having mild, moderate and severe learning disabilities, and does this classification have any usefulness in describing the work you do with clients who have learning disabilities?

6. What particular training in this area have you completed?

7. How did your counselling training help you work with this client group?

8. How do you establish a relationship with a client/s?

---

1. Spaces were left between each question for responses. Here the spaces have been omitted to ease reading.

9. What are the particular difficulties and dilemmas you have found working with this client group? (you may wish to select three key points)

10. What are the particular rewards of working with this client group?
11. Was the client(s) able to attend the sessions alone?

12. What development in mood, behaviour, demeanour, attitude, did you notice during the course of your work together in yourself and your client(s)?

13. How did the client(s) respond to the ending?

14. How easy/difficult has it been for you to get supervision for this work

15. What, if any, are the differences in your work with clients who have learning disabilities and with those who have not?

16. What, if any, are the differences in your feelings in working with this client group, and others?

17. Do you have any other comments that you would like to add?

Would you be willing to meet for a tape-recorded interview of approximately one-hour duration if needed? If so, please give your name, address and telephone number and e-mail address.

Thank you for your time

Appendix 1a

Covering letter for questionnaire

Dear

Thank you for responding to the advertisement in Person to Person, regarding my MA research into counselling people with severe learning disabilities.

The aim of this research study is to investigate the experiences of Person-Centred practitioners who are working with clients who have severe learning disabilities. There is no need to supply your name, as this is an anonymous questionnaire, though if you would be happy to participate in a taped interview, please include your name, address and telephone number. These details will NOT be used in the study. Identifying details should not be included in your responses, so that confidentiality is maintained. In the dissertation, any possible identifying details of yourself or your clients will not be included, or will be changed to ensure that anonymity and confidentiality are preserved.

I enclose an s.a.e. for the return of the questionnaire, and I would appreciate return by May 26th.
Thank you for your time.

Yours sincerely,

Jan Hawkins

Appendix 2

Collated responses to the questionnaires

Please give your responses to the following questions:

1. How many clients with severe learning disabilities have you worked with as a counsellor?

    (a) 4
    (b) 8
    (c) 1 severe and 1 moderate
    (d) 1
    (e) None that I would describe as severe. I tend to be referred those with good communication skills, mild/moderate learning disability
    (f) none with severe; 5 with moderate
    (g) 1
    (h) 9 or more − difficult for me to know how they are labelled so not sure how severe. I believe 2 would be labelled 'severe'

2. How long have you been working altogether as a counsellor, with this client group?

    (a) 1 year
    (b) 3 years
    (c) Since February 1999
    (d) 18 months
    (e) 3 years
    (f) 5 years
    (g) About 7 months
    (h) 5 years

3. How was/were the referral/s made?

    (a) Via social services who were awarded funding for counselling a group of individuals whose behaviour was considered inappropriate for the day centre that they attended
    (b) Various avenues:− direct by a carer; via day centre staff; direct by client themselves at a drop in session; via social services; voluntary sector
    (c) I offered a free counselling service to Mencap residential homes as part of my training
    (d) Mencap
    (e) Referrals come to me thorough the Community team's psychologist. These usually come via a joint meeting with social services. We also take referrals

> *from residential services, day centres etc.*
> *(f) Through staff of the school's 'Support Centre' where I was working*
> *(g) Via the manager of the service I work at (who knew my client and knew she had expressed an interest in counselling)*
> *(h) Through special needs in school an Ed. Psych. One came by herself.*

4. How did you establish the counselling contract/s?

> *(a) No formal contracts were made! Social Services were given some sponsorship money and asked me to partake in the scheme. They gave me free rein to do what I wished . . .*
> *(b) Using a combination of verbal communication with client & depending on the method of the client, using drawings, timetables and written contract. The important element I found was taking things at the client's pace and establishing a relationship based on their level of need*
> *(c) I offered the same boundaries and options as I do with all my clients*
> *(d) Through Mencap home manager in consultation with client*
> *(e) Verbally at the first session*
> *(f) I explained the nature of counselling . . . the limits of the confidentiality and the likely duration in the first session and invited the clients to ask questions and say how they felt about it and what they hoped for*
> *(g) By speaking directly with the client*
> *(h) With the student*

5. How would you say clients are, or can been classified as having mild, moderate and severe learning disabilities, and does this classification have any usefulness in describing the work you do with clients who have learning disabilities?

> *(a) I apply no label to them at all — first and foremost they are individuals in their own right. I feel I do nothing different to what I would do with 'normal' clients*
> *(b) Having to emphasise the communication*
> *(c) I think the classifications are very outdated, as people who are said to have severe l/d often have skills and abilities in certain areas, which do not conform to the stereotype. I think it would be more useful to me, as a counsellor, to know more about a person's abilities to communicate rather than what is perceived to be their intellectual ability*
> *(d) I do not find it relevant and therefore would not try to do so*
> *(e) We classify by clinical impression and I.Q. testing. I would classify (broadly): Mild: those living independently and who are able in everyday living; moderate: those living perhaps in residential care and/or living with some support independently; Severe: those needing 24 hour support, physically severely handicapped or with severe challenging behaviours*
> *(f) The only usefulness of labelling degree of disability is that it can facilitate the*

*process of attempting to provide appropriate support. I have no experience
of students with severe learning disabilities – so assume that these are
excluded from mainstream schools. My clients have had mild–moderate
learning disabilities*

(g) *To be honest I am not quite sure where in this spectrum my client would be
placed. I would guess at moderate, possibly. My client is an adult under 30,
can tell the time only by the hour and with some uncertainty and reads only
a tiny amount. However she can speak clearly and is quite independent in
many areas of her life*

(h) *Little help to me*

6. What particular training in this area have you completed?

(a) *Bugger all – apart from my Diploma in Counselling!*

(b) *I would say that most of what I have has been learned by my direct experience
of the client group, which is about 20 years all in. Counselling training and
all other input with working with people has been relevant*

(c) *I have worked in a Mencap residential home for almost 5 years but have had
no specific l/d counselling training*

(d) *None*

(e) *No training in this particular area. I have combined my experience of working
in Learning Disability for 11 years with my training and practice as a general
counsellor*

(f) *None*

(g) *None*

(h) *None specifically relating to counselling people with severe learning
disabilities*

7. How did your counselling training help you work with this client group?

(a) *Very little, in that although my training involved looking at issues around
disabilities and learning disabilities, I maintained my stance that I considered
them as not 'fitting' into a particular category, but as individuals who should
be accepted as such. I did not take any of their disabilities into account unless
they themselves considered it to be an issue*

(b) *The main usefulness was in going at the client's pace and using whatever
'tools' are required to meet the client need and being prepared to be flexible
and creative in my work*

(c) *I think the Person-Centred Approach is geared towards accepting a client as
they are at any particular point in time, in this respect I don't think additional
knowledge of the client group is necessary. I have found the core-conditions
have been enough, although a flexible approach has been needed and I think
the p/c way of working allows for this*

(d) *It didn't specifically, but the person-Centred Approach puts the client, not
their problem, as the focus. It enabled me to 'be' with the client. I believe she*

felt valued and heard and that I believe is all she really needed

(e) Working with this client group for a long period of time has helped me to adapt other counselling training. I have found It difficult to find appropriate training

(f) Again – no specific exploration of working with learning disability. Counselling training helped because it was person-Centred – based on a philosophy of unconditional valuing and empowerment

(g) I cannot remember issues around learning disabilities being raised in either of the Diploma Courses I have completed. Obviously many other general principles remain relevant

(h) Being person-Centred the whole emphasis on entering another's internal frame of ref.; 'as if' one's own is vital – offering core conditions and struggling to really travel alongside them

8. How do you establish a relationship with a client/s?

(a) I honestly believe I achieve a relationship with clients, regardless of background, race, disability, etc. by being me . . . I don't pretend to stand in judgement, I don't try to ascertain the reasoning behind the sessions. I endeavour to allow the client to be themselves too. It has reinforced my belief in the process of giving the client the core conditions

(b) Allowing client to tell their story and ensuring that I communicate my ability to understand their feeling and concerns in whatever form this may take – verbal, body language, pictures etc. Allowing client to be themselves. Acceptance of them as individuals. Allow for client to gain trust in my ability to stay with them and being willing to stay not knowing until the client is confident and gained trust in me to share the more difficult material – this often takes a very long time.

(c) A preparedness to appreciate that for most people with l/d have rarely experienced confidentiality in relation to their experiences and this takes a long time to be accepted. Provide honesty in relation to how confidential service is

(d) I have found that working with Prouty's pre-therapy approach has been invaluable to help develop the psychological contact with the l/d clients I have worked with

(e) Openness, honesty and treating the client as an ordinary person with rights while acknowledging her particular difficulty; By understanding and asserting in my approach that she was not a monster or subhuman but merely experienced a particular difficulty. By acknowledging that I wasn't perfect either!

(f) In general I feel it takes 3–6 sessions to establish a relationship. I find a lot of the time that confidentiality has to be re-confirmed to create the safety that our clients are not used to. If a client has problems in talking I will ask questions and generally show interest in their life to encourage and relax them

(g) *Gently, responsively and over time. Early days include a considerable amount of self-introduction — a sort of 'this is me . . . who are you?' approach. I attempt to listen hard to what may or may not be being verbalised and to offer non-verbal ways of expressing thoughts and feelings and taking about experience. We draw, model and play (actual and devised/created games)*

(h) *By seeking to meet them where they are, utilising the core conditions in a way very similar to what I would with any client. trust and empowerment. Really being hear for themselves rather than their behaviours. Allowing them to lead. At first all this is hard for them to accept. Therefore I will work in a way to facilitate real contact, sand, playdoh, computer — whatever*

9. What are the particular difficulties and dilemmas you have found working with this client group? (you may wish to select three key points)

(a) *(i) they tended to reach a plateau of learning. It appeared to me that they became aware of certain factors in their lives and their learning to come to a temporary halt (ii) Because of a combination of learning difficulties and mature age, their beliefs rarely changed! One, in particular, thought that women did the cooking and were there for sex (ouch!) (iii) I learnt new levels of patience! They did tend to wander in their thoughts and words . . . the sessions often went onto the latest Rugby scores, football, Christmas presents*

(b) *1. Confidentiality — has always been a big issue for me in that organisations/ local authorities want information and proof of the benefits of counselling which is not always easy to quantify. 2. Other people's doubts of the usefulness of counselling for people with learning disabilities especially those who have no verbal/or little verbal communication. 3. Having an environment that communicates the value of the individual (when not working in an environment of my choosing)*

(c) *Confidentiality has been an on-going issue. I have found that the house staff after ask for a 'progress' report at the end of sessions or want to tell me things about the client before a session. Also where the sessions take place is not ideal, resources for clients with l/d are usually limited and sessions take place in the client's own room. I have found this to be difficult at times and not how I would like sessions to be. There have also been language and communication difficulties, both of my clients have speech impairments and it has taken me a while to 'tune' in to the way in which they speak*

(d) *Lack of social awareness which we tend to take for granted*

(e) *Organisational difficulties and under resourcing are big difficulties. Travel and transport are quite often a problem. Clinically I have found quite often the client needs an advocate, but we have not got an advocacy service in the area. The need at times to talk to staff members involved giving me dilemmas. I overcome this by agreeing with the client the need to do this and involve them*

(f) *Counselling philosophy and practice runs counter to the school's philosophy/*

environment − *It is personally difficult to offer a positive experience and then to hear the client being bellowed at as they leave the counselling room − Working as a minority in a large school is isolating and being viewed with suspicion doesn't help − i.e. regarded as a 'soft touch' . . . 'woolly liberal'*

(g) *The initial challenge was whether I could allow myself to believe that the core conditions were sufficient for her, even given her disability. After this came a consideration around boundaries, concerning where and when it was appropriate for my response to her to be practical, given the limits of her ability to e.g. find out about agencies for herself. Always, though, I need to do this in a way which does not take away from her very real abilities*

(h) *1. Disempowerment of presenting person − usually significant other whose voice is heard. 2. Trust − accustomed to being labelled and sorted and judged. 3. Tiredness − 50 minutes for 2 with health problems in addition − is long*

10. What are the particular rewards of working with this client group?

(a) *There were no expectations from any of the clients − they were selected by their 'key' workers at the day centre they attend. They were very open and trusting toward me which enabled me to appreciate the work I was doing. I suppose the word TRUST is uppermost in my mind . . .*

(b) *1. Identifying points in the work where the 'normality', the non l/d part of the individual, shines bright*

2. Seeing small changes that I know are a result of my willingness to stick with the process − i.e. recognising they are important

3. Seeing results/change that I have instigated i.e. my client moving to a new home and being so happy about it

(c) *I don't think I'm experienced enough to make any judgement regarding rewards, so far I feel equally satisfied about working with l/d and non l/d clients*

(d) *Her emotional awareness, sensitivity and caring nature. Her capacity for fun and a willingness to address the issues at stake*

(e) *Watching them improve their lives and advocate for themselves. Building a trusting relationship*

(f) *Helping some of the most disempowered young people to find their 'voice' and to begin to experience themselves in a positive way − as a unique, valuable individual rather than as a learning disability (in mainstream schools this client group tends to perceive itself as 'thick', 'stupid" and 'failing')*

(g) *My client's simplicity and directness are very engaging. I know that she has very few outlets and that she faces many disadvantages in her life. Even more than with my other clients I am aware that just being there with her is worthwhile*

(h) *The challenge of finding a way to really meet. The joy of the encounter. The growth of their self esteem and capacity to invite ideas and especially humour. A coming alive.*

11. Was the client(s) able to attend the sessions alone?

(a) *unfortunately, one of the Day Service officers was present and this was one of the conditions to the sessions taking place. Apparently this was done for insurance reasons.*

(b) *Yes – never as yet has this been a problem. The only issue I had was when working with a client in their own home and she chose to wander around the house (boundary issues)*

(c) *Yes*

(d) *Yes*

(e) *The majority of clients are brought to the centre by carers but once arrived they attend sessions alone. We also go out to clients where there are travel problems and if a private space can be found in the day centre, home etc.*

(f) *Yes*

(g) *Yes*

(h) *Yes*

12. What development in mood, behaviour, demeanour, attitude, did you notice during the course of your work together in yourself and your client(s)?

(a) *I got angry once! Having been involved with teenagers with learning difficulties here at College on a large scale for a number of years, I felt it would give me an insight into potential behaviour. Having said that, the relationships that were built up were very strong and trusting (again!). the clients felt able to share how they felt about particular subjects, something which up until the sessions started were either ignored, or simply forgotten – no-one had really listened to them before – why should they, they have learning difficulties. My work enables them to share real issues. (Which probably helps to answer the previous question 10 the clients were able to share issues of anger, joy and sadness, in some cases, for the very first time. Initially, there was little display of emotion. After a few sessions, they felt able to start exploring new areas of their personality.)*

(b) *Myself powerlessness to change the client's outside environment. Frustration at the attitude/approach to clients in their everyday world. Anger at the system which doesn't do enough to protect adults with l/d. Continuing change in me – deepening level of empathy. Sadness – lots of feelings of how limited my clients worlds are and lack of power they seem to have over their own lives.*

(c) *I found that as the session progressed, both my client and myself became much more relaxed. It was obvious in my client's speech, which became much slower and easier to understand. I think my client also became more aware and understanding my role in the relationship, she began to see me as the 'counsellor' and not as someone who just came every week for a 'chat'*

(d) *She became more outgoing, positive and confident. Her speech improved in clarity. Her gait became more 'normal' as opposed to the institutionalised shuffle. Her handshake became firmer and she learned to hug! She began increasingly to make decisions for herself*

(e) *I have found that with most clients the process has empowered them to face situations in their lives, this improves confidence and self esteem. In general this client group learn to ignore their feelings or keep feelings under control. As counselling progresses this guard comes down and there is the opportunity to explore and progress. Anger is one most often suppressed I feel.*

(f) <u>Self:</u> *increasing confidence and openness; developed ability simply to 'be' with the client — to trust the Person-centred process and to put less pressure on myself to be <u>doing</u> something (i.e. producing tangible 'results' for the school).* <u>Clients:</u> *Visibly relaxed and gradually began to interact, communicate and be able to 'play' — humour and jokiness often emerged — including their teasing of me (wonderful!). significant trust developed.*

(g) *She has become less tense, frustrated and prone to worry. She also seems to be gradually growing in trust of herself and is consequently more assertive and aware of what she wants. I, too, have become more relaxed, more willing to trust my instincts and be open with her, trusting her ability to find her own way.*

(h) *Confidence grows. Walk differently. Find their voice in other places too.*

13. How did the client(s) respond to the ending?

(a) *One was glad they finished, but it was obvious that the majority were at an interesting stage of their development. It left them feeling that much more could have been achieved. However, because it felt that they had all reached a plateau with respect to their learning, perhaps it was a good time to rest for a while. Unfortunately the funding was then channelled into group work with another group from the same centre*

(b) *Endings to date have felt well timed and the individuals concerned I feel have been ready to end. Some individuals I am working with now I fear the ending may feel like they are being abandoned/rejected and will need very careful handling. With one individual I felt quite overcome with emotion in terms of the communication done via toys, me and her behaviour (client with no speech). I wondered throughout the process if she really wanted to be with me. The ending proved she really did gain something and communicated it.*

(c) *Hasn't happened yet*

(d) *We worked on it together so that she finally chose and agreed it*

(e) *Endings are difficult for the client in the majority of cases. We spend a time on planning the ending with the client, and looking at the future*

(f) *We talked about ending for weeks before it happened and individuals decided what they would like to do (e.g. make cards, record their experiences of our work etc.). There was appreciation, sadness, and anxiety about who they would be able to talk to/receive support from in the future*

(g) *Not applicable yet*

(h) *In school often not a total ending as they can and do return if the need arises*

14. How easy/difficult has it been for you to get supervision for this work?

(a) *No problem as it was a continuation of some of the other work I have been doing at a day centre for people with disabilities*

(b) *I have been very lucky to find a supervisor who is fully aware of the needs of the clients I work with and a very good understanding of the effects of the work on me. I feel without this input I would feel very alone and misunderstood*

(c) *I was very lucky to already have an extremely supportive supervisor who had some previous experience with a similar client group, although not as a counsellor. I found that it was a mutual learning experience for us both*

(d) *My supervisor died just as I started work with this client! I did finally find another supervisor who was at least supportive of my work with her − no specific help however*

(e) *The psychologist on the team provides regular supervision. She is also a gestalt therapist.*

(f) *Easy for me − I suspect this is unusual!*

(g) *I have dealt with this work with my existing supervisor. This has felt satisfactory because he has some experience of working with learning disabilities (albeit more mild than severe) and my client's disabilities are not such that I have felt a strong need for specialist advice/assistance*

(h) *Own supervisor (person-centred) had no problem offering this and has been enormously supportive and creative*

15. What, if any, are the differences in your work with clients who have learning disabilities and with those who have not?

(a) *I feel there is none at all. Each client is an individual. Having worked with people with disabilities, it would be easy to categorise them into those with cerebral palsy, strokes, amputees, etc., etc., etc. I feel it doesn't work like that particularly with the feedback I have had from sufferers of disabilities. They want to be treated as a person, not as a disability, and as a result, I do my utmost to respect their wish. I have found that, although I am counselling a person with disabilities, the issues they bring with them are not tied into the disability itself.*

(b) *The main concern I have is the level of attachment my clients have in relationship to me. I fear what happens when what I am able to offer is no longer available to them. The process I feel takes a lot longer for a variety of reasons: (1) Trust in my willingness to not give up on them (2) Working with individuals who have been so disempowered all their lives (3) Working with individuals who do not communicate on a verbal level and trusting myself that what is communicated in other ways has meaning and sometimes not really knowing if its my interpretation because they can't verbalise it. (4) I see movement/change much quicker in my non learning disabled clients (5) the work is a lot more draining, I feel I have to work so much harder.*

(c) *I think that my basic attitude is the same; I still rely on the core conditions and myself. The biggest difference is in my willingness to be more flexible and patient enough not to assume that the relationship will develop in the same manner and the same speed as with a client without a learning disability*

(d) *I found I had to be more real and therefore congruent. I couldn't get away with 'professionalism' which we may occasionally seek refuge behind! She challenged me to maintain the core conditions uncompromisingly!*

(e) *Clients rather than choosing themselves to have counselling are encouraged by staff/carers around them — Clients need more reassurance on confidentiality — it takes longer to establish a relationship*

(f) *The only significant difference for me has been the challenge of facilitating communication — the necessity of developing non-verbal ways of articulating something (different feelings in particular). I've had to use more imagination and creativity to engage with clients and have developed greater patience — i.e. I may have an idea of where it might be useful for a client to explore, but individuals will do it in their own time and must not be rushed!*

(g) *The process of our work is similar but I feel the demands on me are subtly different. To enter into her world requires me to be able to let go of my own in some ways which are not necessary with other clients. I also have to be more aware of a need to communicate with her in ways that she can understand. This particular relationship has also demanded considerable openness from me — she asks some very unusual questions of me and I have not wanted to hide myself from her. In some respects she is quite childlike but of course she is not a child. The nature of the relationship in this case feels qualitatively different from other clients, perhaps in some ways more relaxed and unconstrained (which I find an interesting observation I will have to consider further). However, as relationships vary with each client I cannot say to what extent this does or does not result from her disabilities*

(h) *Capacity to work while checking their understanding is needed. Their disempowerment encourages them to be compliant therefore need constantly to check where they are. Limited vocabulary/memory mean that sentence construction and sharing of ideas needs to be simple. Keep an eye on making assumptions about their understanding or meanings attached have to work very hard to check out my understanding of their world.*

16. What, if any, are the differences in your feelings in working with this client group, and others?

(a) *I get much more enjoyment from working with these client groups. From feedback, it is obvious that there has been little work with individuals who have been considered 'not to have the inclination to want therapy'. There again it might be because of the lack of funding in this area. But there seems to be a much deeper level of appreciation*

(b) *Feelings of responsibility seem much more apparent. For many clients they have not had a long term attachment of the nature I am offering. They have* not had a trusted individual who really listens and take time to hear their feelings and concerns. I often feel very inadequate in my work with individuals which I think has to do with what they themselves are feeling

(c) I don't think I can comment on this, I don't feel any different but that could be due to my relative inexperience

(d) No difference beyond those mentioned in previous questions

(e) There are no major differences. However I do find I feel more responsible for how the client is progressing etc.

(f) I tend to experience more anger — around the way these clients are treated by others — schools; parents; social workers . . . Empowerment becomes a burning issue, and source of frustration — the odds are stacked against this. I experience a sort of fierce protectiveness (which I don't feel with the same intensity in my work with adults/people without disabilities).

(g) I am aware that my intellectual ability has always formed an important part of my self-concept and was the key to many of the opportunities I have had in my life. To work with and enter into the world of someone whose life is so different in these respects is, I am aware, potentially threatening. Even now I wonder to what extent I have really been able to engage with this in myself — working with this client has, however, been a great pleasure and I have from the beginning felt considerable affection and respect for her.

(h) Their challenge in different ways brings out different emphasis in me. They force me to track my responses carefully. Usually have very close emotional contact once trust has been established. Have to be v. aware of own feelings and not fall into wanting to 'help them'.

17. Do you have any other comments that you would like to add?

(a) I get frustrated that many consider anyone with a disability (mental or learning) as a case for different or specific consideration. The only reason for this would be that they have not been considered before now for straight forward therapy! Having talked with a number of people with physical disabilities, their one wish is to be treated equally as those of us without any form of disability. They don't want 'special' treatment — simply to be accepted as a person with the same feelings and thought processes as everyone else

(b) I feel very privileged in working with all my clients, l/d or not. But I feel the patience and willingness to fully appreciate the needs of this group do not just happen and experience of the needs, the issues involved in terms of inter agency understanding of counselling process and belief in benefits to people with l/d need to be addressed

(c) [blank]

(d) I felt highly privileged. I enjoyed a steep learning curve!

(e) [blank]

(f) Look forward to reading your dissertation! There is definitely a failure in most counselling training to address this area of therapeutic work — non discriminatory practice requires more than lip service!

(g) *I have virtually no contact with people with learning disabilities prior to this. Working with my client has opened my eyes to the many ethical and philosophical issues in this area as well as making me much less likely to be afraid or awkward in interacting with someone with learning disabilities, although of course I have an incredible amount still to learn*

(h) *There is something very special about working with this client group. I feel very privileged when allowed to get close. I often feel humble when I touch their difficult world. Usually enormous warmth and humour. They can begin to grow as adults rather than remain as dependent children. Very exciting — needs enormous patience!*

Appendix 3

Research assumptions

Questionnaires

1. What particular training in this area have you experienced?
It seems there is almost NO specialised training for working with this client group — often people fear that their skills from general counselling training are not relevant, and they fear working with people who have no verbal language.

2. How long have you been working with persons with learning and/or physical disabilities?
This will be an interesting question, especially if I add, 'as a counsellor'.

3. How many clients with severe learning disabilities have you worked with as a counsellor?
I anticipate very few have had experience with clients who had learning difficulties.

4. How would you say clients are, or can been classified as having mild, moderate and severe learning disabilities, and does this classification have any usefulness in describing the work you do with clients who have learning disabilities?
One of the difficulties I anticipate in this research is the different ways of labelling people as having or not having learning difficulties. There is, in some areas, an emphasis on IQ scoring as the determining factor, with those who score less than 50 on a global IQ test being deemed to have severe learning difficulties. At the other end of the scale are those who have 'specific learning difficulties' often with an average or higher than average IQ score (sometimes globally called dyslexia), which affect their abilities in certain academic areas, but not in other areas of life. Those who have 'mild to moderate' learning difficulties often fall anywhere between these two IQ score level, (Sinason, 1992, says between 50–70) and many are now educated in mainstream schools. My own anger about the reliance on IQ testing will need to be held, as it is this kind of test that defines whether people have their needs recognised, often rather than focusing on their functional abilities. *For the purposes of this research I shall define severe learning difficulties as being those for whom most or all areas of their lives are affected by their difficulties in functioning independently. For many of these clients IQ scores will have been either unobtainable or below 50, and many of these clients have either restricted or no verbal abilities.*

5. How was the referral made?
Self-referral is rare in this client group; who makes the referral and their reasoning for it puts a different skew on the beginning of a relationship than

when a client is self-referred. Often, in my experience, the referrer wants and sometimes requires reports on the counselling process, which makes a farce of confidentiality.

6. How easy/difficult was it to establish a relationship with the client?
This may be affected by a number of issues as in any therapeutic relationship — what are the issues in this client group?

7. What are the particular difficulties and dilemmas with this client group?
I have outlined some I have experienced above. The continual demand for reports, results and recommendations is at odds with their relationship with their clients.

8. What are the particular rewards of working with this client group?
Making contact with another human being is, for me, deeply moving — with this client group there is sometimes an incredible sense of meeting a pure soul deeply hidden within a set of behaviours and restricted communication systems, that within the withdrawn, uncommunicative and often challenging person, lies a clear integrity that speaks volumes if only we listen with our entire being instead of simply through our hearing.

9. Was the client able to attend the sessions alone?
Therapists are often required to work with clients within this group with others present, or with other persons with learning disabilities intruding upon the sessions.

10. What differences in mood, behaviour, demeanour, attitude, did you notice?
Therapy can have a significant impact on clients with learning disabilities, which can be seen in changes in their mood, behaviour, demeanour and attitudes; especially when changes are encouraged and supported by carers.

11. How did the client respond to the ending?
Some clients, especially with severe learning disabilities, seem to respond to people as tools, therefore not seem to notice the end of a counselling relationship, whereas others become very attached and find ending very difficult — what effects do these experiences have on the therapist?

12. How easy/difficult has it been for you to get supervision for this work?
There are very few counsellors/therapists who work with people with learning disabilities, and therefore it is more difficult to have access to a more experienced practitioner with the relevant experience for supervision. I have so far never worked with a supervisor who had experience of offering therapy to this client group.

13. What, if any, are the differences in working with clients who have learning and/or physical disabilities and those who have not?
Learning the client's particular mode of communication may take longer than with a verbal client; practitioners may need to be more willing to work creatively with this client group; time boundaries may need to be very flexible with this client group; feedback about the work may be non-existent with this client group so that the therapist must have a strong sense of purpose, and able to recognise subtle cues about whether the client really does want to continue or end the work; progress may be extremely slow; the therapist may feel required to justify their role on a regular basis with funders; therapists may be asked or required to supply reports, recommendations, and/or attend planning reviews which creates an unusual tension

14. What, if any, are the differences in your feelings in working with this client group, and others?
For myself I find I experience extremes of emotions often when working with a client who has severe learning disabilities — my experience of compassion and recognition of the harm done to my clients in the name of 'care' is ever present in the face of the unlikelihood of any real positive changes in their environments. My anger towards those who have inflicted terrible abuses, and complete lack of concern for their emotional needs, both in the past and in the present, needs space in supervision for expression, as there is little hope of changing the world in which the client lives. I am often in awe of the emotional intelligence and clarity shown by people for whom there is no 'side', no impression management — I feel I can come very close spiritually with the wholeness of the person within the disability. Not so different from any other client, but more extreme. I am interested to learn if this is a common experience of practitioners in this field.

15. Do you have any other comments that you would like to add?

References

Adler, A. (1963) *The Problem Child*. New York: Putnam's

Bass, E. and Davis, L. (1988) *The Courage to Heal*. New York: Harper and Row

Bowlby, J. (1969) *Attachment and Loss, Vol 1: Attachment*. London: Hogarth Press

Brown H. and Craft, A. (1992) *Working with the Unthinkable: A Trainer's Manual on the Sexual Abuse of Adults with Learning Difficulties*. London: The Family Planning Association

Corker, M. (1994) *Counselling – The Deaf Challenge*. London: Jessica Kingsley

Corker, M. (1996) *Deaf Transitions: Images and Origins of Deaf Families, Deaf Communities and Deaf Identities*. London: Jessica Kingsley

Cresswell, J.W. (1998) *Qualitative Inquiry and Research Design: Choosing Among Five Traditions*. London: Sage

De Vinck, C. (1989) *The Power of the Powerless: A Brother's Legacy of Love*. London: Hodder and Stoughton

Denzin, N. K. and Lincoln, Y. S. (eds) (1998) *The Landscape of Qualitative Research: Theories and Issues*. London: Sage

Devinsky, O. (1994) *A Guide to Understanding and Living with Epilepsy*. Philadelphia: Davis

Dixon, H and Craft, A., and Nottingham County Council, LDA 669, *Picture Yourself*

DoH/DSS (1989) White Paper: Caring for People: Community Care in the Next Decade and Beyond. London: DoH/DSS

Dreikurs, R. and Cassell, P. (1972) *Discipline Without Tears*. Toronto: The Alfred Adler Institute of Ontario

Dukes, S. (1984) Phenomenological methodology in the human sciences. *Journal of Religion and Health, 23*, (3), 197–203

Finkelhor, D. (1984) *Child Sexual Abuse: New Theory and Research*. New York: Free Press

Goleman, D. (1996) *Emotional Intelligence: Why it can matter more than IQ*. London: Bloomsbury

Hawkins, J., de Vries, M. and Schaffer, C. (1996) *Partners With disAbility*. London: Kith & Kids Publication

Horwood, W. (1988) *Skallagrigg*. London: Penguin Books

Howard, G.S. (1983) Towards methodological pluralism. *Journal of Counselling Psychology, 30*, 19–21

King, D. (1998) The persistence of eugenics. *Genethics News,* 22 (Feb/March), 6–8

Kvale, S. (1996) *InterViews: An Introduction to Qualitative Research*. London: Sage

Lovett, H. (1996) *Learning to Listen: Positive Approaches and People with Difficult Behaviour*. London: Jessica Kingsley

McBrien, J. (1994) In Emerson, E., McGill, P. and Mansell, J. *Learning Disabilities and Challenging Behaviours*. London: Chapman and Hall

Mearns, D. and Thorne, B. (1988) *Person-Centred Counselling in Action*. London: Sage

Mearns, D. and Thorne, B. (1999) *Person-Centred Counselling in Action* [second edition]. London: Sage

Mearns, D. and Thorne, B. (2000) *Person-Centred Therapy Today*. London: Sage

Moustakas, C. (1994) *Phenomenological Research Methods*. Thousand Oaks, CA: Sage

O'Connor, S. (1994) Universal Mother. Ensign Records.

Pörtner, M. (2000) *Trust and Understanding: The Person-Centred Approach to Everyday Care for People with Special Needs*. Ross-on-Wye: PCCS Books

Prouty, G. (1998) Pre-therapy and the pre-expressive self. In: Merry, T. (ed.) (2000) *Person-Centred Practice: The BAPCA Reader*. Ross-on-Wye: PCCS Books

Roe, D. L. and Roe, C. E. (1991) The third party: Using interpreters for the deaf in counselling situations. *Journal of Mental Health Counselling*, 13(1), 91–95

Rogers, C. R. (1951) *Client-Centered Therapy*. London: Constable

Rogers, C. R. (1957) The necessary and sufficient conditions for therapeutic personality change. In: Kirschenbaum, H. and Henderson, V. L. (1990) *The Carl Rogers Reader*. London: Constable

Rogers, C. R. (1978) *On Personal Power: Inner Strength and its Revolutionary Impact*. London: Constable

Sacks, O. W. (2000) *Seeing Voices: A Journey into the of the Deaf*. London: Vintage Books

Sanderson, C. (1995) *Counselling Adult Survivors of Child Sexual Abuse*, 2nd edition. London: Jessica Kingsley

Sinason, V. (1992) *Mental Handicap and the Human Condition: New Approaches from the Tavistock*. London: Free Association Books

Strauss, A. and Corbin, J. (1998) *Basics of Qualitative Research: Techniques and Procedures for Developing Grounded Theory*, 2nd edn. London: Sage

Thompson, T. and Mathias, P. (eds) (1999) *Lyttle's Mental Health and Disorder*, 2nd edition. London: Harcourt

Waitman, A. and Conboy-Hill, S. (1992) *Psychotherapy and Mental Handicap*. London: Sage

Watson, T. S. and Gresham, F. M. (Eds) (1998) *Handbook of Child Behaviour Therapy*. London: Plenum Press

Worden, J.W. (1983) *Grief Counselling and Grief Therapy*. London: Tavistock Publications

Wosket, V. (1999) *The Therapeutic Use of Self: Counselling Practice, Research and Supervision*. London: Routledge

New PCA book from PCCS Books for living and
working with people
with contact impairment

Pre-Therapy: Reaching contact-impaired clients
Gary Prouty, Dion Van Werde and Marlis Pörtner
ISBN 1 898059 34 9 pp.192 £15.00

Developed by Garry Prouty and his associates over 30 years, Pre-Therapy is a method for anyone wanting to work with people whose ability to establish and maintain psychological contact is impaired temporarily or permanently, by illness or injury, whether of organic or psychological origin. This book presents the most complete and up-to-date formulation of Pre-Therapy philosophy, theory and practice.

Applications of the method with the most difficult client-groups — those described with severe psychosis and others with profound learning disabilities — are described by all three authors, with detailed accounts from Dion Van Werde and Marlis Pörtner.

Pre-Therapy has changed the practice of psychologists, psychiatrists, psychotherapists, social workers, counsellors and carers in mainland Europe; now this book introduces its revolutionary ideas to English-speaking readers.

CONTENTS
Part 1   Garry Prouty **The Foundations of Pre-Therapy**
Formative Experiences, Pre-Therapy and Existential Phenomenology, The Theory of Pre-Therapy, The Practice of Pre-Therapy, Pre-Symbolic Theory, Newer Applications of Pre-Therapy

Part 2   Dion Van Werde **Pre-Therapy Applied on a Psychiatric Ward**
Mission Statements, A Contact Milieu,

Part 3   Marlis Pörtner **Pre-Therapy in Europe**
The Pre-Therapy Project at Sint-Amandus, Further Evolutions of Pre-Therapy

UK customers call for discounts 01989 77 07 07
or visit www.pccs-books.co.uk

New PCA book from PCCS Books for living and working with people with special needs

Trust and Understanding: the person-centred approach to everyday care for people with special needs
Marlis Pörtner
ISBN 1 898059 27 6, pp.128 £12.00

'So many care institutions operate from a service or systems led approach. Vulnerable people requiring care can very often find themselves in oppressive and harmful situations if they do not happen to fit into a particular category or box. Person-centred approaches offer individuals alternative ways forward within a human rights context. These approaches provide people with styles of personal care which allow them to make choices and take control of all aspects of their lives. This is vital if full citizenship and social inclusion are to become a reality for all people.

The descriptions of the person-centred concept and styles of implementation found in these pages, taken from a global field of experience, help us to develop our own understanding and sensitivity towards the needs of others.

The author offers a vision of how to develop trust and understanding, qualities which create a climate of empowerment and increases self-worth. I am pleased to recommend this book to all of us who endeavour to increase our trust and understanding in our relationships with others.'

Mandy Neville, Chief Executive, Circles Network, UK

CONTENTS
Creating living spaces; Fundamentals of the Person-Centred Approach; Guidelines for everyday work; Specific care for people with special needs; Consequences for carers; Institutional attitudes to the person-centred concept; The person-centred concept and families; Pre-therapy; The Person-Centred Approach in different professional fields; Similar approaches in nursing; A hopeless case? Implications for education and training; Outlook.

CL

UK customers call for discounts 01989 77 07 07
or visit www.pccs-books.co.uk

362.
309
41
HAW